Problems

in

Trial Advocacy

2017 Edition

PROBLEMS

IN

TRIAL ADVOCACY

2017 EDITION

Anthony J. Bocchino

Donald H. Beskind

NITA®

NATIONAL INSTITUTE FOR TRIAL ADVOCACY

FOR LYNN AND WENDY

CONTENTS

Section III: Impeachment and Rehabilitation

Section IV: Adverse Examination

Section V: Expert Witnesses

ACKNOWLEDGMENTS

Grateful acknowledgment is given to Kenneth S. Broun, Steven Lubet, John M. Maciejczyk, Louis M. Natali, James H. Seckinger, Edward R. Stein, Warren Wolfson, Deanne C. Siemer, and Frank D. Rothschild who authored earlier versions of many of these problems and provided their wisdom and insight in preparing these materials.

The authors also acknowledge the extensive contributions of Ms. Beth Targan, Professor Bocchino's research assistant. Her work was exemplary, and evidenced insight and maturity beyond her years.

INTRODUCTION

The problems in this book simulate actual courtroom situations and are designed to develop the basic skills necessary for all trial lawyers. The situations are realistic and in many cases are based, in whole or in part, on actual trials. They involve a variety of both civil and criminal cases.

The book is designed so that fact patterns used for direct and cross-examination problems contain two witness examinations per fact pattern and are also used for other exercises in the course (e.g., exhibits, impeachment, etc.). As a result, you can spend less time learning fact patterns and more time developing your skills as a trial lawyer. You can also learn to appreciate that a trial is not merely a collection of segments, performed independent of each other. Rather it is the process of developing—through opening statements, direct and cross examination of lay and expert witness, introduction of exhibits, witness impeachment and closing arguments—a well-conceived, planned and delivered case theory. An effective case theory will be one that supports a judgment in your favor as a matter of law, answers the question of what really happened and why for the fact finder, and persuades the fact finder that your client should prevail as a matter of fairness and justice.

For each problem then, your first task should be to decide on your theory of the case. Then consider the role of the assigned exercise in proving that case theory. Finally, you should plan the execution of the exercise so as to present all those points essential for the effective proof of your case theory.

For each fact pattern the names and gender (as implied from the names) of the witnesses are provided. The witness role may, however, be played by either a man or a woman. The roles are gender neutral, and the gender of the witness is never crucial to the proper handling of the case.

Just as in trial, the quality of your performance of these exercises will depend on the quality of your preparation. At a minimum, you should be well versed in the facts of each problem and have outlined the exercises for which you are assigned.

Copies of the exhibits are available online at:

http://bit.ly/1P20Jea

Password: PITA2017

SECTION I

DIRECT AND CROSS-EXAMINATION

For substantive instructions on these subjects, please refer to any of NITA's texts on the art and science of trial advocacy.

BURDEN = π

Problem 1

Nita Liquor Commission v. Cut-Rate Liquor and Jones

(James Bier)

The Liquor Commission has charged the defendants with a civil violation of Nita Liquor Commission Regulation 3.102 for knowingly selling intoxicating beverages to an intoxicated person. Violation of this regulation carries a maximum penalty of $1,000 for a business and $100 for an individual defendant. The business can also lose its retail sales permit.

The elements of the civil complaint under Regulation 3.102 are:

1. Knowing (defined as knew or should have known)
2. Sale
3. Of intoxicating beverages (beer, wine, fortified wine or spirits)
4. To an intoxicated person (one who is appreciably impaired).

Because this is a civil case, the plaintiff Liquor Commission has the burden of proving each element of Regulation 3.102 by a preponderance of the evidence. Defendants have requested a jury trial.

The Liquor Commission's complaint alleges that Dan Jones, an employee of Cut-Rate Liquor, knowingly sold a bottle of Thunderbird wine to Walter Watkins, who was at the time intoxicated. Jones and Cut-Rate deny the allegations of the complaint.

π: experience

The chief witness for the Liquor Commission is Investigator James Bier. Bier is a seven-year veteran of the Liquor Commission. Before serving in this position, he was a police officer for eight years. During his career as a Liquor Commission Investigator, he has investigated the full range of potential violations of the Nita Liquor Commission Regulations.

In answer to discovery requests, the plaintiff provided to the defendants the investigative report that Bier filed on the evening of June 5, 2016. The text of that report is as follows:

> Undersigned investigator assigned with partner, Donald Smith, to investigate the complaints by citizens that the Cut-Rate Liquor Store at the intersection of Seventh and Jackson in Nita City was selling liquor to intoxicated persons and to minors. Surveillance begins at 7:30 p.m. on June 5, 2016. Set up surveillance on the east side of Jackson Avenue, across the street and south of the Cut-Rate Liquor Store. From this position could see the entirety of the intersection, and also could see into the subject place of business through a plate glass window that extends most of the frontage of the subject business along Jackson Avenue. View into business somewhat obstructed by advertising in the window.

Δ question view

From 7:45 p.m. until approximately 8:45 p.m., no unusual activity noted. Several customers enter store, make purchases, and exit store. Store clerk, later determined to be Dan Jones, is only one operating the business. At approximately 8:45 p.m., subject, later determined to be Walter Watkins, is observed on the northwest corner of the intersection leaning on lamppost. He appears disheveled, and he is wearing dark pants, white shirt, sneakers, and a wrinkled lightweight tan raincoat. Watkins pushes self off post and proceeds south across the intersection. Watkins staggers badly as he crosses street, and in the center of the street he stumbles, but catches self before falling. Watkins proceeds to curb on southwest corner where he stumbles again and trips while stepping up onto the curb in front of subject store, at which time he puts both hands out in front of himself to brace for the fall, and he manages to regain his balance without actually hitting the pavement.

After tripping and falling at the curb, Watkins straightens himself up, and he walks to the entrance of the Cut-Rate Liquor store, where he pauses for a moment in front of glass door to subject business. He then enters the store. He proceeds to counter where the clerk, Jones, is standing and appears to have a conversation with him. While Watkins is in the store, we can see him and Jones from the shoulders up, due to the obstructing advertising in the window. No other obstructions noted. After brief conversation, Jones turns away from Watkins and goes out of sight for a brief period of time and then returns to the counter in the area of the cash register. After completing his transaction, Watkins exits store holding a brown paper bag that was not in his hand at the time he entered the store.

Partner and I approach Watkins and physically detain him outside the store. From distance of three feet, note an odor of alcohol about the person of subject and note that eyes are glassy and bloodshot. Ask for identification, which is provided. On questioning, subject provides name and address. Note that speech is somewhat slurred. Take bag from subject. Bag contains unopened and sealed bottle of Thunderbird wine. No receipt found in bag. Subject responds to question as to where he purchased the wine and states that it was from the Cut-Rate Liquor store. Perform field sobriety tests. Subject is unable to walk heel-to-toe in a straight line, pick up coins from sidewalk, or touch finger to nose from arms extended out to the side. Subject Watkins is arrested for public intoxication.

Proceed inside store to issue citation to clerk, Dan Jones, and the Cut-Rate Liquor store for a 3.102 violation of knowingly selling intoxicating beverages to an intoxicated person. Jones makes no statement. Note that the entry door to the store is plate glass with steel security bars and alarm system, only decal on the door lists the store hours of operation, and that wall of store facing

Seventh Street is also plate glass with some advertising. From vantage point of counter can see northwest corner of intersection and both Seventh and Jackson Streets. Note also the width of the counter (approximately two-and-a-half feet), location of the cash register, and that store sells Thunderbird wine, which is stored on a shelf, approximately fifteen feet behind counter. Return to vehicle and transport Watkins to Nita City police station for processing. (Diagram attached to report.)

Signed: [*Signed*]

James Bier, Investigator, NLC

Further investigation of the case revealed that Watkins was found guilty of public intoxication in a bench trial and paid a $25 fine. Investigator Bier testified at that hearing consistent with his report.

Dan Jones and the Cut-Rate Liquor Store deny all of the allegations in the complaint and assert that Walter Watkins did not appear to be intoxicated on the evening of June 5 when he was in their store.

Dan Jones was deposed by the plaintiff and gave, in part, the following information:

My name is Dan Jones, and I live at 12 Chelsea Court in Nita City. I work as the night manager (4:00 p.m. to 12:00 a.m.) at the Cut-Rate Liquor store at Seventh and Jackson. I am a high school graduate, fifty years old, and have worked for Cut-Rate since getting out of the Navy in 2011.

I was working the four-to-twelve shift on the evening of June 5, 2016. I don't know Walter Watkins. I have been shown his picture, and he looks familiar to me. I cannot say that I remember him as ever being a customer on June 5 or any other time. At the same time, I can't say that he never was a customer of mine. He might have been. I did sell a bottle of inexpensive wine to a gentleman within ten or fifteen minutes of the investigator coming into the store that might have been Watkins. I don't remember that it was Thunderbird. The man was a little disheveled, but he didn't appear intoxicated to me. If he had, I would have turned away his business. Our policy is not to serve people who are visibly intoxicated. Our determination is based on observation—looking for typical signs of intoxication, usually slurred speech, odor of alcohol on the breath, bloodshot eyes, uneven gait, stumbling, or staggering.

The evening of June 5, 2016, was moderately busy from 4:00 p.m. to 10:00 p.m. I made a number of sales during that period of time. At no time on that date did I sell liquor to someone who appeared to be drunk. That is against company policy, and I can be fired for doing so. Several years ago I sold

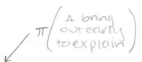

some wine to someone who was arrested later for DUI after he hit another car. He wasn't drunk when I sold him the wine. It was handled by the insurance company. I think they settled for what they called nuisance value. That experience made me very careful about who I sold liquor to at the store. I understand that a couple of our other stores had problems, but I've never had any other problems from the Nita Liquor Commission.

On June 5, 2016, I did receive a citation from an Investigator Bier for knowingly selling intoxicating beverages to an intoxicated person, but I deny making such a sale. Bier gave me the citation and asked me if I wanted to make a statement to him. To be honest, he surprised me, and I almost did talk to him, but I remembered our policy at Cut-Rate to make no statements to liquor investigators if ever confronted with an allegation of a violation of liquor regulations. I just accepted the citation and passed it along to my employer.

Signed: [*Signed*]

Dan Jones

It has been determined that Walter Watkins is no longer in the jurisdiction and will not be available to testify. Investigator Smith is also unavailable.

The case is now at trial. Investigator Bier is the first witness for the Liquor Commission.

Part A

For the plaintiff, conduct the direct examination of Investigator Bier.

For the defendant, conduct the cross-examination of Investigator Bier.

For the plaintiff, conduct any necessary redirect examination.

Part B

For the defendant, conduct the direct examination of Dan Jones.

For the plaintiff, conduct the cross-examination of Dan Jones.

For the defendant, conduct any necessary redirect examination.

Exhibit 1

Diagram of Intersection

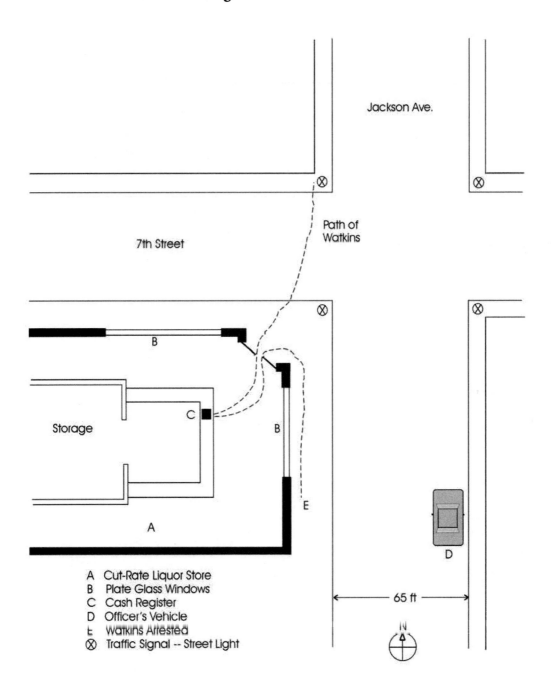

Jackson Ave.

Path of Watkins

7th Street

B

Storage

C

B

A

E

D

65 ft

A Cut-Rate Liquor Store
B Plate Glass Windows
C Cash Register
D Officer's Vehicle
E Watkins Arrested
⊗ Traffic Signal -- Street Light

N

Brown v. Byrd

(Robert Byrd) (Kenneth Brown)

Fact Summary

Kenneth Brown brought suit against Robert Byrd for damages arising out of a collision between their cars on April 20, 2015, near the intersection of 12th Avenue and East Main Street in Nita City. Brown alleges that Byrd was following him too closely and failed to keep a proper lookout. Brown is seeking to recover damages in excess of $250,000 for his neck, back, and closed-head injuries, which he claims were caused by Byrd's negligence. Byrd denies liability and asserts that the impact was caused when Brown stopped short after initially starting through the intersection, and in the alternative, even if the accident was his fault, the impact was not sufficient to cause, and did not cause, any physical injury to Brown.

The accident was investigated at the scene by Officer David Pierce of the Nita City Police Department. Officer Pierce was called to the scene of this accident by radio dispatch at 3:40 p.m. and conducted an investigation. He interviewed the two drivers involved in the accident and inspected the scene. The accident was, in his opinion, unavoidable. That, coupled with the fact that there were no injuries either visible or complained of by either party, resulted in no citations being issued for this accident.

Brown alleges that as a result of being rear-ended by Byrd's car he suffered a back injury. He further claims that the injury precludes him from engaging in any strenuous exercise or activity and that the muscle relaxant prescription drugs he is required to take prevent him from drinking any alcoholic beverages, even beer. Brown asserts that his back injury, the pain and suffering from his back and head injuries, and the deprivation of his activities warrant substantial compensation. Brown is also asking for lost wages.

Byrd's insurance carrier asked one of its investigators, David Randolf, to review and verify Brown's alleged injuries. After an investigation, Randolf filed a report with the insurance carrier disputing the extent of the injuries claimed by Brown. Randolf began his investigation by identifying Brown by reference to a picture provided by the insurance company and by setting up a surveillance of Brown's home on June 24, 2015. He noted no unusual activity on the first day of the surveillance. On June 25, Randolf followed Brown to the Nita Country Club. This was just over two months after Brown's alleged injury. At that time, Randolf observed Brown play two sets of tennis and then consume four or five beers, both at the tennis court and at the nearby outdoor patio bar. Randolf took photographs of Brown playing tennis and drinking afterwards.

SUMMARY OF KENNETH BROWN DEPOSITION

My name is Ken Brown, and I am thirty-three years old. I am single. For the past five years I have worked as an institutional stockbroker here in Nita City at Golden Investments, located at 637 12th Avenue. I live at 5 Scott Place in the southern part of town. I grew up here and graduated from South Central Nita High School. I was on the swim team and the tennis team while in high school and concentrated on tennis while in college, competing on the collegiate level at UCLA, where I played both singles and doubles. Even though I was not good enough to turn pro, tennis played a big part in my life after that, not only because I like the game and it helps me keep in shape, but also because it opened a lot of doors for me professionally in landing accounts and keeping customers happy. I joined the Nita Country Club, in fact, soon after taking my current position with Golden Investments.

I was driving home at the time of the accident. I had left work at the same time as usual. I have to be at work before 6.00 a.m. because the stock market opens at 9:30 a.m. East Coast time, which is 6:30 a.m. out here. David Wilkins, who handles after-hours trading, came in about 2:00 p.m. to cover me, and I briefed him about where the market stood when it closed at 4:00 p.m. East Coast time and what we traded up to that point. I have known David since college—he was my doubles partner on the tennis team. At any rate, I left shortly after 3:00 or so. My office is just six blocks up 12th Avenue from Main Street, and I take the same route every day when I head home. I am always especially careful as I near Main Street because the elementary school is right on the corner and a lot of youngsters are out and about at the school using the playground all year-round. On the day of the accident the school was just letting out at around 3:15 or 3:30, and there were a lot of kids out. There were also some crossing guards, and I think there was an ice cream truck on one corner of the intersection. As I approached the intersection I was extra cautious with the kids in the area. Because the light was green, I intended to go through the intersection.

I was traveling south at no more than twenty miles per hour as I approached the intersection. Just before I got to the crosswalk, the light turned yellow. Because I travel this same street five days a week, I know this light has an especially quick yellow. At the same time I saw a kid running towards the intersection near the crossing guard. Because of the shortness of the yellow light and the kid, I knew I would never be able to safely make it through the intersection, so I applied my brakes and stopped almost immediately. I didn't realize the clown behind me had speeded up from a safe distance behind me to right on my tail, and the instant I stopped, he smashed into my car.

<u>Page 17</u>

1   Q: Where was your car, in relation to the crosswalk, when you were hit?

2   A: I had just come up to the crosswalk.

3   Q: No part of your car was in the crosswalk at all?

4   A: I was just into the crosswalk when I got smashed, but he pushed me

5   through the crosswalk and into the intersection.

6   Q: Where was the front of your car in relation to the crosswalk when you

7   got out of the car?

8   A: I was just through the crosswalk into the intersection.

9   Q: How far did your car move forward after you were hit from behind?

10 A: I'm not sure, the width of the crosswalk, maybe ten feet.

I didn't feel hurt at all after the accident. It's funny how you hear about other people in accidents who feel fine with the rush of adrenalin right afterwards and only later start to feel bad. That's what happened to me. The police officer was there in a matter of minutes, and I told him I felt fine and didn't need any medical assistance. It was obvious who was at fault because the other guy rear-ended me. When it came time to explain what actually happened, the officer didn't have time for us. He spent ten minutes getting down all the basic information like name, address, license numbers, and so on, but then he got called to another accident and left. We never got to tell him what happened. I was shocked that he didn't give Byrd a ticket. He just rushed off without fully investigating our accident. He seemed like a real rookie, too. Nice enough guy, but still wet behind the ears, if you know what I mean. He couldn't have been older than twenty or twenty-one.

The next day my neck and back got worse and worse. I was in so much pain I had to see my doctor, Dr. Gomez. He sent me to the hospital to get an x-ray and an MRI. I was told that they didn't show anything other than some degenerated disc problems at L4–5. The doctor told me that this was probably from years of playing tennis and probably not from the accident. He said that there was little he could do for me and recommended that I rest and take ibuprofen for pain. I decided I'd see a chiropractor, Dr. McCullough, who has an office in his house near my home. Dr. McCullough recommended we treat the condition conservatively, meaning with regular adjustments, hot baths, ibuprofen, and massage for the first week. When this didn't do much to relieve the pain that first week, he then prescribed the muscle relaxants I've been taking ever since just to marginally function. I also got a prescription for pain medication for when it just got too much to handle, but I use them sparingly. I also had some really bad headaches for a few weeks and got dizzy spells for a short time. The headaches came on about every afternoon. I only get a headache now about once a week.

It was very difficult for me mentally as well, trying to handle the loss of my physical life and wondering if my back problem would ever go away so I could feel normal again. The nights were the worst time because I found it hard to find a comfortable position, and I didn't sleep nearly as soundly as I used to. And I would wake up stiff as a board and have to take pills all day to make it through. At the suggestion of my lawyer, I kept a diary about how I was feeling. (That diary was produced at the deposition as Exhibit 3.) In the past two months I have had some improvement, and although I still can't play tennis, I can do the stretching I used to do religiously every morning, and I'm getting better. My back gave me problems at work as well. I often had to work standing up. Since I've been stretching regularly in the past several months, I've been OK at work. I do get tired a lot faster than I used to. By the end of work, it's all I can do to get home and put my feet up to rest. I am hopeful that I'll be able to start playing tennis again in the future. Dr. McCullough says I've made progress and that if I continue my treatments, tennis is not out of the question, although I'll probably never get back to the level I was at before the accident. Overall, I'd say my back is about 80 percent of what it was before the accident. The real problems lasted for about six months, and since then I've been making pretty steady progress.

Getting better

Page 49

1	Q:	Do you drink alcohol?
2	A:	Not now, I don't.
3	Q:	What about before the accident, did you drink then?
4	A:	Well, I never have much been a big drinker, I would have an occasional
5		beer or two after work with a client or friend, or often after playing
6		tennis, or wine with a date. Nothing much.
7	Q:	Would you drink three or four beers in one get-together?
8	A:	No, just one or two at the most.
9	Q:	After the accident, did you drink at all?
10	A:	No, that's been cut out of my life as well because of strict orders from
11		my doctor not to mix alcohol with my medications.
12	Q:	Have you followed those orders exactly at all times?
13	A:	I followed those orders to a T. I don't drink at all anymore, not even
14		beer.
15	Q:	You never drink anything alcoholic now, not even a beer or two?
16	A:	No, I don't. I can't drink so much as a single beer on this medication.

Yes, this photo marked as Exhibit 1 is a picture of me playing tennis. I recognize the court as one at the country club. Yes, this photo marked as Exhibit 2 is a picture of me drinking a beer. Exhibit 2 looks like just outside on the courts. Also at the club. So what? Who took these? I have no idea when they were taken. They couldn't have been taken since the accident because, like I said, I haven't been able to play tennis or drink beer.

No, you're right, there was that one time just a couple months after the accident when I foolishly tried to see if I could handle a game of tennis. I was so frustrated that I just had to try and play, I missed it so much. I played with my doubles partner, David Wilkins, who I also work with. I took a bunch of muscle relaxants, and I felt okay during the couple of sets we played. I was so excited I probably had a few beers just to celebrate being back out on the courts and feeling so alive. David had driven, so I wasn't worried about driving home. And did I pay for it later that day and for a couple of weeks after that. My chiropractor was really upset with me and said I probably set my treatment back a month. But that was the one and only time I tested myself that way. I learned my lesson the hard way.

This accident has also hurt me financially. I was not as good at my job during 2015 because I was distracted by pain. I was the top earner in my group in 2014, and I made a little over $250,000. In 2015, I was eighteenth out of twenty people in the group and made over $60,000 less than in 2015. My income for 2015 was approximately $190,000, as compared to $250,000 in 2014. Fortunately I have been feeling better this year, and my earnings are back up, so I'm currently second in the group for 2016.

You have shown me a notebook marked as Exhibit 3, and I recognize it as a diary I kept of times when I felt pain after the accident. It isn't complete because I didn't start it until I was advised to do so two weeks after the accident by my lawyer, and I wasn't always diligent in making notes. You have also shown me a document marked as Exhibit 4. I recognize Exhibit 4 as the first quarter 2015 work evaluation I received at my job at Golden Investments. I don't agree with the evaluation, but it is what I received from my supervisor, Alyssa Hoffman.

I have read this deposition, and it is complete and accurate.

[*Signed*]

Kenneth Brown

November 15, 2016

DEPOSITION SUMMARY OF ROBERT BYRD

My name is Bob Byrd. I am thirty-five years old, and I live at 104 East Main Street in Nita City. I am married with two children—Mike, age eight, and David, age six. I work as a salesperson for an auto parts supply company, Nita Automart. I have been sued by Kenneth Brown for a car accident I had with him.

<u>Page 18</u>

1	Q:	Where were you going at the time of the accident?
2	A:	I had an appointment at Ferguson Auto Body.
3	Q:	Where is that located?
4	A:	In South Nita City.
5	Q:	What time was the appointment?
6	A:	Four.
7	Q:	Why were you going there?
8	A:	They're a client of mine. I had an appointment to meet with the Parts
9		Manager, Bill Cheswick. He's hard to get an appointment with.
10	Q:	How long does it take to get to Ferguson's from where the accident
11		happened?
12	A:	I know I was cutting it close, but if it wouldn't have been for this
13		accident, I would have gotten there in time.

Cross

As I said, the accident involved a man, who I now know as Ken Brown, at the intersection of 12th and East Main in Nita City on April 20, 2015. The accident occurred at 3:30 in the afternoon. The weather was clear and dry.

As I approached the intersection of 12th and Main, I was traveling south on 12th Avenue at about twenty-five miles an hour, which is the speed limit on that part of 12th Avenue. Mr. Brown's Honda sedan was about two car lengths ahead of me.

The light was green, but Brown slowed a bit as he came to the intersection. On the northwest corner of that intersection is the Nita Elementary School. Because school was letting out at that time, I was being especially careful watching the schoolchildren near the intersection on the northwest corner. I saw a crossing guard bending over and talking to a little boy, who looked like my David, on the northeast corner of the intersection. There were also some children, I'd estimate about eight or ten of them, crowded around an ice cream truck parked just east of the intersection, facing west on East Main Street.

Page 35

1	Q:	Tell me how the accident happened.
2	A:	I was driving behind Mr. Brown's car, maybe fifteen feet behind him,
3		going no more than twenty. When I got about twenty feet from the
4		crosswalk on 12th, the light turned yellow. By then I was ten feet
5		behind him because he had slowed some. I look up, and his brake lights
6		were off and he seemed to be speeding up, so I assumed Mr. Brown
7		would continue through the intersection.
8	Q:	Where was Mr. Brown's car at the time the light turned yellow?
9	A:	Just into the crosswalk.
10	Q:	Not into the intersection?
11	A:	Well, just about.
12	Q:	But not there yet?
13	A:	Not yet, but I assumed he would continue through.
14	Q:	Why did you make that assumption?
15	A:	It was the only intelligent thing to do.
16	Q:	Why's that?
17	A:	Well, otherwise he would have to have jammed on his brakes and stop
18		suddenly.
19	Q:	What's wrong with that?
20	A:	Obviously, it can cause someone following behind to run into you.
21	Q:	Which is what you did?
22	A:	My point exactly.
23	Q:	Had Mr. Brown continued as you assumed, what were you going to do?
24	A:	I planned to follow him right through the intersection. In my opinion,
25		it was safer to go through the light, even if it changed while I was in the
26		intersection, than jamming on my brakes.
27	Q:	Even if the light turned red?
28	A:	Yes, even if it turned red.

At any rate, I glanced left and right as I got to the intersection. Instead of going through, Brown suddenly slammed on the brakes and stopped. He must have been almost through the crosswalk when he braked. That's why I thought he was going through. I hit the brakes as hard as I could, but I still ran into the rear end of Brown's car. I have marked on this diagram the location of Brown's car and the location of my car when the impact happened. I'm sure Brown was through the crosswalk and into the intersection when I hit him. When I hit him, I was doing no more than ten miles an hour. In fact, the damage to my car, a 2015 Volvo, was minimal. There was a hardly noticeable ding in the back of Brown's Honda. The impact was so minimal that neither of our air bags inflated.

Brown jumped out of his car and came towards me. I asked him why he stopped short, and he said he had a red light and the wreck was all my fault. I didn't want to get into an argument with him, so I didn't respond, but to my way of thinking, this accident was his fault. It is unsafe to stop so quickly. The yellow light is a caution light, not a stop light, and he should have driven appropriately and gone through the intersection with caution, especially when he didn't brake until the last possible second after he was in the crosswalk. I did ask him if he was hurt, and he said that he wasn't.

A cop came and investigated the accident. I told him I couldn't avoid hitting Brown. He obviously agreed with me because I didn't get a ticket.

I have read this deposition, and it is complete and accurate.

[*Signed*]

Robert Byrd

November 18, 2016

The case is now at trial. The plaintiff has presented his case-in-chief and rested. The defendant's midtrial motion for judgment as a matter of law has been denied.

Part A

For the plaintiff, conduct a direct examination of Kenneth Brown.

For the defendant, conduct a cross-examination of Kenneth Brown.

Part B

For the defendant, conduct a direct examination of Robert Byrd.

For the plaintiff, conduct a cross-examination of Robert Byrd.

Exhibit 1

Playing Tennis

Exhibit 2

Drinking Beer

Exhibit 3

5/7

Pain in back and neck starts after arrival in Chicago 4/20 Up all night with back and neck pain. Also terrible headache — doesn't respond to Tylenol or ibuprofen. Saw internist next day. Told pain is definitely from car wreck, though didn't seem hit that hard. Stayed home from work rest of week. Returned to work but not able to work full shift. Dr Gomes prescribes rest and ibuprofen. Informed if not better in couple of days try heat and massage treatment, maybe chiropractor. Pain still nagging in back, headaches are not as frequent by 5/5. Made appointment with Dr McCullough who has office in neighborhood, recommended by Arnie down the block. Treatment gives temporary relief from pain. Treatment schedule discussed. Pain not quite as bad but enough to notice today — unable to work full day.

5/10

Stretching a little in morning helps stiff back. Worked full day — pain distracting at work — by 6:00 back very painful. Called for McCullough appointment.

5/11

Back still bothering me — dull aching pain — had to leave work early. Set up regular treatments with Burmeister Clinic for heat, massage, hot bath therapy.

5/15

Burmeister helps but still stiff every morning — worked 6 hour days this week.

5/20

Sharp pain today reaching for a notebook at work — stays all day until I get to Burmeister.

Exhibit 3 (con't.)

5/30
Continuing dull pain in back —
missed two days work this week
first bad headache in two weeks.

6/8
Dull ache continues though a
little better — sharp pain, needed
massage, reaching for pan in
kitchen — still distracting at work

6/15
Had a pretty good week. Back
still hurts but not as bad.

6/25
Tried to play tennis today — big
mistake — back feels as bad as
right after accident.
See Dr. McCullough — ordered to
stay home and rest for week —
take vacation week.

7/4
Back to work — ok today for
first time — back sore tonight
really hurts at work — affects
concentration a lot.

8/10
Pain has been up and down, but
getting better — Burmeister appointments
seem to be helping. Less distracting
at work.

8/25
First bad day in couple of weeks.
Stayed in one position too long at desk,
got back spasms. Ok after stretching.

10/15
Pretty good for almost a month —
every once in a while, like today,
I move too fast and get sharp
pain. Today lasted for a couple
hours and Tylenol didn't help.

10/17
Saw Dr. McCullough — he sees
good deal of improvement but
warns not to try too much.

11/20
Doc okays light tennis —
beginning with 20 minute
sessions.

Exhibit 4

GOLDEN INVESTMENTS
FINANCIAL ADVISORS

Member
Nita Stock Exchange
16 Bull Boulevard
Nita City, Nita

March 30, 2015

TO: Ken Brown
FROM: Alyssa Hoffman, Vice President
RE: Quarterly Review

For the period 1/1/2015 through 3/31/2015

Salary: $20,000
Commissions: $23,256
New Clients This Quarter: 11

As the above numbers show, there is some reason for concern in your performance during the first quarter of this year. Although there has been a small slowing in the market, compared to the last quarter of 2014, your commissions for this quarter are less than half for the last quarter of 2014 when your commissions were $49,500. Similarly, while your client base was reduced by the death of your best investor, you have only eleven new customers in this quarter, when compared to the thirty-one new customers in the last quarter of 2014. The comparison of the first quarter of this year with the first quarter of last year is also disappointing. Your commissions for the first quarter of 2014 were $40,075 and new clients for that quarter were twenty-three.

I am sure you share our disappointment concerning your performance, especially after your personal record year of 2014. Ken, we all go through these droughts, especially after a big year. It's time to get back to work in earnest. With your talent, I expect that you can rescue this year if you just put your mind to it. I expect that we will see significant improvements in the next quarter.

If you need any assistance, please feel free to make an appointment with my personal assistant.

Exhibit 5

NITA CITY POLICE DEPARTMENT
Accident Report

1. Investigating Officer: D. Pierce		2. Badge No: 2157
3. Date: April 20, 2015	4. Time: 3:40 p.m.	5. Place: Nita City
VEHICLE # 1		
6. Operator: Kenneth Brown	7. Address: 5 Scott Pl. N. C.	8. Vehicle Title #: G18M4443798
9. Year: 2013	10. Make: Honda	11. Model: Sedan
12. Lic. Plate: GSB 356	13. State: Nita	14. Insurance: State Farm
15. Pol. #: 00528–24–2234	16. Towed: Driveable	17. Damage: Rear bumper and trunk
VEHICLE # 2		
6. Operator: Robert Byrd	7. Address: 104 E. Main, N. C.	8. Vehicle Title #: IP644W5772
9. Year: 2015	10. Make: Volvo	11. Model: Sedan
12. Lic. Plate: KJM 044	13. State: Nita	14. Insurance: USAA
15. Pol. #: 3001–17750–1440	16. Towed: Driveable	17. Damage: Front fender
18. Principal Road: 12th Avenue	19. Speed Limit: 25	20. Intersecting Road: E. Main

21. Injuries:
None - minor accident

22. Narrative:
Interviewed both drivers. Vehicle #1 was traveling south on 12th Avenue. When he neared intersection of E. Main light was green. Light changed to yellow and #1 stopped short and was rear-ended by Vehicle #2. #2 appeared to be traveling within posted speed limit of 25 mph and to have his vehicle under control. #2 may have been following too close, but accident was made unavoidable by the sudden and unnecessary stop by #1. Note also that timing of yellow light was short as previously noted. In light of all of above—No Citations—Both vehicles driveable—No injuries.

23. Investigating Officer Signature: [*Signed*]	Date: 4/21/2015

Exhibit 6

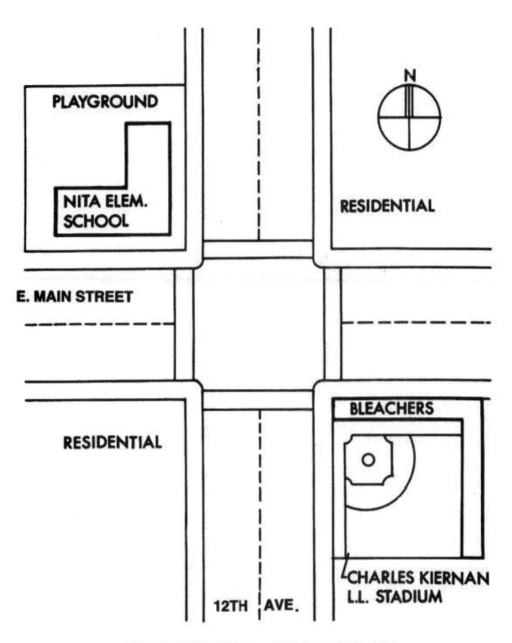

INTERSECTION — 12TH & E. MAIN

PROBLEM 3

State v. Lawrence

(Gale Fitzgerald) (James Lawrence)
VICTIM   ACCUSED

Fact Summary

James Lawrence has been charged with assault and theft as a result of a purse-snatching incident on the evening of Friday, July 1, 2016. The victim was Gale Fitzgerald, a twenty-eight-year-old woman who works as a paralegal for a law firm in Nita City.

On Friday, July 1, 2016, Fitzgerald was at the end of a long week preparing for trial and had worked late. She left the office at 9:15 p.m. and was on her way home from work. She got off the bus at the corner of Fifth and Main at 9:45 p.m. and walked east on Main toward her apartment at 406 Main. At about the middle of the block on which her apartment building is located, she heard footsteps behind her and felt a sharp pull on her purse. She struggled briefly with her attacker. He threw her to the ground and ran off with the purse across the street and back toward Fifth Street.

Ju. 1

Fitzgerald reported the crime to the police on the evening it happened and gave a statement that evening to Officer James Wright. She visited the police station at Wright's request on July 5, 2016, and looked at mug books, which included a photo of Lawrence taken two years before, but she was unable to identify anyone. A report of that meeting was prepared by Officer Wright.

Jul. 5

On July 15, 2016, Lawrence was arrested in an attempt to snatch the purse of an off-duty police officer, Sonia Henderson. A current mug shot was duly made, and Officer Wright called Fitzgerald to come to the station and look at the current mug shot of Lawrence together with four photos of other white males. Fitzgerald identified Lawrence. A video was made of the procedure, and a transcript was prepared.

Jul. 15

?

When arrested for the Henderson purse snatching, Lawrence was given his *Miranda* warnings and chose to waive his right to remain silent and gave a statement. That statement was video recorded and transcribed. He told police that he was on a movie date on Friday, July 1, 2016. When the movie was over, he took his date to her house and kissed her goodnight. He denied any involvement in the Fitzgerald purse snatching. When contacted by Officer Wright, Chelsea Williams said that she was at a movie with Lawrence that evening and that he took her home, but she could not remember exactly when she reached home.

The defense brought a successful motion in limine with respect to Lawrence's attempt to snatch the purse of the police officer. Lawrence's previous arrest for assault on April 3, 2016, resulted in a guilty plea to a misdemeanor, for which he received a six-month suspended sentence with ten days to serve.

The case is now at trial. The first witness for the State is Gale Fitzgerald.

Part A

For the State, conduct a direct examination of Gale Fitzgerald.

For the defendant, conduct a cross-examination of Gale Fitzgerald.

Part B

The last witness in the case is James Lawrence.

For the defendant, conduct a direct examination of James Lawrence.

For the State, conduct a cross-examination of James Lawrence.

Exhibit 1

NITA CITY POLICE DEPARTMENT
Nita City, Nita

INVESTIGATIVE REPORT

1. Complaining Witness Gale Fitzgerald	**2. Address** 406 Main Street, Nita City, NI
3. Phone 449–5237 (home) 889–9000 (work)	**4. Complained of Offense** Theft, Assault (purse snatching)
5. Date July 1, 2016	**6. Place** 400 block of Main Street Nita City

7. Narrative

Complaining witness interviewed at her apartment at above address. States that upon exiting bus at 5th and Main and walking towards her apartment was grabbed from behind by unknown assailant. Struggle ensues. Assailant stole purse belonging to complaining witness containing personal articles, including wallet and $400 in cash. Witness agrees to come to station on 7/5 on lunch break to attempt mug shot ID and to sign statement (see attached statement).

7/5/2016
Complaining witness comes to station at 1300 hours. Reviews and signs statement given three nights previous. Shown several mug books of known purse snatchers. Not able to make positive ID. Purse containing wallet with ID for Gale Fitzgerald found in mailbox at 814 Main Street. Purse identified by Ms. Fitzgerald as hers. States that everything but money still in the purse. Reviews and signs supplemental statement (see attached supplemental statement).

7/15/2016
Interview with James Lawrence at city jail. Lawrence being held on attempted theft and assault charges for trying to steal by force the purse of off-duty police officer, Sonia Henderson. Advise suspect of investigation of July 1 incident and other purse snatchings. Advised of his Miranda rights. Waived. (See signed waiver form attached.) Suspect says he has an alibi for July 1 incident. Went to movies with Chelsea Williams, 1013 Elm Street, Nita City. Gives signed statement (attached).

---

10. Investigating Officer—Name and Signature

[Signed]
James Wright, Badge #007

NITA CITY POLICE DEPARTMENT
Nita City, Nita

INVESTIGATIVE REPORT

1. Complaining Witness Gale Fitzgerald	**2. Address** 406 Main Street, Nita City, NI
3. Phone 449–5237 (home) 889 9000 (work)	**4. Complained of Offense** Theft, Assault (purse snatching)
5. Date July 1, 2016	**6. Place** 400 block of Main Street Nita City

7. Narrative

7/16/2016

Complaining witness called to station. Suspect who meets description given by Ms. Fitzgerald arrested on 7/15 in attempt to snatch purse of off-duty police officer.

Ms. Fitzgerald shown array of photos including recent photo of suspect, James Lawrence. Positive ID made. Obtain purse from Ms. Fitzgerald as evidence in the case against Lawrence. This officer notes that photograph of suspect was among those included in mug books complaining witness viewed on 7/5/2016.

7/20/2016

Contact alibi witness, Chelsea Williams, at job. Arrange for interview at police station on 7/21 before she goes to work.

7/21/2016

Meet with Chelsea Williams at 0900. Agrees to give signed statement This officer notes that Ms. Williams lives no more than a ten minute walk from the crime scene in this case.

10. Investigating Officer—Name and Signature
[Signed]
James Wright, Badge #007

Exhibit 2

STATEMENT OF GALE FITZGERALD

My name is Gale Fitzgerald. I am twenty-eight years old. I am single and live in an apartment at 406 Main Street in Nita City. I work for Harry Loomis, a personal injury lawyer, as a secretary and paralegal. His offices are in the Public Ledger Building in downtown Nita City.

On July 1, 2016, I worked late. Harry was in the middle of a trial, and we had been at the office until at least 9:00 p.m. every night for the week before July 1. I left the office at 9:15 p.m. and got lucky and caught a bus right away outside the building. The bus, which travels up Fifth Street, let me off at the bus stop at the corner of Fifth and Main Streets at about 9:45 p.m. I got off the bus and started to walk east on the sidewalk toward my apartment. There are street lights on the corners of the intersection and some small lights on the houses on that block. I would say that the visibility was fairly good given that it was nighttime.

As I walked towards my apartment, I completed the 500 block and entered the block my apartment is on. As I got to a fire hydrant at about the middle of the block, I heard fast footsteps behind me. Before I could turn around I felt a sharp pull on my purse, which I was carrying on my right shoulder. The tug on the purse turned me around, and I was facing my attacker. I know it was stupid, but I struggled with him. I had taken $400 out of the ATM in our building just before I left for the night, and I didn't want to lose it. I also had in my purse a letter I received at the office from a good friend that I hadn't yet had a chance to read.

We struggled over the purse for what seemed like a long time, but I guess was less than fifteen seconds, until he threw me to the ground. Somehow the strap broke on my purse, and my attacker ran off with my purse across the street and in the direction that he came from, toward Fifth Street. My attacker was a white man, approximately 5'8" to 5'10" in height, 160–175 pounds, with dark hair (dark brown or black), wearing dark pants, a white tank-top shirt, and running shoes.

As soon as I got into my apartment I called the police. Officer Wright came to my apartment soon afterwards, where I am now giving this statement. That's all I can remember. I am very upset by this. I've never been attacked before.

Signed: [*Signed*]

          Gale Fitzgerald

          July 5, 2016

Exhibit 3

SUPPLEMENTAL STATEMENT OF GALE FITZGERALD

I have come to the police station today at the request of Officer Jim Wright. Officer Wright returned my purse to me, which he told me was recovered from a mailbox in the 800 block of Main Street.

The purse has a torn shoulder strap. All of my personal belongings and my wallet with all my identification are still in it. All of my money, including the money I took out of the ATM before going home on the day of the mugging, is gone.

I have been shown several books of mug shot photographs and have not been able to identify my attacker among them.

Signed: [*Signed*]

Gale Fitzgerald

July 5, 2016

Exhibit 4

<table>
<tr><td colspan="2" align="center">**NITA CITY POLICE DEPARTMENT**
Nita City, Nita

WAIVER OF RIGHTS</td></tr>
<tr><td>**1. Complaining Witness**
Sonia Henderson</td><td>**2. Address**
Nita City Police Department</td></tr>
<tr><td>**3. Phone**
889–9000 (work)</td><td>**4. Complained of Offense**
Theft, Assault
(purse snatching)</td></tr>
<tr><td>**5. Date**
July 15, 2016</td><td>**6. Place**
Sixth & Davenport St.
Nita City</td></tr>
</table>

I am *James Lawrence* I have been given my rights. I understand that I do not have to make any statement whatsoever, that I have a right to remain silent, that I have a right to have a lawyer present, and that anything I say should I give a statement could be used against me in a court of law. Knowing those rights, I am freely and voluntarily agreeing to talk with an officer of the Nita City Police Department and waive those rights with regard to the matter described on the top of this form.

[*Signed*]

James Lawrence

[*Signed*]

James Wright

WITNESS NAME

July 15, 2016
DATE

Exhibit 5

STATEMENT OF JAMES LAWRENCE

Taken by Officer James Wright

Wright: It's July 15, I'm Officer James Wright of the Nita City Police Department. It's 10:30 p.m. The suspect, Mr. Lawrence, has chosen to give a statement. We are recording this statement in an interview room at the Nita City Police Department by use of video. The proceedings will be transcribed for Mr. Lawrence's signature. All right then, let's begin.

Wright: What is your name and address?

Lawrence: James Lawrence, 523 Maple Street, Nita City.

Q: You understand that you are under arrest for the attempted robbery of Sonia Henderson, do you not?

A: Yes.

Q: And you've been given your *Miranda* rights and are voluntarily choosing to speak with me, is that correct?

A: Yes.

Q: Just to be clear, sir, I am showing you a document that's titled "Waiver of Rights," and it has a signature on it. Is that your signature?

A: Yes.

Q: What is your height and weight?

A: I'm just over six feet tall and 175 pounds.

Q: I want to ask you about another assault and purse snatching that happened in the recent past.

A: I've never done this before. I don't know anything about any purse snatches.

Q: Let me ask you this, sir, where were you on the evening of July 1 at approximately 9:30 to 10:00 p.m.?

A.   Was that a Friday?

Q: Yes, it was.

A: Let's see. Friday a couple weeks ago. I was with my girlfriend, Chelsea Williams. We went over to get something to eat after her work and then down to the movies. We saw *To Kill a Mockingbird* at the Varsity Theater near her apartment. Then I walked her home. I stayed with Chelsea until sometime between 9:30 and 10:00. Then I walked home.

Q: Do you ever use public transportation to get from Chelsea's apartment to home?

A: Yeah, if the weather's really bad, or if I'm in a hurry. I'll take the number 9 bus, which goes down Elm to Fifth, and then goes down Fifth to where I get off at Maple, which is just a half block from my apartment.

Q: How did you walk home on July 1?

A: I always go the same way. She lives down Tenth and Elm. I walk over to Eighth Avenue, down Eighth to Maple, and then over to my apartment at 523 Maple. I like to walk down Eighth Avenue because there are some interesting stores, and I like to window shop. I can't really afford the stuff in those shops, but it's nice to look.

Q: Have you ever been to a bar near Eighth and Main called Dorothy's?

A: I'm not a regular or anything. It's pretty expensive, but I've been in there. I don't drink much, maybe a beer or two, but that's it. Especially at those prices.

Q: Were you at Dorothy's on the evening of July 1 of this year?

A: I might have been, but I don't think so. I was really short of money a couple of weeks ago. I had just paid my rent, and my customers—I do lawns and yard clean-up for people—had been slow in paying. I couldn't even afford to pay for Chelsea's meal at some fast-food place that night, so I doubt if I stopped into Dorothy's.

Q: Do you know a woman named Gale Fitzgerald?

A: No, never heard of her.

Q: Have you ever been to her neighborhood, at Fourth and Main?

A: I might have. It's only a couple blocks from my apartment, but I have no reason to go to that block.

Q: Do you know any reason why Ms. Fitzgerald would identify you as the man who stole her purse and shoved her to the ground on July 1 of this year at about 9:45 p.m.?

A: No. If she said so she must be mistaken, and it's dark at 9:45 at night, and there are lots of trees in that neighborhood. Just houses, no stores. There aren't many street lights either.

Q: Come on, Jim. You needed the money, you saw this poor woman. You ripped her off just like Officer Henderson.

A: I don't have to take this. That's all a bunch of bullshit. I want to see my lawyer.

Q: It'll go easier on you if you just confess. Let's clear this up today. There's no need to drag it out. It really will. . . .

A: That's it. I want to see a lawyer now. You said I could have one if I wanted. Well, I want one now.

Q: OK. Your loss, pal. This ends the statement of James Lawrence on July 15. Off record.

I have read the above three-page transcript, and it is a true and accurate transcription of my statement to Officer James Wright given on July 15, 2016.

[*Signed*]

James Lawrence

Witness: [*Signed*]

            James Wright

Exhibit 6

TRANSCRIPT—GALE FITZGERALD—7/16/2016

Officer Wright:	The time is 5:18 p.m., the date July 16. We are in the Nita City Police Department conference room with Ms. Gale Fitzgerald. Ms. Fitzgerald, we're recording this session with your knowledge and permission, is that correct?
Ms. Fitzgerald:	Yes, that's true.
Officer Wright:	We've again asked you to come to the station to help us in our investigation of the mugging that took place on July 1, in which you were the victim. We have several photographs we'd like to show you. Please tell us if any of these five photos is of the man who attacked you and took your purse.
Ms. Fitzgerald:	Why yes, that's him, number 4. Oh yes, how did you know? What's his name? Has he done this before to others?
Officer Wright:	I can't tell you, ma'am, any details about our investigation. Are you certain this is the man who attacked you on July 1?
Ms. Fitzgerald:	Well, I wouldn't put my life on it, it was dark you know, but I definitely recognize the tattoo on his right arm. His arm was right next to me. The face . . . there was barely enough light for me to see his face, and it was only for a few seconds. This looks like the guy. No, I'm sure this is the guy. It must be.
Officer Wright:	Thank you very much, Ms. Fitzgerald. We'll be letting you know when you're needed for trial.
Off record.	

Exhibit 7

SUPPLEMENTAL STATEMENT OF GALE FITZGERALD

July 16, 2016

I have come to the Nita City police station today at the request of Officer Jim Wright for the purpose of participating further in the investigation of the attack on me on July 1, 2016.

I have been shown a series of five photographs. Photograph #4 is a photograph of an individual who I can positively identify as my attacker. I had never seen this man before July 1, when he attacked me. I am informed that the name of my attacker is James Lawrence.

At Officer Wright's request, I am returning my purse, which I haven't yet had the time to repair, to be kept as evidence in the case.

Signed: [*Signed*]

Gale Fitzgerald

July 16, 2016

Exhibit 8

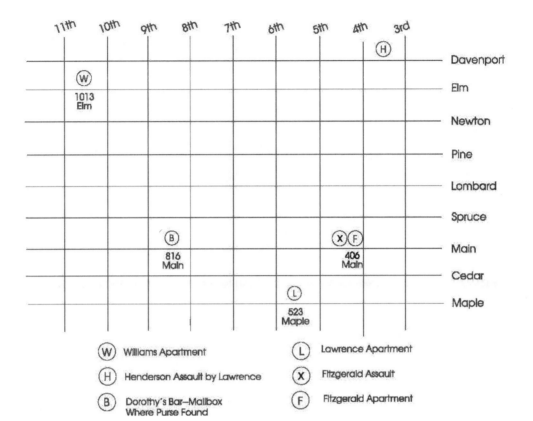

11th 10th 9th 8th 7th 6th 5th 4th 3rd

Ⓗ Davenport

Ⓦ Elm
1013
Elm

Newton

Pine

Lombard

Spruce

Ⓑ ⓍⒻ Main
816   406
Main   Main

Cedar

Ⓛ Maple
523
Maple

Ⓦ Williams Apartment   Ⓛ Lawrence Apartment

Ⓗ Henderson Assault by Lawrence   Ⓧ Fitzgerald Assault

Ⓑ Dorothy's Bar—Mailbox   Ⓕ Fitzgerald Apartment
Where Purse Found

Exhibit 9

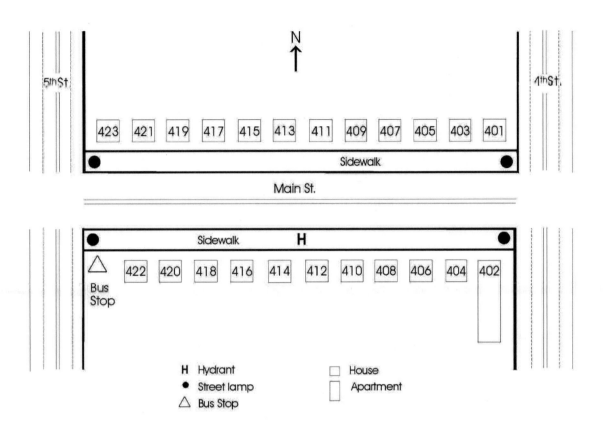

PROBLEM 4

McArthur v. Rogers

(Kathryn McArthur) (David Rogers)

The plaintiff, Kathryn McArthur, has sued the defendant, David Rogers, for injuries sustained in a fall on December 28, 2015. At that time McArthur was renting a rustic ski cabin from the defendant for the week following Christmas in 2015. The plaintiff claims that the defendant was negligent in failing to properly maintain the handrail and steps leading up to the back deck and main entrance to the cabin. She further claims that she slipped on the deck and tried to break her fall by grabbing the handrail and that the handrail broke, allowing her to be thrown off the deck. As a result, the plaintiff broke her left femur below the hip, which required insertion of a rod and screws to repair the fracture. The plaintiff claims she sustained $35,000 in medical bills and lost wages of $40,000. She has sued for $500,000.

The defendant claims that the plaintiff was negligent in running on the snowy deck and further that he, defendant, had no notice of the alleged defective condition of the handrail as he had hired PBA Management to manage his rental property.

Relevant excerpts from the depositions of the plaintiff and the defendant follow.

DEPOSITION OF KATHRYN MCARTHUR

My name is Kathryn McArthur. I am forty-two years old, married with two children, and work as a real estate broker at Reliance Real Estate in Nita City. I am an avid skier, and each winter, my family and I take a ski vacation in the mountains of northwest Nita during the week following Christmas.

For the years 2012 through 2015, we rented a ski cabin in Bear Valley, Nita, from David Rogers. It is a three-bedroom cabin with a large common area and perfect for our family vacation. You have shown me a diagram that has been marked as Exhibit 5, and it shows the basic floor plan of the cabin. As you can see, the main entrance to the cabin is off a deck on the back of the cabin. You get to that deck by the stairs that are marked on the diagram.

As I said, we had been renting that cabin for three years before this accident happened. The cabin was pretty rustic, but with one exception was in good shape. The one exception was the handrail and stairs that led up to the back deck of the cabin. They were in pretty bad shape. We noticed during our vacation in 2014 that the stairs were starting to rot away and the handrail was wobbly. In fact, after our vacation in 2014, we complained to the real estate agent about the condition of the stairs and the handrail. When we arrived on December 25, 2015, we noticed that the stairs had been partially repaired, but the handrail was still in its same old wobbly condition or a little worse.

The vacation was going great, but we were having some problems with animals overturning our garbage cans that were located on the ground to the side of the stairs that led up to the back deck. The garbage cans were where they are shown on Exhibit 5. It was a pain to have to pick up the garbage each morning, so on the night of December 27 we placed some logs on top of the cans to try and keep the animals out of the garbage cans.

Just before dawn on the morning of December 28, I was awakened when I heard some rustling outside the cabin. I figured that it was some animal trying to get at the garbage, so I put on some moccasins, threw on my parka, rushed out the back door, and started toward the stairs. It had snowed the night before, and I slipped a little on the deck, so I reached out to the handrail to keep from falling. It broke out under my weight, and I fell off the top of the steps to the ground, from about eight feet high. As it turned out, I broke my leg pretty bad. The break was to my left upper leg, between the hip and the knee joints.

We, of course, ended our vacation early. I had to have surgery on my leg to insert a rod with surgical screws. My medical bills were over $35,000 and have been covered by my medical insurance, but I missed two months of work as a real estate broker at Reliance Real Estate. My annual income as a real estate broker is approximately $250,000, so I estimate my lost earnings for the two months I wasn't able to work as approximately $40,000. Exhibits 1–4 show my earnings at Reliance Real Estate for years 2013 through 2016. The rehabilitation for this injury was fairly difficult and painful. I was off my feet for about a week, and the rehabilitation period was four months. Fortunately, I have recuperated very well and was able to ski at our Christmas vacation in 2016.

DEPOSITION OF DAVID ROGERS

My name is David Rogers. I am fifty years old. I am an attorney, and I specialize in personal injury cases. I live at 2130 Ridge Pike in Nita City, Nita. I have a wife of twenty-three years and two daughters—Katie, age eighteen and Brenda, age twenty. I am the owner of a rustic cabin in Bear Valley, Nita. I thought about selling the pro   perty in 2014, but changed my mind. The cabin is my pride and joy. I do not live there now because my law firm is in Nita City. I hope to someday retire to my cabin in Bear Valley, but for now I rent it out in order to help with the costs associated with maintaining the property. Exhibit 5 is a diagram of my cabin.

I am pretty hands-off when it comes to the management and maintenance of my property. In order to save aggravation, I have hired a management company, PBA Management (PBA), to handle everything with the renters. PBA deals with everything from booking different renters throughout the year, creating rental agreements with the renters, and responding to any complaints from renters. PBA is supposed to respond to any complaints by getting the appropriate people to fix any problems on the property, if need be. PBA is also supposed to inspect the property for defects after each renter leaves the property.

Since I am an attorney, I know the importance of documenting everything. Therefore, I created a system with PBA whereby they log every single telephone call made in connection with my property. The log is done in a specific log book that only contains information about my Bear Valley property. The agreement that we made was that the company would document all complaints.

I review the log book biweekly and sometimes more often when someone from PBA thinks that I should be aware of something that is more serious in nature. I did not remember ever reading or hearing about a complaint from Ms. Kathryn McArthur. Since the inception of this lawsuit, I have scrutinized the log book and have found only phone calls regarding the rental agreement and the dates that she wanted to rent. Since I knew that the McArthur family had been renting for three years, the lack of more phone calls from Ms. McArthur in the log should have raised a red flag for me, but at the time I assumed that Kathryn McArthur had no problems, and if she had I would have expected it to have been in the log book. I fully trusted PBA until the inception of this lawsuit, so I did not think to question or second guess the way in which they were handling the property. Further, there were not any complaints in the book about the handrail and the stairs that led up to the back deck of the cabin where Kathryn McArthur was unfortunately injured.

I have read Kathryn McArthur's complaint and am very sorry for her injuries and the suffering that it has caused her. PBA never documented the alleged complaints that she made about the property. Further, PBA never documented any phone calls made from other renters about the handrail in question. I pay PBA to maintain the property and make sure that it is safe for the renters. I did everything I could to make sure that PBA kept copious records and kept me informed. I cannot be expected to be responsible for PBA's negligence. Because I was not told about the problem, I believe that the responsibility of Kathryn McArthur's injuries is in the hand of PBA due to her own negligence in running onto a snowy deck.

David Rogers read and signed the deposition making no corrections.

The case is now at trial. The plaintiff calls Kathryn McArthur as its first witness.

Part A

For the plaintiff, conduct a direct examination of Kathryn McArthur, assuming all of the exhibits have been stipulated to be admissible during the pretrial conference, and may be used in the examination of the witness.

For the defendant, conduct a cross-examination of Kathryn McArthur.

For the plaintiff, conduct any necessary redirect examination.

Part B

For the defendant, conduct a direct examination of David Rogers.

For the plaintiff, conduct a cross-examination of David Rogers.

Exhibit 1

2016 Commissions per Agent (thousands $)

Sales Agent	Jan	Feb	Mar	Apr	May	June	July	Aug	Sept	Oct	Nov	Dec	Total 2016	Avg/ Month
Bamber	4.1	5.3	5.5	6.2	7.3	7.1	8.3	10.5	9.2	7.1	5.1	4.3	80.3	6.6
Gumm	5.2	7.4	8.1	9.8	10.6	12.4	13.1	14.5	13.2	11.7	10.4	9.3	125.7	10.4
Kane	6.3	8.6	10.7	13.8	17.9	19.5	21.3	24.7	23.2	18.6	16.9	14.3	195.8	16.3
McArthur	0	0	8.7	11.5	16.7	20.7	26.4	28.9	24.4	17.5	15.4	14.2	184.4	15.3
Quinn*	0	0	0	5.9	6.2	8.7	11.6	12.4	9.3	8.1	7.9	5.6	75.7	6.3
Ruff	5.6	6.7	8.5	10.9	12.1	15.6	19.2	17.4	15.8	11.6	7.1	5.3	135.8	11.3

*Quinn started with the agency in March 2016.

Exhibit 2

2015 Commissions per Agent (thousands $)

Sales Agent	Jan	Feb	Mar	Apr	May	June	July	Aug	Sept	Oct	Nov	Dec	Total 2015	Avg/ Month
Bamber	5.5	6.3	8.4	9.1	9.6	10.3	12.4	11.5	9.7	7.6	5.3	4.7	100.4	8.3
Gumm	7.1	8.4	9.5	11.6	13.8	16.4	19.5	17.1	13.6	9.5	7.4	6.3	140.2	11.6
Kane	13.8	15.3	17.9	19.4	20.6	22.3	24.9	20.5	17.6	13.3	10.7	9.2	200.5	17.1
McArthur	13.3	11.5	14.7	17.5	20.0	21.5	27.9	29.9	24.2	17.1	15.1	14.1	226.8	18.9
Parcell*	15.3	16.7	18.9	21.8	25.4	27.8	0	0	0	0	0	0	125.9	10.4
Ruff	6.9	8.2	9.7	13.4	15.8	16.5	19.7	17.2	12.6	10.3	8.6	6.7	145.6	12.1

*Parcell left the agency in July 2015.

Exhibit 3

2014 Commissions per Agent (thousands $)

Sales Agent	Jan	Feb	Mar	Apr	May	June	July	Aug	Sept	Oct	Nov	Dec	Total 2014	Avg/ Month
Bamber	0	0	4.4	5.7	6.1	7.2	9.3	8.4	5.8	5.3	4.1	3.5	59.8	4.9
Gumm	4.2	5.7	6.3	9.6	10.2	12.8	13.3	15.7	13.4	10.2	8.6	5.8	115.8	9.6
Kane	9.5	10.3	13.7	15.9	17.2	19.6	22.4	24.1	18.3	16.8	12.5	10.6	190.9	15.9
McArthur	11.3	9.5	12.7	15.5	18.0	19.5	25.9	27.9	22.2	15.1	13.1	12.1	202.8	16.9
Parcell	10.4	12.3	15.6	17.2	20.9	22.5	23.8	24.2	22.7	19.5	17.3	14.1	220.5	18.3
Ruff	5.2	7.4	8.6	10.8	11.5	14.9	16.4	15.7	13.3	11.2	8.8	6.5	130.3	10.8

*Bamber sta ted with the agency in March 2014.

Exhibit 4

2013 Commissions per Agent (thousands $)

Sales Agent	Jan	Feb	Mar	Apr	May	June	July	Aug	Sept	Oct	Nov	Dec	Total 2013	Avg/Month
Coughlin*	10.9	13.7	16.6	17.5	19.7	22.9	23.5	25.8	0	0	0	0	150.6	12.5
Gumm	4.3	5.1	5.9	6.2	8.1	9.4	11.1	12.3	10.2	9.6	7.2	6.1	95.5	7.9
Kane	6.3	8.5	11.6	17.8	19.5	20.7	21.9	22.8	20.1	18.6	9.7	5.5	183.1	15.2
McArthur	9.4	7.4	10.8	13.4	16.1	17.4	24.0	25.8	20.3	13.0	11.2	10.0	178.8	14.8
Parcell	10.6	12.6	13.8	15.3	18.9	20.4	23.1	24.7	20.4	17.6	16.3	12.2	205.8	17.1
Ruff	5.1	6.4	7.1	8.3	9.5	11.9	13.6	14.5	12.7	11.6	10.3	9.4	120.4	10.0

*Coughlin left the agency in August 2013.

Exhibit 5

Ski Cabin

PROBLEM 5

State v. Benjamin

(Mark Warden) (Alan Benjamin)

Alan "Al" Benjamin, age fifty-five, of 30 Hillside Lane, Nita City, who is a local pawnbroker, has been charged with receiving stolen property. To convict Benjamin the State must show that Benjamin had:

(1) actual control of the property;

(2) that the property belonged to another;

(3) that the property was stolen; and

(4) that Benjamin either knew or should have known that the property was stolen.

[handwritten: ELEMENTS]

He was arrested on December 14, 2016, at his place of business, Al's Pawnshop in nearby Middlebury, Nita. Seized at the time of the arrest were several items, including an engagement ring and wedding band set later identified as belonging to Kathy Strickland.

Strickland will testify, and has done so at the preliminary hearing in this case, that her diamond engagement ring and wedding band were stolen from her home on November 27, 2016, while she was out on a fourteen-mile run, training for the Boston Marathon. At the preliminary hearing, she identified the two items, State's Exhibits 1 and 2, as being her jewelry. The investigating and arresting officer in the case is Detective Sam Fletcher. He will testify that he went to the Strickland residence on November 27, after being called by the patrol officers who responded to Strickland's 911 call.

Fletcher found that the sliding glass doors facing the patio at the rear of the residence showed signs of forced entry. He took fingerprints. Later comparison with known prints of Mark Warden showed that those latent prints were a clean match, with more than the required minimum number of points of comparison. Warden, fortuitously, had been caught during a residential break-in in a nearby neighborhood on November 29, 2016. When Warden's apartment was searched, property from more than seven robberies was recovered, among them several items taken from the Strickland residence. During questioning, Warden stated that Mrs. Strickland's wedding band and engagement ring had been sold to the defendant, Benjamin.

[handwritten: FINGERPRINT MATCH]

[handwritten: SOLD TO BENJAMIN]

At the time of his arrest and the search of his house, the Nita police believe that someone other than Warden ran a gang responsible for the robberies. For years they suspected that Benjamin, a pawnbroker in Middlebury, Nita, was running such a ring. Middlebury is about fifteen miles from Nita City. Every time they located stolen merchandise at Benjamin's business, it increased their suspicions. However, he always had a plausible reason for claiming the goods were not stolen and could not successfully be prosecuted. In addition, an attempt to fence stolen goods to Benjamin in a sting operation had failed when Benjamin refused to believe the seller that the goods were not hot.

In an effort to obtain Warden's cooperation against Benjamin, Detective Fletcher and Assistant District Attorney Jane Devon went to see Warden and his attorney, Mike Grayson, at the jail on December 2. Devon's proposal was simple—he told Warden that if he had truthful information and gave testimony against Benjamin that led to his arrest and prosecution, he could plead to one count of felony breaking and entering an unoccupied dwelling. That charge carries a presumptive sentence of three years. His alternative, if he did not cooperate, was seven counts of felony breaking and entering, carrying a presumptive sentence, if convicted, in excess of twenty years.

After consulting with his lawyer, Warden agreed to cooperate and provided the following statement.

PLEA DEAL

CROSS
- impeach w/ other motive
- pretty bad alternative

FRE 410
- bars use of statements in plea negotiations
- Fairness Exception: if open the door

STATEMENT OF MARK WARDEN

12/2/2016

I am Mark Warden. I'm thirty-two years old. After I graduated from high school, I was in the Army for about eight months until I got a dishonorable discharge for drugs. After that I've knocked around and never had any one job for too long. For the past couple of years, I've been a pretty heavy user of methamphetamine.

Hitting houses has been how I got the money for my drugs. I picked nice neighborhoods where people have good stuff, but not the kind of stuff that you protect with those expensive alarms that automatically call the police. I always stayed away from houses with alarms or dogs.

I did the seven houses you asked me about. I tried to steal mainly stuff I could easily move—jewelry, cash, and silver. I stayed away from the big things like TVs. Cash I used for drugs. Jewelry and silver I had to fence. I used a lot of different people, but when I was desperate for money, I went over to Al's Pawnshop in Middlebury. He didn't pay me as well as the other fences. He always asked where I got the stuff, but didn't seem to care what my answer was. Other pawnshops paid better, but they were much further away.

I know you want me to say that Al Benjamin was the guy who put me up to these break-ins from the questions you've asked, but he wasn't. I did them myself and for myself. He bought a lot of stuff from me and maybe he knew the stuff was hot, but he never asked me to steal nothing. He never turned me down either. He was always ready to take my stuff, but at his price.

I took the two rings you showed me to Al's Pawnshop the day after I hit that house—the one where the lady went out running every day and was gone for hours. I figure the diamond was better than a carat and that both rings were platinum. When I came in, Al had me wait until there were no other customers in the store. When he saw the rings, he asked me where I got them, and I told him I won them in a card game. That seemed to satisfy him. He got out the thing he sticks in his eye and looked at the ring for the better part of a minute. When he looked up, he said the stone had flaws and the most he could give me for the two rings was $450. I told him he was ripping me off and that they were worth thousands, but I needed the money for drugs and took his deal. Two days later I went to Al's to sell some stuff I had from another job. I saw that he had the rings he bought from me for $450, priced at $5,800. I took my business to another shop. I haven't been back since.

I have read this statement and I swear that it is true.

|Signed|

Mark Warden

12/2/2016

GRAND JURY TESTIMONY OF ALAN BENJAMIN

After being duly sworn to tell the truth, the witness testified to the following:

My name is Alan Benjamin, and I live at 30 Hillside Lane in Nita City. I am fifty-five years old, married to Gloria, my wife of twenty-five years. We have two grown children—Alan, Jr., who is twenty-four, and Mary, who is twenty-two. I operate a number of pawnshops and check-cashing establishments in and around Nita City. There are ten stores in all. It is a good business, but sometimes, unfortunately, you get dragged into accusations such as this. I have been arrested before on charges of receiving stolen property and always been acquitted. I have no criminal convictions. I have waived my Fifth Amendment rights to testify here today against the advice of counsel. I want to clear this whole thing up as soon and as easily as possible and get the police off my back.

I do own an establishment at 145 Clairmont Street in Middlebury, Nita, which is about fifteen miles from Nita City. The name of the establishment is Al's Pawnshop. I also run a check-cashing business out of that same location. I run a legitimate business. I have never purchased property from anyone when I even thought that it might be stolen. Owners of pawnshops are the constant target of the police, and accusations such as the current one against me are bad for business and expensive to defend, what with the cost of lawyers and the time missed from my businesses. It's just not worth it to take risks about what you're buying.

I recognize the photo you have shown me of Mark Warden. I admit that I bought some jewelry from him on one occasion sometime in late November or early December of 2016. It might have been an engagement ring and wedding band—I think it was some ladies jewelry, I just don't remember. To my knowledge I never did any other business with him.

[handwritten margin note: only remembers this one instance?]

Warden may have done other business at my Middlebury store, I don't know. I don't usually work there, but my manager was ill and needed some surgery after Thanksgiving in 2016, and I ended up working that store for a couple of weeks until he could return.

I don't recall anything specific about my transaction with Warden other than it was some jewelry that he brought in and that he said he had won gambling. I do recall that he was a little disheveled and looked like he might be strung out on drugs, but you see all kinds of people in my business who are down and out on their luck. That's why they come to a pawnshop. I don't know what I paid Warden for the jewelry, but I'm sure I tried to get as good a deal as I could. It was his option to take the price I offered, try to negotiate, or go someplace else. From looking at him and hearing his story, I didn't figure him to be an expert on jewelry.

Did I take advantage of him? Maybe, but like I said, it was his choice. Do I normally sell items I purchase for over ten times the purchase price? Sure, if I can. It's a business, not a charity. Lots of the items I purchase go unsold for a long time, and just because I try to make a big profit doesn't mean I will. I'm always marking down my prices when things aren't moving the way they should.

No, I never do anything but the most perfunctory check of the people who sell me items. I always ask where they got the items, and so long as their stories seem reasonable, I'll try to make a good purchase.

I've been in this business a long time, over thirty years, and I never purchased an item I believed to be stolen. Some may have been stolen, like Mrs. Stickland's rings, but I'm really a victim in all this. I gave Warden good money for those rings, and now I don't have the money or the rings.

I have nothing further to add. I hope this clears these unfounded accusations up.

End of transcript.

The case is now at trial. The State has presented its first two witnesses, Kathy Strickland and Detective Fletcher. The next witness for the State is Mark Warden.

The defendant is the last witness in the case.

Part A

For the State, conduct a direct examination of Mark Warden.

For the defendant, conduct a cross-examination of Mark Warden.

For the State, conduct any necessary redirect examination.

Part B

For the defendant, conduct a direct examination of Alan Benjamin.

For the State, conduct a cross-examination of Alan Benjamin.

PROBLEM 6

State v. Carroll

(Paul O'Rourke) (Amanda Jones)

Evelyn Carroll is charged with theft of confidential information in violation of Nita Criminal Statutes 18 Nita Code § 794. Carroll is an employee of Pear Electronics, an emerging producer of microchip technology in Silicon Valley, Nita. She was arrested as part of an ongoing investigation by the Nita Bureau of Investigation (NBI) into a series of thefts of microchip designs from Pear and other chip makers. Paul O'Rourke, a Special Agent for the NBI, had been working on the investigation for several months before Carroll's arrest. He has been a Special Agent since graduating from the Nita University School of Law in 2008. He has specialized in the investigation of industrial espionage cases and has taken numerous courses in advanced surveillance techniques. As a result of the investigation, O'Rourke had identified George Moore as the prime suspect in the thefts. Moore was known by O'Rourke for several years as a reputed broker of stolen electronic technology. It was believed that Moore had systematically recruited mid-level employees at numerous companies in Nita's Silicon Valley who, in turn, provided him with stolen technology. O'Rourke's report follows.

REPORT

November 14, 2016: Pursuant to court approved interception of George Moore's home telephone (see transcript attached) learned that within the next three days a prototype of Pear Electronic's new "Platinum" chip would be passed from a Pear employee, identity unknown, to George Moore. Drop was to be made at an ATM[1] next to the Cove Bar & Grill at 1201 Front Street in Nita City.

November 15, 2016: Set up surveillance with Special Agent Richard Robinson outside Cove Bar. Robinson took 8:00 a.m. to 8:00 p.m. shift. I was on surveillance from 8:00 p.m. to 8:00 a.m. Position taken up in unmarked vehicle some sixty feet from drop. Vehicle parked facing south on the west side of Front Street. Inspected ATM for anything unusual. ATM found clean. No unusual activity observed on this shift.

November 16, 2016: Surveillance continues. No unusual activity observed.

November 17, 2016: Surveillance continues. No unusual activity on Robinson's shift. At 8:00 p.m., I resume surveillance after checking the ATM, which is still clean. At 2:00 a.m. on 11/18 subject sighted. Subject approaches from north of

---

1. At some point prior to the transaction, the ATM surveillance camera had been spray-painted over so that no image from it is obtainable.

the ATM, walks up, looks around furtively, places small container in envelope compartment of the ATM, turns and proceeds north in direction of approach. Subject is female, 5'5", approximately 125 lbs., wearing tan trench coat.

Surveillance continues. At 2:10 a.m. Moore arrives in black, late model domestic sedan, parks in front of drop, walks up to the ATM. As Moore leaves the ATM, he is apprehended and searched. Recovered a small metal container containing microchip with Pear logo. The item seized was in the lining of raincoat.

November 18, 2016: Attempted to interview Moore, but he insisted on counsel and refused to sign waiver. Proceeded to Pear Electronics. Spoke with head of security, Stephen Ketaineck. Informed he had a suspect. I was shown a photograph of subject. I made positive ID of woman who made drop. Located and arrested Carroll. After full explanation of her rights, she knowingly waived the same and submitted to an interview by this special agent. She denied taking anything from Pear and denied ever being at the ATM on Front Street. Suspect claims she was home with her sleeping child at time drop was made.

[*Signed*]

Paul O'Rourke, SA
Nov. 18, 2016

During his investigation O'Rourke believed that George Moore had systematically recruited midlevel employees at numerous companies in Nita's Silicon Valley, who, in turn, provided him with stolen technology.

The following is a statement from a friend and coworker of the defendant, by the name of Amanda Jones.

STATEMENT OF AMANDA JONES

My name is Amanda Jones. I am a thirty-five-year-old single mother of my son Jimmy. I work for Pear Electronics, and I have for four years. I was under investigation for stealing confidential information and then giving it to a man by the name of George Moore. I do not know George Moore. No formal charges were ever made against me, so I assume they realized I had nothing to do with stealing anything from Pear.

Evelyn Carroll also works at Pear Electronics, and she has worked there for three years. She came to the company directly out of school where she got her associates degree in computer technology. To the best of my knowledge, she did not have any previous employment in the field of technology. Pear Electronics has been her one and only job in this field.

Evelyn and I are both single mothers and have developed a friendship throughout the time that she has been working at Pear Electronics. Because of family and work obligations, neither of us has a lot of spare time. However, the free time that we do have we tend to spend together. We spend our workdays together, and when we can, we share a babysitter and go out socially. We talk both about work and about personal situations that arise in our everyday lives. We are each other's confidants. I know that recently Evelyn has been concerned about her finances because her son's father was behind on his support payments.

Pear Electronics is a large company that employs over 300 employees. There are many female employees that work at Pear Electronics. I'm sure many of them had access to the chip that was stolen.

On the evening of November 17, 2016, Evelyn and I got a sitter and went out to a couple of clubs. Given Amanda's money situation, it was my treat, but as it turned out there were a couple of guys who bought us drinks, so it really didn't cost much. I brought my son Jimmy to her home where the sitter was and left him there. We then went out to a club and danced some. Evelyn had several drinks as I was the designated driver. I know she said she was very tired when I dropped her off and picked up my son at 11:30 p.m. No, I didn't see or talk to her after that until the next morning. I then drove the sitter home and was at my apartment at about 12:15 a.m. I did see Evelyn the next morning at work. We chatted about our evening out. She did not appear unusual in any way, although she seemed a little groggy. I kidded her about having too much to drink.

I heard from Evelyn the night of November 18, and she told me she had been arrested for stealing a computer chip. She told me they said she dropped the chip on Front Street at about 2:00 a.m. on November 18, 2016. That's impossible; she was home with her son. I'm sure she never stole anything. She's not that kind of person. You have just informed me that she was previously arrested and convicted for a misdemeanor of passing a bad check in 2011, but that doesn't change my opinion of her. I have no reason to think that she would do anything dishonest now.

Amanda Jones read and signed the deposition, making no corrections.

* * *

Attached to this problem is a diagram of the waterfront area where the surveillance occurred. Assume that this is a part of O'Rourke's report and was drawn by him.

Moore has refused to testify, and his case has been severed. Carroll has pleaded not guilty, and her case is going to trial first. Assume that the trial judge has ruled the wiretap of Moore is admissible. Assume further that the metal container and the Pear computer chip are also admissible.

The case is now at trial. The State calls Special Agent O'Rourke as its first witness. The first witness for the defendant is Amanda Jones.

Part A

For the State, conduct a direct examination of Special Agent O'Rourke.

For the defendant, conduct a cross examination of Special Agent O'Rourke.

For the State, conduct any necessary redirect examination.

Part B

For the defendant, conduct a direct examination of Amanda Jones.

For the State, conduct a cross-examination of Amanda Jones.

WIRETAP TRANSCRIPT
Subject: George Moore
Location: Moore residence, 38 Brighton Road, Nita City
Date: November 14, 2016
Time: 8:00 p.m.

Moore:	Hello.
Unknown:	George?
Moore:	Yeah.
Unknown:	Do you have a line on the Pear chip yet?
Moore:	Yeah.
Unknown:	When's it comin' in?
Moore:	Two, three days max.
Unknown:	Are you using the same drop?
Moore:	What's it to you?
Unknown:	We really need this chip, and I don't want you and your guy getting caught.
Moore:	Front Street, near the Cove has worked for the last six months. It will work this time, too. You worry about the money; I'll worry about the chip.
Unknown:	You're the boss. I'll be in touch.

End of transmission.

Exhibit 1

Front Street and Four Buildings

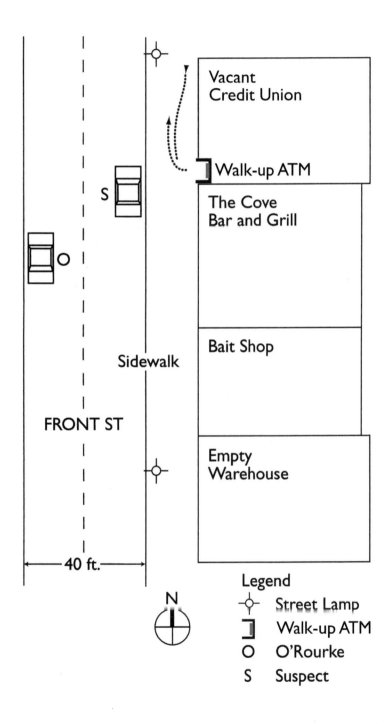

Problem 7

Manning v. Carleton

(Melvin Carleton) (Doris Manning)

On May 5, 2016, Melvin Carleton, a graduate student in social work at Nita University, was at home studying for final examinations. Carleton lives in Apartment 2A of the Coventry Court Apartments in Nita City. On the evening of May 5, and the early morning hours of May 6, Carleton claims that he heard a child being beaten in Apartment 2C, which at that time was occupied by Ms. Doris Manning and her four-year-old son, Robby. Carleton reported the alleged child beating to his landlord, Bruce Hill, telling him that Manning was a drunk and that she was beating her son. As a result, Manning was evicted from her apartment. Manning has sued Carleton for slander, claiming in excess of $50,000 in damages. Carleton defends, saying that his statement was true.

The following are the relevant excerpts of the deposition of Melvin Carleton and Doris Manning.

Deposition of Melvin Carleton

My name is Melvin Carleton. I am twenty-three years old and live at the Coventry Court Apartments, Apartment 2A, in Nita City. I am a second-year graduate student at the University of Nita School of Social Work. In May of 2016, I was just completing my first year of a two-year program leading to a master's degree in social work.

I first met the plaintiff, Doris Manning, when I moved into the Coventry Court Apartments in September of 2015. She and her son Robby, who was four years old in the spring of 2016, lived in Apartment 2C. The diagram you showed me, which is marked as Exhibit 1, shows my apartment and the Manning apartment. It also shows Apartment 2B, which is an efficiency apartment that's been vacant the whole time I've lived in the complex.

Robby Manning was the only small child who lived in Building 2 in the apartment complex. I noticed Ms. Manning and her son around the apartment complex from time to time and usually spoke with her casually when we met. I didn't think much about it at the time, but several times I saw Robby with a band-aid on his face, a bruise, or some kind of relatively minor facial injury. I remember once he had a black eye, and when I kidded him about it, Ms. Manning was quick to volunteer that Robby had run into the corner of the kitchen table. He also frequently had bruises and scrapes on his legs and arms. I don't want to overstate his injuries because at the time I put them off to his being an active boy who was a little careless, but I now believe there were other, more serious problems.

In the late winter of 2015, my friendly relationship with Ms. Manning changed. At that time, she began dating a man named Billy Parrish. At first he and I were cordial, saying hello as he came or went from Ms. Manning's apartment, but problems developed from two sources.

First, Parrish would often park in my assigned parking space. Because parking was at a premium at the Coventry Court Apartments, this was a problem for me, especially when I had groceries to bring up to the apartment. I spoke to him about the problem, and he promised to be more considerate, but from time to time he would park in my space. Second, once Parrish was on the scene, he and Ms. Manning would stay up late, drinking and playing loud music. I complained to them several times over the phone, and they would tone it down a little each time, but the same thing happened over and over again and, quite frankly, disturbed my studying. In fact, I complained to the landlord, Bruce Hill, several times about the noise, and each time it seemed to help for a while, but in the end, nothing helped.

On May 5, 2016, I was in my apartment studying for final exams at my kitchen table. I looked out the window at about 9:00 p.m. and saw Parrish walking on the walkway carrying a bag that looked, from the size and shape, like it contained a couple of liquor bottles. I called out the window to him to try and keep it down that night because I was studying for an exam, but he ignored me.

At about 11:00 p.m. the noise from 2C became distracting. I could hear Ms. Manning and Parrish laughing and talking louder and louder. I could see them drinking and dancing in the kitchen and could hear the stereo as it got louder as time went on. I called Ms. Manning to complain, and she told me to "lighten up," but she did turn down the stereo. I could still hear them laughing and talking, but when I concentrated, it didn't hurt my studying.

At about 12:30 a.m., I decided to get some sleep. I had just fallen asleep when I was awakened by loud music coming from 2C. It was then that I also heard a whacking sound and a child crying. I knew it had to be Robby Manning, because he was the only kid in my building. This really disturbed me because my fieldwork for that semester was with the Child Abuse Project for the Department of Social Services in Branford, Nita, which is the next town over from Nita City. Robby stopped crying in a few minutes, but I remember thinking about all his cuts and bruises. I was able to put it out of my mind when the crying stopped so quickly, and I went back to sleep.

A little later, I was again awakened. My watch showed it to be 2:30 a.m. This time I could hear raised voices that sounded like Ms. Manning and Parrish, then the whacking sound and Robby screaming and crying. This went on for another hour. I thought about calling the police, but knew from my field placement that there was little the police could do. At that time I went into the living room and went to sleep on the couch.

The next morning I got up early because I had an exam. While I was sitting in the kitchen watching the *Today* show, I noticed Ms. Manning taking out some garbage. Both liquor bottles I saw going in with Parrish were going out, and they were both empty. I took my exam in Social Welfare Policy later that morning. Because I was so tired, I could tell that I wasn't doing well in the exam. As it turned out I got a "C" on the exam, which was by far the lowest grade I ever received in any school. I graduated from college with a 3.6 GPA and my GPA at social work school was 3.4 for the first year, even with the "C." My next lowest grade was one "B," and every other grade was "B" or better.

When I got home, I went to Bruce Hill's office and told him about the night before. I remember saying, "It was bad enough when Ms. Manning and Parrish were just noisy and drunk all the time, but now she's beating her kid. You've got to do something about it." I guess Hill had enough as well, because Ms. Manning was evicted from her apartment at the end of that month.

Carleton read and signed his deposition without making any corrections.

Deposition of Doris Manning

My name is Doris Manning. I am thirty-two years old, the single mother of my son Robby who is now six years old. I live at 213 Harding Street in Nita City. Until June of 2016, we lived at the Coventry Court Apartments, Apartment 2C. I work as a teacher's aide at Nita Central Elementary School, where Robby is in the first grade.

I first met the defendant, Melvin Carleton, in September of 2015 when he moved into the Coventry Court Apartments. He moved in Apartment 2A, which was one apartment away from ours on the second floor of the two-story apartment building. Apartment 2B was vacant at that time. I have looked at the diagram of the apartment complex (Exhibit 1), and it accurately shows the layout of our building and the relative position of the apartments.

Carleton seemed nice enough when I met him, but a little bookish and immature. At first I got the feeling that he was interested in me, but he was really not my type. No, he never actually asked me out, but when you're my age, you know when someone is interested. In the same way, I made it clear to him that I wasn't interested in dating him. He was also about ten years younger than me, and I am attracted to more mature men. As I said, Carleton was friendly and would stop and chat with me whenever we ran into each other around the complex. He was also nice to Robby and would chitchat with him.

I found out that Carleton was a social work student of some sort at Nita University and he was a very serious student. He seemed to be studying all the time. Whenever I'd go by his apartment on the way to mine, I would pass by his kitchen window, and he always seemed to be sitting at his kitchen table (which was right next to the window) with books and papers all over the place. For the first three or four months I would describe our relationship as cordial. That all changed when I started dating a gentleman by the name of Bill Parrish.

Carleton really didn't like Bill, and I'd say the feeling was mutual. Carleton was hostile towards Bill from the first time I introduced them to each other. Bill's response was to ignore Carleton. Frankly, he thought Carleton was sort of a nerd and pretty weird. As a result, the two hardly spoke at all.

The real problems between Carleton and Bill arose when Bill parked his car in Carleton's space (Bill had bought me a stereo and was carrying it upstairs so it was easiest to park in the space nearest the stairs), and Carleton got really pissy about it. It was his space, and he did pay for it as part of his rent, but the space for 2B was almost always available because nobody lived in that apartment. The two of them had several arguments about the parking space, and that was just the beginning.

The problems got worse over the stereo. Bill and I like to play our music on the loud side. When I could get a sitter, we'd go out dancing, but because it was hard to find someone to watch Robby, most of the time we'd play music and dance at my apartment. Yes, we did have an alcoholic drink from time to time, but never more than one or two. I would usually have work in the morning, and Bill would have to drive home, so we never got what I would call drunk. More times than not, when we were playing music and dancing Carleton would call and ask us to turn the music down. If it was late (after 10:00 p.m.) or on a weekday, we'd usually turn the stereo down when he complained, but on weekend nights (Friday and Saturday) I felt that I had just as much right to enjoy and use my apartment as Carleton did his, and I'd play the stereo on the loud side and up until about 11:00 p.m. When Carleton complained over the phone on the weekends (he never came in person although I caught him looking into my kitchen window from outside his apartment several times), either Bill or I would tell him to lighten up and not bother us.

I know Carleton complained about the noise to Bruce Hill, the apartment manager, several times. Hill came by and talked to me about the stereo and told me that he had gotten several complaints. I assume it was Carleton because no one else ever complained. At any rate, I promised Hill to try and keep it down during the week, but he agreed with me that I could have people over and enjoy myself on weekend nights.

By the late spring there was a lot of tension between Bill and Carleton, especially as exams approached. I think it was all made worse by the fact that Bill and I weren't getting along very well, and it was clear to me that we were heading for a breakup. It seemed that Carleton or Bill were always trading nasty comments when they came across each other.

I know that Carleton accused me of beating Robby. That's just plain crazy. I'll admit that I've spanked his bottom from time to time, but never with anything other than my hand and always through his clothes. If this happened more than twice or three times in any month, I'd be surprised. Robby has had his falls and bumps and bruises over the years. He was not very athletic as a toddler. But I don't think that he was much more prone to hurting himself than lots of other boys. He did get a black eye once when he ran into the corner of our kitchen counter when he wasn't looking where he was going, but only that one time. I've never had to take him to the hospital for an injury of any kind. No, he's never had any stitches either.

I know what Carleton said I was doing to Robby on the night of May 5. There is absolutely no truth to his claim that I was hurting my son. No, Bill never laid a hand on him, either. In fact, I wouldn't let Bill discipline Robby at all. That was one of the issues between us.

I will admit that on that night Bill and I were playing music and dancing and the music got a little loud. We may have had a drink or two—I can't remember. Carleton did call and complain saying that he was studying for an exam, and although I may have made a smart comment to him, I did turn down the music. I remember that Bill got upset when I turned the music down because he wanted to continue to enjoy himself. Actually, because the music was down or off, it gave us a chance to talk out our differences in the relationship. That was the night that we eventually broke up.

I know that Carleton claims that he heard a whacking sound and Robby crying about 12:30 a.m. There was no whacking in my apartment, but Robby did wake up with a nightmare, and he was crying. He had watched some DVD that scared him, but I was able to calm him down in a couple of minutes, and he went back to sleep. Bill and I then went back to our conversation that went on for quite a while and got pretty emotional. It was a couple of hours later when we were really into it, and I guess our voices were raised, because it woke up Robby and scared him all over again and he was crying. Bill got upset that I left in the middle of our argument and shouted after me, and I told him, in no uncertain terms, to back off. As I said, that was the end of my relationship with Bill. I haven't seen him since. Anyhow, that's what Carleton probably heard.

The next day, Hill came to me and told me about Carleton's accusations. Hill was really worried about the cops being called. I think he actually believed Carleton. He asked me if I could leave by the end of the month, but made it clear that he wanted me out. I didn't want a fight, so I started to look for another place to live. At first I had trouble getting a place when I gave them my Coventry Court address and Hill as a reference. Things would look good, and then I'd get a call saying the apartment wasn't available. One manager told me that Hill had told him about Carleton's complaints and that he couldn't rent to me under those circumstances, that the apartment complex was a quiet one where people had to get up early. As it turned out, I was able to rent the little house we live in now when I told them I was moving out of my parent's home and gave them as a reference. It's a better place for Robby because there are other kids in the neighborhood and there's a yard for him to play in.

Carleton's accusations are a complete lie. I would never hurt Robby. He's the most important thing in my life. I don't know why Carleton did this to me, but he did, and I think he shouldn't be able to get away with it.

Manning read the deposition and signed it without correction.

The case is now at trial. The first witness for the defendant is Melvin Carleton.

Part A

For the plaintiff, conduct a direct examination of Doris Manning.

For the defendant, conduct a cross-examination of Doris Manning.

Part B

For the defendant, conduct the direct examination of Melvin Carleton.

For the plaintiff, conduct the cross-examination of Melvin Carleton.

Exhibit 1

Apartment Complex

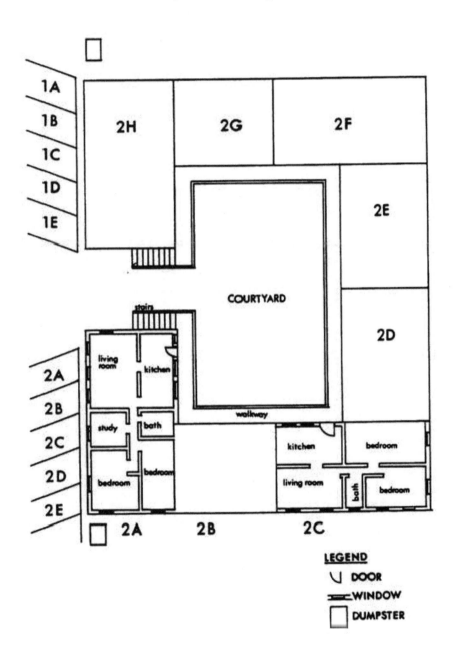

Problem 8

NitaSport, Inc. v. Nita Slugger Corp.

(Thomas Devine) (Paula Blanchard)

NitaSport, Inc., the plaintiff, is a chain of seventeen discount sporting goods stores owned and operated by Tom Devine. One of their suppliers is the defendant, baseball bat manufacturer Nita Slugger Corp., run by Paula Blanchard. This case involves a claim by NitaSport that Nita Slugger failed to fill an order for baseball bats and that NitaSport suffered losses when it had to buy more expensive replacement goods elsewhere.

The following are the relevant excerpts from the depositions of Paula Blanchard and Tom Devine in the case of *NitaSport, Inc. v. Nita Slugger Corp.*

Deposition of Paula Blanchard

My name is Paula Blanchard. I am forty years old. I live in Nita City. I am the president of Nita Slugger Corporation. I have been the president of this company for five years. The company supplies bats and other baseball equipment to retailers.

I met Thomas Devine in Fort Lauderdale. I was attending spring training for Nita's major league baseball team, the Nats. It was March of 2015. Mr. Devine and I met while we were in line to check out of our hotel in Florida. I do not remember how we began talking, but we soon realized that there was the potential for us to do business together.

When I returned from Florida, I called Mr. Devine and offered to sell him a new line of bats. The offer was for ten gross at $1,836 per gross. The total was $18,360, plus the cost of shipping. I explained to him that the offer would stay open for thirty days and that Mr. Devine could accept within that time either in writing or over the telephone. I also told him that if he accepted, I would need 10 percent of the money within ten days and upon receipt of the money I would start to ship the order. The shipping costs and the rest of the payment for the order were due within thirty days of Mr. Devine's receipt of the bats. Mr. Devine called me and left a message with my secretary. I called him back, and he told me that he wanted to go through with the previously mentioned deal. After I received the check for 10 percent, I began fulfilling the order. I sent the order through UPS immediately. Everything went smoothly with this deal.

Because the deal went well and Mr. Devine seemed like an honest businessman, I sent him a letter offering to sell him more bats. Because the demand for bats was higher, I quoted him a price 5 percent over the price of the first deal. Shortly after, on January 6, I received a phone call from Mr. Devine. We negotiated and went back and forth over the price for a little bit. Finally, I decided that in order to keep Mr. Devine's business I would allow him to order the bats at the 2015 price, but told him that the same rules applied as the first order, that he needed to notify me within thirty days and a 10 percent deposit was due before I would begin shipping. He said that he would contact me if he wanted to go along with the order. That was the last time that I heard from or spoke to Mr. Devine within the previously mentioned thirty-day window. I assumed that he did not want to go through with the order, and in my mind the deal was off.

I never got a voice mail message from Mr. Devine on January 25 stating that he wanted to make the deal. My secretary, who is very diligent and takes her responsibility seriously, gets my voice mail messages for me and writes them down on a yellow legal pad. She places the pad on my desk, and I return all of my phone calls from the legal pad. There was never a message that Mr. Devine called me since the phone call that I told you about. I have never had a customer or any other person that I do business with complain that I did not return their telephone calls. I was expecting Mr. Devine's call because I thought that he was going to go through with the order, but I never received that call. As far as I know, the voice mail system has never lost my messages. In my business, customer relations are very important, therefore, I take the task of returning my calls very seriously.

I also never received a letter from Mr. Devine. My secretary also gets my mail and leaves it on my desk for me. I never saw a letter confirming the order from Mr. Devine. Whenever I get a letter from a customer of mine, I give the letter to my secretary to make a copy and put it in the customer's file. I have no such letter from Mr. Devine accepting my offer.

I did, however, receive a check and a letter dated February 15, 2016. The check was for the previously discussed 10 percent, and the letter was confirming the order. The check and the letter surprised me because it was past the thirty-day deadline that Mr. Devine and I had discussed. Since the offer was no longer on the table, I returned the check to him via regular mail. Also, the warehouse of one of my main competitors burnt down, and I could sell my bats for more money. Since the thirty days had lapsed, I knew that I could sell these bats at a higher rate. I would have honored the contract with Mr. Devine, but he did not fulfill the obligations that the contract was contingent upon.

I am aware that Mr. Devine's company was being audited, and the rumor around town is that his business is not doing so well. He needs the bats as cheaply as possible, and he is falsely accusing me of ruining our deal.

[*Signed*]

Paula Blanchard

Deposition of Tom Devine

My name is Thomas Devine. People call me Tom. I am forty-four years old and live in Nita City. My wife Kathy and I founded NitaSport, originally called Nita Sports Authority, in 1997. After the business took off, Kathy realized her lifelong ambition in 2003 and went to law school. I've been running the business ever since. Kathy works as a lawyer in the Nita City Public Defender's Office.

I first met Paula Blanchard of Nita Slugger Corporation in March of 2015 in Fort Lauderdale, Florida, where we were both attending spring training for the Nita Nats. The Nats are Nita's major league baseball team. Our meeting was a chance encounter while we both were in line waiting to check out of our hotel. I remember Blanchard started the conversation by complaining about how slowly the checkout line was moving. Before long, we were talking about our respective businesses, and I realized that she was a potential supplier of baseball bats for our stores.

About a week after I returned to Nita, on March 20, 2015, I had a call from Blanchard reminding me how we had met in the checkout line and telling me she had a new line of bats coming out. She offered to sell me ten gross of the new bats at $1,836 per gross for a total of $18,360 plus shipping. She explained in the phone conversation that the price was good for thirty days and that I could call or write any time within that period to accept. Once I accepted, she said I had to have a 10 percent deposit to her within ten days, and then she would begin shipping the order. She also said that the other 90 percent of the purchase price plus the shipping costs were due within thirty days of our receipt of the shipment.

After I spoke with Blanchard I called around to several of our stores and talked with our managers. The consensus of the managers was that Nita Slugger made excellent bats and their new product would be a big seller. After these conversations, I decided to place an order with Blanchard. On March 25, 2015, I dialed her number (which I had jotted down during our first phone conversation) and asked for Blanchard. The secretary told me she was out. I had a choice between voice mail and leaving a message with her secretary. I left a message with the secretary asking Blanchard to call me back.

When Blanchard called back later that day, I told her we wanted ten gross of bats shipped immediately via UPS to our warehouse and told her our check for the deposit would be sent out that day. I remember getting a check from the bookkeeper and mailing it to the address Blanchard gave me during that conversation. She must have received my check because the bats arrived within a week. They sold well, and we paid for them within thirty days.

I planned to buy more bats from Blanchard in 2016, but before I got around to making the order, I got a letter from Blanchard offering to sell me some more baseball bats. Exhibit 1 is the letter I got from Blanchard. The price quoted for the bats was higher than the previous year, so I gave Blanchard a call.

I called Blanchard on January 6, the day I got her letter. After some small talk, Blanchard asked if I got her letter, and I told her I had. I said I was interested in buying some more of her bats, but wanted to discuss the price. Blanchard's initial proposal was 5 percent over the 2015 price. I countered saying that American Bat, Blanchard's biggest competitor, was willing to sell a comparable bat for less than Blanchard's 2015 price. Actually, I had never spoken to American Bat and was just bluffing, guessing that Blanchard's 5 percent increase was soft. Blanchard responded by saying that even if American Bat's price was less, Nita Slugger's "major league" product was a substantially better bat. After some back and forth, Blanchard said that to keep our business, she would hold the price at the 2015 level if we bought twelve gross of their bats. As with the first order, Blanchard said the price was good for thirty days and required a 10 percent deposit before shipment started. Not wanting to appear too eager and because we had a cash flow problem at the time, I did not order the bats during this conversation.

I called Blanchard's office on January 25, 2016, to accept the offer for twelve gross for a total price of $22,032. After being told that Blanchard was out, I left a message on her voice mail. My message was something like "Paula, this is Tom. We'll take twelve gross at last year's price. We're going through an audit right now, so it will take two to three weeks for our check for $2,203 to reach you." The voice-mail machine was making some funny noises, so I wasn't confident that my message got taken down. Rather than calling again and leaving a message with her secretary, I decided to write her a letter to confirm my order. Exhibit 2 is a copy of that letter. I typed the letter myself on my computer, and printed out a copy of the letter for our files when the original was mailed, either on January 25 or 26. Exhibit 2 shows the address that I mailed the letter to. My mail is sent out twice a day by my secretary, who drops letters in the mailbox outside our offices when he goes to lunch and in the afternoon on his way home. Exhibit 3 is a copy of my outgoing phone log for January 25. The third entry shows my call to Blanchard.

During the second week in February of 2016, I read in the *Nita Journal* that American Bats' plant and warehouse had been destroyed by fire. Although I was sorry for them, I remember being glad that I had ordered from Nita Slugger at the price we agreed on. As American Bats was a major player in the industry, I was sure that the price for bats would sky-rocket.

As promised, I sent Blanchard my check three weeks after the phone call and letter, on February 15. Exhibit 4 is the letter that I sent to Blanchard along with the check. After she got my check, Blanchard called and said since I had not accepted her offer within thirty days, she would not honor our order. She said that American Bats' plant and warehouse had burned to the ground, as I already knew, and that bats had nearly doubled in price. I told her that I had left a voice mail, and it was her problem if she hadn't gotten it. I also told her that I sent her the letter as a backup. She denied receiving either the phone message or my letter. I remember being outraged by her attempt to up the price. I told her in no uncertain terms that I expected better treatment and would take my business elsewhere. Eventually we found another supplier, Power Bats. However, because of the shortage, we had to pay them $3,125 per gross, a total of $37,500. Our loss was the difference of $15,468 between the amount we were to pay Nita Slugger for the bats and the amount we had to pay Power Bats.

Devine read and signed his deposition making no corrections.

* * *

In her deposition, Blanchard claimed she never got the voice mail message and that she would have remembered it if she had. She also said the voice mail system has never lost a message that she was aware of, and that she doesn't believe Devine ever called. She also denies ever receiving Devine's letter. She opined that she thought Devine got caught up short after American Bats manufacturing plant burned to the ground and was trying to salvage a bad situation at her expense. Blanchard acknowledges getting a $2,203 check from NitaSport on February 18, 2016 along with a letter from Devine (*see* Exhibit 4). The check surprised her, she says, because she assumed since she had not heard back from Devine that he had decided not to go ahead with the order. She returned the check to Devine.

Devine has filed suit against Blanchard for breach of contract seeking $15,468, plus interest, in damages. The case is now at trial. The plaintiff calls Tom Devine as its first witness.

For the plaintiff, conduct a direct examination of Tom Devine; assume that all of the exhibits have been stipulated to be admissible during the pretrial conference and may be used in the examination of the witness.

For the defendant, conduct a cross-examination of Tom Devine.

For the plaintiff, conduct any necessary redirect examination.

For the defendant, conduct a direct examination of Paula Blanchard.

For the plaintiff, conduct a cross-examination of Paula Blanchard.

Exhibit 1

NITA SLUGGER CORPORATION

"The Bats of Champs"

Three Williams Plaza
Williamstown, NI 99992
Ph: 101-555-1717
Fax: 101-555-1700

January 4, 2016

Mr. Tom Devine, President
NitaSport, Inc.
1800 Riverside Drive
Nita City, NI 99992

Dear Tom:

I hope this letter finds you happy and well in the new year. As the new year begins, I am pleased to announce that NITA SLUGGER is introducing, for 2016, a new line of bats. The "Major League" model is one of our finest products in the long history of NITA SLUGGER.

We are pleased to offer the "Major League" bats to NitaSport at the introductory price of $1,928.00 per gross when you order a minimum of five gross of bats. We are confident that these bats will be an excellent seller for the upcoming season, and we encourage you to make your order early.

Tom, I hope that you can take advantage of this fine offer. I hope that we can speak about an order soon, or at the latest, at spring training for the NATS.

Sincerely,

[*Signed*]
Paula Blanchard
President

Exhibit 2

NitaSport, Inc.

1800 Riverside Drive
Nita City, NI 99992
Ph: 102-444-1000
Fax: 102-444-1019

January 25, 2016

Ms. Paula Blanchard, President
Nita Slugger Corporation
Three Williams Plaza
Williamstown, NI 99992

Dear Paula,

I am writing to accept your offer of January 6, 2016, to purchase a dozen gross of your new "Major League" line of bats at the price of $1,836.00 per gross for a total price of $22,032.00.

As we are currently going through an audit here at the home office, it will be several weeks before I will be able to get you the deposit check of $2,203.00. If this is a problem, please let me know.

Unfortunately, I won't be able to make it to spring training this year. I hope to see you next year.

Sincerely

[*Signed*]

Tom Devine

COPY

Exhibit 3

NitaSport, Inc.

Tom Devine

Outgoing Phone Log

Date: January 25, 2016

	Person Called	**Telephone #**	**Purpose**
1.	John Chambers Univ. of Nita Athletic Director	443-8001	Called re: supplying equipment for 2016 football season—Same deal as last year
2.	David Lange Nita Sports Films	441-2424	Obtained film for Chamber of Commerce Meeting on 2/2
3.	Paula Blanchard Nita Slugger	555-1717	Called to order 12 g. bats @ $1,836— left message
4.	Ray Roman Nita State Athletic Director	555-6000	Confirmed order of new uniforms for women's field hockey team—Ship by 8/1
5.	May Cravitz Lyman Hall H.S	446-9423	Called re: 2016 equipment order for baseball team; she will get back to me with order by 2/1
6.	Tony Bello Nita NATS Ticket Office	441-NATS	Called to renew season tickets for 2016 season—same seats as last year 10% price increase
7.	Greg McDermott McDermott Dodge Service Dept.	443-5100	Repairs on van will be completed by 1/25 & delivered to Ridge Pike Store. Cost Estimate—$265

Exhibit 4

NitaSport, Inc.

1800 Riverside Drive
Nita City, NI 99992
Ph: 102-444-1000
Fax: 102-444-1019

February 15, 2016

Ms. Paula Blanchard, President
Nita Slugger Corporation
Three Williams Plaza
Williamstown, NI 99992

Dear Paula,

Enclosed is our check for $2,203.00 as the deposit on our order of January 25, 2016.
After being held hostage by our audit, we are back to normal business operations.

We look forward to your shipment of a dozen gross of your "Major League" line of bats.
I'm sure they will be a big seller for us.

Thanks for your patience on this matter. I hope to see you at the Nats' spring training next
year, if not before. If you're in town for a game, please give me a call.

Sincerely

[*Signed*]

Tom Devine

PROBLEM 9

Quinlan v. Kane Electronics

(Roberta Quinlan) (Brian Kane)

Fact Summary

Roberta Quinlan is a business broker who specializes in the buying and selling of electronics manufacturing and sales firms. Business brokers are agents for buyers or sellers of businesses, and they generally work on a commission basis. Quinlan has been a broker in the electronics industry for ten years. Kane Electronics was a family-owned chain of retail electronics outlets with twenty-six locations throughout the State of Nita. Its president, founder, and sole shareholder was Brian Kane.

On August 4, 2016, Kane Electronics was sold to Nita Computer World, a national retailer of computers and other electronic business equipment, for $10 million of Nita Computer World stock. Roberta Quinlan claims that she served as the broker for this transaction and that she had an agreement with Brian Kane to do so. She claims that the agreement was reached during a business meeting held at Kane's house on June 12, 2016, and was set out in a confirming letter that she mailed to Kane the next day, June 13; she also maintains that she contacted Cliff Fuller of Nita Computer World on behalf of Kane Electronics and was responsible for putting Nita Computer World and Kane together, which is what business brokers do. She has sued Kane for $300,000, 3 percent of the closing value of Kane Electronics, per her agreement with Kane.

Kane and Quinlan have known each other for about ten years, mainly as golf partners. Kane admits that he decided to sell his business in early June and that he told Quinlan of his decision during a round of golf on June 11. Kane admits he invited Quinlan to his house the next day to talk about the sale of his business. Kane admits he had several conversations with Quinlan about the possible sale of his company over the years, but he says they were all preliminary and brainstorming in nature. Kane denies there was an agreement between him and Quinlan for her to act as his agent. He denies ever receiving a confirming letter of agreement from Quinlan. He admits that when he was first contacted by phone by Cliff Fuller of Nita Computer World on June 27, 2016, Fuller said he had been referred by Roberta Quinlan. He also admits that he did not know Fuller or of Nita Computer World's interest in his company before the Fuller phone call. Kane maintains he negotiated his own deal with Nita Computer World and does not owe Quinlan a commission.

DEPOSITION OF ROBERTA QUINLAN

My name is Roberta Quinlan. I am forty-eight years old and a lifelong resident of Nita City. I am married to William Feldman, who is a partner with the law firm of Parker & Gould in Nita City. We have two children who are grown and on their own. I have both a BS and an MBA in business from Nita University. I began my career as a business broker once the kids were in middle school. My job is to put buyers and sellers of businesses together and help them reach sales agreements. Over the past fifteen years I have developed an expertise in companies and businesses involved in the electronics industry, both manufacturers and retailers of these products.

I have known Brian Kane for about ten years. We met in 2006 when he asked me to play in a mixed foursome golf tournament with him at the Rolling Green Golf Club, where we both are members. We are both avid players, and since that time, we have regularly entered tournaments together as well as playing together socially. I have played since college. Even though Brian took up the game later in life, he is a natural athlete and fierce competitor, so we make a very good team and have been quite successful. These photos you have shown me, marked Exhibit 7 and Exhibit 8, are of Brian and me playing in the club championship round in the early summer last year before all this happened.

About five years ago Brian, who is now in his early fifties, started talking to me about possibly selling his business, Kane Electronics. Of course I already knew all about his business, including that he started it on a shoestring in 1986 after working for Business Machines Incorporated for a few years and that he had expanded to twenty-six retail outlets throughout the state of Nita. He too knew about my business and my expertise in the electronics industry. These conversations usually occurred either on the golf course or at lunch after our game. He seemed really torn between his love for his work and a strong feeling of guilt at not spending more time with his family.

On June 11, 2016, Brian told me during a round of golf that he had finally decided to sell his business. I knew by then that he and his wife were having troubles, and he told me he desperately wanted to be able to spend more time with his family and get his marriage back together. I told him I would be pleased to discuss the sale and give him some advice on how to proceed. As I said, Brian knew all about my business, but there was no talk of retaining me at that point. Instead, he asked that I come by his house the next day, which was a Sunday, so that we could talk more about the sale of his business.

I got to his house about noon. We immediately went to the study and met for about four hours. We first talked about the value of the company. He had already obtained appraisals and based on those said that he hoped to get somewhere in the neighborhood of $8 to $10 million for his business. Based on the appraisals of his company and my knowledge of the industry, I told him that $8 million was low and that $10 million was a realistic goal for the sale. We then talked about the possible forms such a sale could take. I explained that because he was the sole owner of the company, the sale could be accomplished by selling all of the stock to the buyer for cash, by selling all of the assets of his company to the buyer for cash, by exchanging his stock for shares of stock in a corporate buyer, or by some combination of these methods. As it turned out, his preference was to exchange his stock for stock of the buying company if he could find a growing company as a buyer.

Page 35

1	Q:	As I understand it, you talked with Mr. Kane at his house in June of last
2		year, not at his office?
3	A:	Yes, he wanted to meet right away on Sunday, so he suggested his home,
4		which was more convenient for both of us.
5	Q:	The two of you discussed various options on how he might sell his
6		business?
7	A:	Among other things, yes.
8	Q:	What else did you talk about?
9	A:	As I said, we went over the appraisals and my advice on the
10		appropriate selling price. We also talked about what I would charge
11		as a brokerage fee.
12	Q:	Who brought up the topic of fees?
13	A:	I did. I told Brian that the range of fees for a deal such as what he
14		was interested in was 3 to 5 percent, depending upon the level of
15		involvement by the broker.
16	Q:	What did he say to that?
17	A:	Nothing really; I think we just moved on to another topic.
18	Q:	What was that topic?
19	A:	We talked about the kind of buyer we would be looking for—stable,
20		on the rise, that sort of thing. I told him I had a lot of contacts in the
21		industry, and I was sure I could find an appropriate buyer.
22	Q:	What was his reaction?
23	A:	He said, "I'm aware of your reputation, Roberta." I assured him that
24		I would do some checking around on his behalf that next week. At that
25		point, Brian's wife came in and reminded him of a social engagement,

26   and we cut our meeting short. As I was leaving, I told him I'd call him

27   next week or so. I believed that Nita Computer World was a potential

28   buyer and intended to check that out.

29   Q: When at his house, you did not tell Mr. Kane that you had someone

30   in mind who might be interested, did you?

31   A: No. I didn't want to raise premature expectations.

32   Q: Did Mr. Kane ask you to check with your contacts in the industry?

33   A: No, but he didn't say not to.

34   Q: And he didn't say that you should do some checking either, did he?

35   A: Not in so many words, no.

36   Q: Did you believe that Mr. Kane had contracted for your services at that

37   point?

38   A: Not formally, that's why I wrote him that same day.

39   Q: But he never said "You're hired," or "I want to hire you to help sell my

40   business," or anything like that, did he?

Page 36

1   A: Brian never said we had a deal explicitly, but he also didn't tell me not

2   to go forward on his behalf, either.

As I was leaving, I told Brian that given the excellent shape his company was in, I felt as though we could proceed fairly quickly to a desirable conclusion. I knew that Nita Computer World was actively acquiring smaller retail outlets and thought that they were a potential buyer for Brian's company. I was familiar with Nita Computer World because my husband had handled a number of acquisitions for them in late 2015 and early 2016.

While I would have preferred it, the fact is we didn't sign a contract that day, but it was clear to me we had a deal. When I got home that evening I wrote and mailed a letter to Brian setting out our agreement. The letter marked as Exhibit 2 is dated June 12, 2016. I kept a copy for my files. The other letter in my files to Kane, also dated June 12, 2016, and marked as Exhibit 3, is a copy of my first draft of my letter to Kane. After I read it over, I realized it wasn't accurate as to our agreement so I wrote and sent Exhibit 2. I don't even know why I kept Exhibit 3—I should have discarded it with the original. I also talked with my husband that night about Nita Computer World as a possible purchaser, and he suggested I call Cliff Fuller, general counsel at Nita Computer World, whom I had met recently at a social event at my husband's firm. Exhibits 9 and 10 are photos of Cliff and me at that event.

The document you have shown me with the heading "Broker Agreement" at the top, Exhibit 5, is a form contract that I usually use in signing up clients. My husband's law firm prepared this for me so that the terms of the agreement with the client would be clear. In Brian's case, given our relationship as friends, I decided to use a letter instead of the form contract. I don't remember any other recent deal in which I used a letter, but my relationship with Brian outside of business was unique among recent clients. I regard a letter as being just as good as a contract.

When I didn't hear back from Brian wanting to change our agreement as spelled out in my letter, I arranged that next week for Cliff Fuller to call Brian. Exhibit 4 is my phone log for June 24, 2016. It shows that call, and the call I made to Brian telling him to expect a call from Cliff Fuller. I keep a log on my computer that I fill in as I'm making phone calls, and this is a printout of that log for that date. While I didn't actually talk with Brian that day, I did leave a message on his voice mail saying to expect a call from Fuller. I tried to call him again later that day, as shown by my phone log, but this time I spoke with his secretary, who said, after checking, that Brian wasn't in. I decided not to leave another message other than that I had called.

I found out through my husband that Cliff Fuller did call Brian and that there was mutual interest right off the bat. I called Brian several times after that, but he didn't return any of my calls. No, I don't have phone logs for those calls. I have looked for logs, but I couldn't find them. I must have called from someplace other than the office, perhaps on my cell phone. I am told they started working on a deal immediately and that the negotiations went smoothly. I was not involved at all in these negotiations, but I was responsible for putting Fuller and Kane together. That's what a broker does. It's for that reason that I deserve the minimum fee that I set out in my contract letter to Brian. Usually the broker will be more involved in the negotiations, but I have had other deals like this where the principals do their own negotiations. It's for that reason that once Kane and Fuller were talking I didn't insert myself into the proceedings. I was always available if needed. I did not have to do a lot of work, obviously, but in my business it's often the work you've done over the years and whom you know, not how much work you do on the particular assignment, that makes or breaks a deal. Brian Kane got top dollar for his business, consistent with my advice to him, and if I had not called Cliff Fuller, the deal would never have happened.

Now Brian doesn't want to pay me for what I've earned. I know he claims he never got my letter, but I mailed it out myself on my stationery, and it was never returned to me by the post office, so I'm sure he got it. He had plenty of time to call or write or fax me calling off the deal, but he never did. It's unfortunate that this has happened and that I have to sue a former friend to get the fee I deserve, but Brian should pay me what I'm owed.

I have read this deposition and it is complete and accurate.

[*Signed*]

Roberta Quinlan

12/28/2016

Deposition Summary of Brian Kane

My name is Brian Kane. I am fifty-four years old and have lived here in Nita City all my life. My wife Elvira and I are currently separated, and she has our three beautiful teenage daughters living with her. After I graduated from Nita University in 1983, I worked three years for Business Machines Incorporated at their Brookline, Massachusetts, facility before deciding to set out on my own in the retail electronics business. I moved back to Nita City, and with the help of some friends and family and a bank, I scraped together enough money to open my first retail electronics store in 1986. Through a lot of hard work and good timing, the business expanded over the years to where I ended up with twenty-six locations all over the state. I was the president, founder, and sole shareholder of the company during all the years before I sold it.

For the first fifteen years of being in business, my life was my business. I had little time for outside activities, even dating. Then in 1998 I met Elvira, a customer who wanted to register a complaint with the "boss" of the company. We married not long afterwards. Bianca, our first child, was born in 1999. Rachel was born in 2001, and Terry in 2003. Not long after Rachel's birth, I decided I needed something to take my mind off of the grind of work, so I took up golf, and it became a real passion.

It was through golf that I met Roberta Quinlan. After I joined Rolling Green Golf Club in about 2006, I remember seeing her on the driving range hitting balls and was very impressed. She could really hit a golf ball. Not long after, I asked her if she would be my partner in a mixed foursome tournament, and that started a long friendship centered around golf. She was a lot of fun to play with and had the same kind of competitive spirit that I have, which resulted in a number of trophies for us both. Exhibits 7 and 8 are photos of Roberta and me at the club.

I was also impressed with Roberta's knowledge of business. We often talked about both our businesses, and I would pick her brain with ideas I had for expansion and the occasional thought of selling my business so I could do something else. Over the years, talk of my selling out was more frequent as I became more disenchanted with being unable to spend quality time with my family and Elvira's discontent with that fact. Like the many other real estate and business brokers that I had dealt with over the years, however, Roberta tended to be a little too aggressive in her own self-promotion. My experience with brokers over the years has been that they are at best a necessary evil, but I never have liked the way they hit you up and try to push you into giving them business.

In early 2016 I started having serious problems in my marriage. I began to reevaluate my life and decided I had been spending far too much time at the office and not enough with my family. My daughters only had another few years before they would be out of the house and in college, and if there was to be any chance of salvaging my marriage, I needed to make some changes. By May I had committed in my own mind to sell out. I hired a couple of appraisers to value my company, did some research on my own, made a few calls to people I knew in the industry, and put out feelers. Although I hadn't been successful as of then, my business was in good shape, in an expanding market, and I was sure I could find a buyer in time.

The next time I saw Roberta, at a golf game in mid-June, I told her of my decision. She got all excited and wanted to talk about nothing else the rest of the day. She urged me to let her broker the deal, wanted to spend a few hours meeting with me after our round of golf, and on and on. Just to get her to calm down and let me enjoy the golf game, I told her we could talk about it the next day at my house. Even though I had no intention of hiring her because I had decided to do this deal myself, I still felt as though I might learn something talking with her and I didn't want to hurt her feelings by abruptly cutting her off and telling her she had no chance of getting this business. I now regret that decision.

When she came over the next day, June 12, a Sunday, we went straight to my study, which is where I work when I am at home. Exhibit 11 is a diagram of the layout of my house and it shows the study where we met. Roberta was more than her usual aggressive self in trying to get me to sign on the dotted line, so to speak, and make her my agent for this deal. I kept putting her off, saying I had to think it all over. I must admit that I was trying to learn as much as I could from her about how she thought the deal might be structured and how she saw things working out best for me. But I had picked her brain for years on business deals without ever hiring her. I definitely did not hire her at this meeting. We just talked. There were many options discussed. At one point I do remember that she told me that her fee for helping me would only be three to five percent, and I tried to make her feel as though I thought that was very reasonable. Of course, what I was really thinking was that by handling the sale myself, with the help of my lawyers of course, I would be saving anywhere from $250,000 to $500,000 by bypassing a broker such as Roberta.

Page 22

1	Q:	Why didn't you just flat-out tell Mrs. Quinlan that you didn't want her
2		as your agent on this sale?
3	A:	I didn't want to seem rude or harsh with my longtime friend and golf
4		partner.
5	Q:	But didn't she tell you she'd be looking around for a buyer for your
6		business?
7	A:	Yes, but I never told her she should. I thought that was just all part of
8		her sales pitch.
9	Q:	Did you tell her not to?
10	A:	No, I didn't.
11	Q:	Did you encourage her to keep a lookout?
12	A:	No, I didn't actively encourage her.
13	Q:	What did you do then?

14   A: I learned long ago in business to keep my options open. I thought, who

15   knows what she might come up with, so I said nothing.

16   Q: What did you think she'd do based on this meeting?

17   A: Well, had I thought about it, I guess I should have known Roberta, as

18   aggressive as she is in business, would try to find someone to buy my

19   business and get the sizeable commission for the deal, but I never hired

20   her to do that for me. She took that upon herself without my approval.

Fortunately, my wife came into the study and reminded me of a social engagement. I was very glad to end that meeting with Roberta. First she was very pushy, then she tried to guilt trip me into hiring her, talking on and on about her contacts in the industry. That's what they all say, you know. It felt like someone trying to get you to change phone companies, and I wanted no part of it.

I remember telling my secretary, Margaret Edmondson, the next day that if Roberta Quinlan called, she was to say I wasn't in. I really didn't like dealing with this side of Roberta's personality, and I was having enough trouble with one woman in my life and didn't need Roberta hassling me too. Exhibit 1 is a telephone slip with my secretary's handwriting on it. I don't remember getting this, but it is consistent with my instructions.

I understand that Roberta claims to have sent me a so-called confirming letter after our meeting. There was nothing to confirm, and besides I never received any such letter from her. Had I received such a letter, I am sure I would have replied instantly, telling her as nicely as I could that I didn't want her services for this transaction. Having since read the copy of the letter she claims to have sent (Exhibit 2), I wonder how one can have a deal when even the commission is totally loosey-goosey.

In late June I got a call from Cliff Fuller, the general counsel at Nita Computer World. I didn't know him at all, nor did I have any idea that they might be interested in my company. Exhibit 6 is a note I made about Fuller's call. I did know the company, however, as a major player in the electronics field and recognized that they were large enough to be able to pay top dollar for my business. Cliff told me in that first call that he had been told by Roberta to call me. It never occurred to me that Roberta would expect to be compensated for this phone call. We arranged to meet for lunch. I don't recall whether Fuller suggested that Roberta join us. He might have, but there was no reason for her to be there. Once Cliff and I talked, I handled everything myself just as I had planned, and after some back and forth and meetings with the lawyers, we arrived at a mutually agreeable arrangement whereby Nita Computer World bought my company in exchange for $10 million of their stock. We probably had ten meetings in all, all without Roberta. It's true that Roberta discussed that form of sale with me, but in the end, it was my tax lawyers who persuaded me to close the deal in that form. The deal closed on

August 4. I was ecstatic. Finally I would have time to be with my kids, and try to make things right with Elvira, and then this lawsuit got filed.

It's not the money that she's asking for that troubles me so much; it's the principle of the thing. If I had wanted Roberta to be my agent, then I would have hired her and signed an agreement specifically setting out our arrangement. That's how I have always done business—in writing. That's the only safe way to proceed I quickly learned some thirty years ago. I never agreed to hire her; instead she's trying to foist herself on me and my company, and I don't like it. And this has ruined a perfectly good golf team, too.

I have read this deposition and it is complete and accurate.

[*Signed*]

Brian Kane

12/29/2016

* * *

The case is now at trial. The first witness for the plaintiff is Roberta Quinlan.

For the plaintiff, conduct the direct examination of Roberta Quinlan, assuming that all the exhibits have been stipulated to be admissible during the pretrial conference, and may be used in the examination of the witness.

For the defendant, conduct a cross-examination of Roberta Quinlan.

For the plaintiff, conduct any necessary redirect examination.

For the defendant, conduct a direct examination of Brian Kane.

For the plaintiff, conduct a cross-examination of Brian Kane.

Exhibit 1

```
┌─────────────────────────────────────┐
│      IMPORTANT MESSAGE               │
│ For  Brian                           │
│ Day  6/24      Time 2:30     A.M.    │
│                              P.M.    │
│ M  s. Quinlan                        │
│ Of                                   │
│ Phone  225 · 6482                    │
│ FAX   Area Code    Number   Extension│
│ MOBILE                               │
│       Area Code    Number   Extension│
├──────────────┬──────────────┬────────┤
│ Telephoned   │✓Returned your│ RUSH   │
│              │  call        │        │
│ Came to see  │ Please call  │Special │
│ you          │              │attention│
│ Wants to see │ Will call    │Caller  │
│ you          │ again        │on hold │
├──────────────┴──────────────┴────────┤
│ Message   Told her you               │
│      were not in —                   │
│      as per your                     │
│            instructions              │
│                                      │
│ Signed    Peg                        │
│ Universal 48023      LITHO IN U.S.A. │
└─────────────────────────────────────┘
```

Exhibit 2

ROBERTA QUINLAN

Business Broker

12 Meredith Lane
Nita City, NI 99992

June 12, 2016

Mr. Brian Kane
One Kane Plaza
P.O. Box 626
Nita City, NI 99992

Dear Brian:

It was a pleasure to visit with you this afternoon, and I write to confirm our understanding.

You, as the sole shareholder of Kane Electronics, desire to dispose of your stock holdings in the company by way of an exchange of shares of a corporation with a good investment future. If I arrange for such an exchange, which is acceptable to you, Kane Electronics will pay me a fee calculated at between 3–5 percent of the closing value to you, dependent upon my time and effort necessary on your behalf.

If I do not hear from you, I will assume that this arrangement is acceptable to you. I already have a prospect in mind and will be in touch with you in the near future.

Warm regards,

[*Signed*]

Roberta Quinlan

rq/s

COPY

Exhibit 3

ROBERTA QUINLAN

Business Broker

12 Meredith Lane
Nita City, NI 99992

Mr. Brian Kane
One Kane Plaza
P.O. Box 626
Nita City, NI 99992

Dear Brian:

It was a pleasure to visit with you this afternoon concerning the sale of Kane Electronics. As I told you, I am confident that I can find an appropriate purchaser of either the assets or the stock of the company, although I understand that you are also open to an exchange of your stock in Kane for stock in a company with a good investment future.

During our conversation, we agreed that I would use my best efforts and contacts (which are many) to find a suitable purchaser of Kane Electronics. Upon consummation of any sale, regardless of its nature or form, which results from my efforts, Kane Electronics will pay me an amount to be decided upon at a later date, but in no event less than 3 percent of the net closing value to the seller.

I will be in touch with you from time to time.

Warm regards,

[*Signed*]

Roberta Quinlan

rq/s

COPY

Exhibit 4

Roberta Quinlan

Business Broker

Outgoing Phone Log

Date	Person Called	Telephone #	Business Purpose
6/24	Cliff Fuller NCW	287-440	Called re: potential interest in Kane Electronics. Says NCW looking to acquire companies like Kane. Thinks Kane may already be on their list of potential acquisitions. He will call Kane.
6/24	Brian Kane Kane Electronics	877-2893	Called to tell him to expect call from Cliff Fuller at NCW. Left message on voice mail.
6/24	Brian Kane Kane Electronics	877-2893	Called again. Secretary claims isn't in. I hope he isn't ducking me to try to get out of our agreement (don't be paranoid).

Exhibit 5

BROKER AGREEMENT

AGREEMENT made this   day of _____, by and between Roberta Quinlan, Business Broker, 12 Meredith Lane, Nita City, NI 99992, hereinafter "broker," and _____, hereinafter "customer."

In consideration of the mutual agreements hereinafter contained and other good and valuable consideration, the sufficiency and adequacy of which are hereby acknowledged, the parties hereto agree as follows:

1.   The term of this contract is six months (180 days) from the date appearing above.

2.   Customer hereby retains the Broker to locate a buyer or seller as appropriate for the requirements of the Customer.

3.   Broker hereby undertakes to use best efforts to locate a buyer or seller as appropriate for the requirements of the Customer. Broker makes no guarantee or warranty of success with respect to any such efforts.

4.   If the Broker locates a willing buyer or a willing seller as appropriate for the requirements of the Customer, the Broker has completed performance under this Agreement and is entitled to the fee described in paragraph 3.

5.   Customer hereby agrees to pay to Broker a fee of ____% of the total selling price for the business, including the fair market value of any stock, stock options, warrants or other consideration of any kind, at the closing of the sale, in cash, by certified check, or by wire transfer.

6.   This agreement shall inure to the benefit of, and shall be binding upon, the parties hereto and their successors and assigns. This Agreement shall be governed by the laws of the State of Nita. This Agreement may be executed in one or more counterparts, which, taken together, shall constitute the whole agreement, and there may be duplicate originals of this Agreement.

IN WITNESS WHEREOF, this Broker Agreement has been duly executed by the parties hereto as of the date first above written.

WITNESS:

_____   _____
                                         Roberta Quinlan, Broker

_____   _____
                                         Customer

Exhibit 6

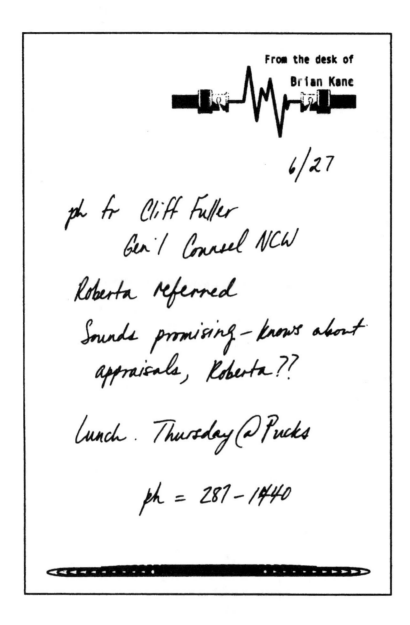

From the desk of
Brian Kane

6/27

ph fr Cliff Fuller
    Gen'l Counsel NCW

Roberta referred

Sounds promising – knows about
appraisals, Roberta??

Lunch. Thursday @ Pucks

    ph = 287 - 1440

PROBLEM 10

State v. Williams

(Joseph Williams) (Alex Clark)

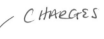

CHARGES

Joseph Williams has been charged with vehicular assault and leaving the scene of an accident. The State alleges that on September 26, 2016, the defendant struck and severely injured Martin Higgins with the right front of his car. At the time of the incident, the victim was involved in a protest against a controversial proposed pipeline construction project in front of the First Union National Bank (FUNB) building in downtown Nita City that houses the Nita Oil Company offices.

Several witnesses have testified that at approximately 12:45 to 1:00 p.m., the victim was involved in the protest that overflowed from the sidewalk in front of the FUNB building onto Main Street. At that approximate time, the victim was standing in Main Street and was struck by the right front of a car traveling southbound on Main Street. After striking the victim, the car sped off, continuing south on Main Street. The police attempted to give chase, but were slowed by onlookers from the demonstration and lost track of the car.

The car was described by witnesses as a white, late model, domestic, four-door sedan. One witness testified that the car had a Nita license plate that contained the letter "J" and the number or letter "0" and that he believed that the "J" was the first figure on the plate, but could not place the "0." He also noticed what he thought were university parking decals on the car.

The same witness who had seen the car hit the victim called the police on September 27 and informed them that he believed that he had seen the same car that struck the victim parked near the law school on the Nita University campus on that morning. After some investigation with the Nita University Campus Police, the police found that the defendant drove a car of the same description as the one involved in the hit-and-run incident and further found that the car had a dent in the right front. A warrant was issued for his arrest, and the defendant was arrested at his home at 6:00 p.m. on October 1, 2016.

ARREST DATE

The case is now at trial. The government has introduced all of the evidence noted above. In addition, the government has shown that the defendant's license plate number is JAW-007. No witness has been able to positively identify Williams as the driver of the car, but several witnesses have testified that Williams looked like the driver of the hit-and-run car, even though they could not be sure he was the one.

NOT CERTAIN ABOUT ID

Further evidence has been received from Mike Calhoun, who knows Williams and is the director of Nita Legal Services. He places Williams in downtown Nita City at the time of the incident. Calhoun testified that Williams had attended a meeting with him and one of his associates, Alice Ratliff, from approximately 11:30 a.m. to 1:00 p.m. in downtown Nita. The meeting began at the Legal Aid office at 610 Main Street and continued over lunch at Sudi's Restaurant at 925 Main Street. Calhoun testified that he noticed the demonstration in front of the First Union National Bank building and that he and the defendant commented on the demonstration. Calhoun, Ratliff, and the defendant walked to the restaurant from the Legal Aid office. After walking back to the office, the three said their goodbyes, and the defendant walked towards his car, which was parked on Main Street in front of the Legal Aid office, facing north, while Calhoun and Ratliff went back into their office.

The following is the statement Williams gave to the police on the night of his arrest. The defendant waived his right to be silent and right to have an attorney present.

STATEMENT OF JOSEPH WILLIAMS

My name is Joseph Williams. I live at 12 Scott Place here in Nita City. These charges are absurd. I did not hit anyone with my car on September 26 or any other time. Before I give this statement, I want to protest being arrested at my home in front of my children. There was absolutely no reason to upset them. I would have come in voluntarily.

I am employed as a professor of law at the University of Nita Law School. I attended law school at Nita University. After a year's clerkship with a Federal Circuit Court of Appeals judge in Washington, DC, and three years with a large Washington, DC, law firm, I returned to the faculty of the Nita University Law School. I have been on the faculty for ten years, and I am tenured. I teach in the areas of contracts and commercial law.

You have asked me about the dent in the right front of my car. That damage was incurred on September 29, 2016, when I was leaving the law school parking lot. I was tired and in a hurry to get home, and as I was backing out I hit a post that had been alongside the right rear fender of my parked car. I guess I oversteered the car as I was backing out to leave the lot. My car wasn't damaged very much, so I haven't even thought about getting it fixed yet. I was alone at the time, but I know I mentioned it to my wife that night and to others at the law school the next day.

On September 26, 2016, I arrived at the law school at 8:55 a.m. for a 9:00 a.m. meeting with Professor Sparks concerning curriculum matters. The meeting ended at 10:50 a.m., and I returned to my office to prepare for my Contracts class. We were going to complete the first section of the course that day, and the students had been assigned to prepare some review problems. I wanted to be very well prepared.

At 11:10 a.m. I received a call from Mike Calhoun of the Nita City Legal Aid Society. We arranged to meet concerning my doing a series of lectures on recent trends in consumer protection law for his lawyers and some community groups. I have done this sort of pro bono work with them and other public agencies in the past, as I view it as my duty as a lawyer to provide free legal assistance to those who can't afford expert legal help. I drove to Calhoun's office in my 2014 white Ford four-door sedan. My license plate number is JAW-007. It is a vanity plate with my initials that was given to me by my children. Apparently I am the seventh person with those initials to get a vanity plate, which explains the number. I arrived at 11:35 a.m. and parked in front on the Legal Aid Office, facing north on Main Street. I then met with Mike and one of his associates, Alice Ratliff.

Our meeting continued through lunch at Sudi's, which is located several blocks north of the Legal Aid office. We walked to the restaurant. As we entered the restaurant I noticed a demonstration going on in front of the First Union National Bank building on Main Street. I do my banking there and was a bit surprised to see a demonstration. Alice explained that it was a demonstration protesting a proposed oil pipeline, and that the Nita Oil Company had its offices in the bank building. I had planned to order some new checks while I was downtown that day, but given the demonstration, I decided to put off that errand to another day.

We finished lunch at 12:45 p.m. and walked the three blocks back to the Legal Aid office. We said goodbye, and Mike and Alice went back into their office. I was about to get into my car when I saw a white compact car go speeding by me, going south on Main Street. The car was headed in the general direction of the university. I didn't notice anything else about the car except that it had some university parking decals on the back bumper like hundreds of cars in Nita, including mine.

I then got into my car, drove one block north and made a right turn onto Seventh, turned right again onto Tower View Road to Main Street and drove back to the University. At 1:20 p.m. I was back in my office, preparing for my 3:00 p.m. class when I started to feel ill. As it turned out, I had to cancel my class and go over to the Faculty Health Clinic, where I saw my doctor, Dr. Lester. I had to wait to see him, but after looking me over and talking with me he told me that it looked like a mild case of food poisoning and that I should go home and take it easy for the rest of the day.

I got home at about 4:15 p.m. The kids—Joe, Jr., and Mary—were there with the housekeeper. My wife Ann got home at about 5:00 p.m. As I said, I don't know anything about this hit-and-run. I have told you everything I remember about that day.

Signed: [*Signed*]   Date: October 1, 2016

Joseph A. Williams

Witness: [*Signed*]

Officer Nancy Kelly

STATEMENT OF ALEX CLARK

My name is Alex Clark. I am a twenty-six-year-old male. I work for the Peace Corps. I just got back from Africa, where I was stationed and working for two years. I live in Nita City now. On September 26, 2016, I was protesting against the proposed oil pipeline that will cross sensitive lands. The protest was outside of the First Union National Bank building in downtown Nita City. The protest was at that location because the Nita Oil Company offices are in that building. The protest got a surprisingly good turnout and expanded onto the street around the building. I was really happy about all of the people that were demonstrating about this important issue.

I remember that at approximately 12:45 or 1:00 p.m. one of the protestors was hit by a car on Main Street. The car was going west on 11th Street, turned southbound on Main Street, and hit the protestor with the front of the right side of his car. It was pretty scary. The car did not stop after it hit the protester. It sped off in the same direction that it was traveling. The car had a Nita license plate with the letter "J," which I think was the first letter on the plate, and the letter or number "0" as well. I'm not sure of the placement of the "0." It also had a bunch of parking decals that looked like they were from the University of Nita. The police saw the man get hit, but could not catch the person driving the car because there were so many people in the street protesting.

I was totally shocked when I saw this man get hit by a car. I was able to see that the car was a white, late model, domestic, four-door sedan. It was driven by a middle-aged Caucasian man with dark hair. The picture you have shown me of Mr. Williams looks like the driver, but I can't be sure. I did not have enough time to make more observations, the whole thing happened so quickly. Because I thought that the man that was hit could have been seriously injured, I was more concerned about him than the car. I assumed the police would catch the man that hit him. They were right there. The next day I was on the university campus, and I saw a car like the hit-and-run car parked near the law school. I called and reported that to the police.

[*Signed*]

Alex Clark

* * *

The case is now at trial. The state calls as its first witness, Alex Clark. The defendant's midtrial motion for a directed verdict of acquittal has been denied. The defense calls as the last witness, the defendant Joseph Williams.

Part A

For the State, conduct a direct examination of Alex Clark.

For the defendant, conduct a cross-examination of Alex Clark.

Part B

For the defendant, conduct the direct examination of Joseph Williams.

For the State, conduct the cross-examination of Joseph Williams.

For the defendant, conduct any necessary redirect examination.

Exhibit 1

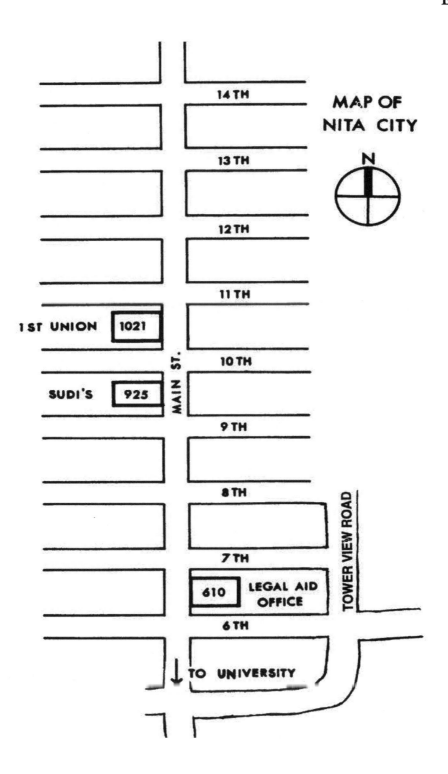

PROBLEM 11

Myers v. Nita Day School

(John Myers) (Emmy Beskind)

The parents of John Myers, an eleven-year-old, are suing Nita Day School for negligent supervision of Johnny while he was a student at the school. They claim that Johnny, then nine years old, received multiple lacerations of his face as well as a concussion when he was allowed to slide headfirst down the slide at recess. They allege that in the few minutes before his injury, he had repeatedly gone down the slide headfirst and that 1) the teacher on duty should have seen him and stopped him, or 2) there should have been enough teachers on duty so that one of them should have seen and stopped him. In addition, they allege that the children were not adequately instructed on the safe use of the slide.

The school's defense is that it did everything that reasonably could be done to prevent the injury. Witnesses for the school say that all students were told on many occasions not to slide headfirst down the slide in general instructions on the use of playground equipment by their teacher, Mr. Colwin, and by the director of the school, Ms. Rodriguez. In addition, the school posted a sign at the foot of the slide warning "Headfirst sliding is strictly prohibited." Under Nita law, a child between seven and fourteen years of age is presumed not to be negligent, but the presumption can be rebutted.

Johnny was injured during a supervised recess on the school's playground at about 10:45 a.m. on Thursday, April 2, 2015. During his deposition, Mr. Colwin, the plaintiff's teacher, testified that at that time he was the only teacher supervising forty students (two classes) at recess. The teacher for the other class had gone to the teacher's lounge to take a break. Colwin also testified that Johnny had been using the slide with several other children for about ten minutes before the incident in question occurred. He remembers seeing Johnny use the slide properly at least three times before he injured himself. He says he never saw Johnny slide headfirst.

Colwin also testified in his deposition that he did not see Johnny until after he had started down the slide headfirst. Until then, his attention was on some other children who were playing kickball and having an argument about the rules. He looked back to the slide when he heard another child yell, "Johnny, stop it." By the time Colwin turned toward the slide, Johnny was on his way down the slide, headfirst. Colwin ran to stop the plaintiff from hurting himself, but got there too late.

At the scene, Colwin immediately realized Johnny's cuts were serious and helped the dazed child to the nurse's office. The school's director called an ambulance. Johnny has had no problems other than a bad headache from his concussion, but his lacerations required over 100 stitches and the scars on his chin, nose, and forehead are permanent, although later plastic surgery might improve their appearance.

On April 3, 2015, David Randolf, an investigator for the Nita Fire and Casualty Company, Nita Day School's insurer, came to the school and investigated the incident. He took the statement of another student, Emmy Beskind, who saw the whole incident. Her statement and a diagram prepared by the investigator follow.

Deposition of Emmy Beskind

My name is Emilia Beskind, but everyone calls me Emmy. I am nine years old and in Mr. Colwin's fourth-grade class at Nita Day School in Nita City. I saw the accident on Thursday when Johnny Myers hurt himself. It was his own fault. He's always doing things he's not supposed to do.

Johnny's been in my class since kindergarten. Every year he gets in trouble. He's bossy and not nice. He always picks on the other kids. He does stuff like pulling on their clothes and bumping into them in line. One time, he even took my book and threw it in a mud puddle. I got in trouble for it, but it wasn't my fault. That was just a week ago. Johnny can be really mean. He always wants to be first. He cuts in the lines and doesn't wait his turn. The teachers always have to tell him to behave. On the playground, he's always running around acting crazy. When the teachers tell him to behave he listens for a while and then acts even worse.

We've been using this playground since kindergarten. Every year at the beginning, the principal, Ms. Rodriguez, has an assembly. She goes over the playground rules. There are only three rules about the slide: wait your turn, only one kid on the ladder at a time, and no head-first sliding. Mr. Colwin goes over the same rules with us all the time, and everybody knows what they are. There used to be a sign on the slide, but I don't know if it was there when Johnny hurt himself. It said something about the slide, but I can't remember what.

The slide is on the playground right next to where we play kickball. We also have a swing set, climbing gym, a go-round, and some see-saws. The drawing you showed me looks like where things are.

Just before this happened, I was on the see-saw with my best friend, Mara. We got off to go to the slide. We got in line alongside the slide. Mara was ahead of me. Colleen was ahead of her, just at the bottom of the ladder. Ben was at the top of the ladder about to go down.

Ben went down the slide the way he was supposed to. Colleen was just about to go up the ladder when Johnny pushed her out of the way. I yelled at him to stop it, but he didn't listen to me. He ran up the ladder and slid down headfirst real fast. He was going so fast he couldn't stop at the end and his head hit the sand at the bottom. He just stayed there. Some of the kids were laughing. They just thought he was playing a joke.

Mr. Colwin ran up to Johnny and turned him over. There was blood all over his face. Mr. Colwin told me to run and get Ms. Rodriguez. I did. I didn't see where Mr. Colwin came from.

After that I went back to class. Mr. Colwin told us that Johnny was going to be OK.

Signed: [*Signed*]

Emmy Beskind

DEPOSITION OF JOHN MYERS

My name is John Myers. I am eleven years old. I go to Nita Day School. I am in fourth grade, and my teacher's name is Mr. Colwin. I got hurt on the playground April 2, 2015, when I was playing on the slide. I went down the slide headfirst and got a lot of injuries to my head and face. Even though the teachers said not to slide down headfirst, everyone did it. When the teacher saw us sliding down headfirst, they never said anything. It was not the first time I slid down headfirst, and no one ever yelled at me before.

When I got hurt, there wasn't a sign on the slide. There is a sign there now that says "Headfirst sliding is strictly prohibited," but that sign wasn't there when I got hurt. There is usually only one teacher watching the whole class at recess. Everyone goes down the slide headfirst. Sometimes the teacher sees us, and sometimes the teacher is busy watching other kids on the playground.

I usually follow instructions, but nobody uses the slide the right way. It was much more fun to use the slide headfirst.

Emmy Beskind hates me. She tried to kiss me once on the playground, but I wouldn't let her. I do not like her. Ever since that day, she has been really mean to me. She talks about me to everyone. She says that I am really mean. She is always telling my best friend Brad that I'm mean. She tattles on me to the teachers, even if I am not doing anything wrong. She is always trying to get me in trouble. Emmy was not even near the slide when I got hurt. She was on the seesaw with her friend Mara. I knew where she was because I often keep my eye out for her. I like to know where she is because she is always out to get me.

Since everyone else went down the slide headfirst without getting in trouble by the teachers, I just did what everyone else did. I just wish that I didn't get hurt so bad.

[*Signed*]

John Myers

* * *

The case is at trial. The plaintiffs have presented their evidence and rested. The defendants' midtrial motion for judgment as a matter of law has been denied. The first witness for the defense is Emmy Beskind.

For the defendant, conduct a direct examination of Emmy Beskind.

For the plaintiff, conduct a cross-examination of Emmy Beskind.

For the defendant, conduct any necessary redirect examination.

For the plaintiff, conduct a direct examination of John Myers.

For the defendant, conduct a cross-examination of John Myers.

Exhibit 1

Diagram

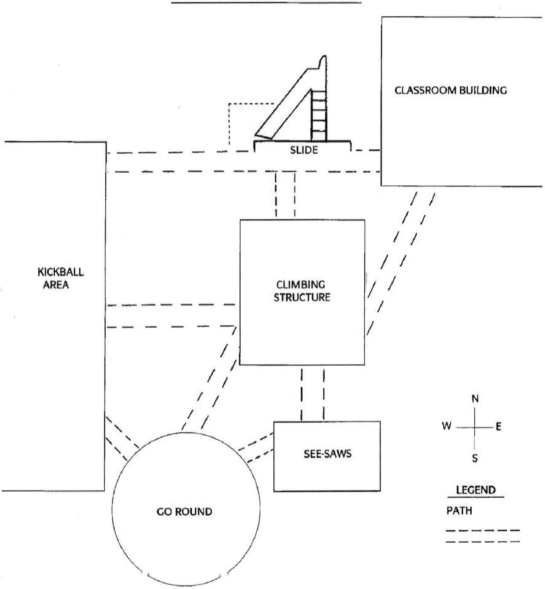

NITA DAY SCHOOL PLAYGROUND

SECTION II

EXHIBITS

For substantive instructions on the topic of exhibits, please refer to any of NITA's texts on the art and science of trial advocacy.

PROBLEM 12

Brown v. Byrd

(Surveillance Photographs)

For the basic facts of this case refer to Problem 2.

The plaintiff has alleged that as a result of being rear-ended by the defendant's car that he has suffered a permanent back injury. He further claims that the injury precludes him from engaging in any strenuous exercise and that the muscle relaxant prescription drugs he is required to take prevent him from drinking any alcoholic beverages, even beer. The plaintiff asserts that his permanent back injury, his pain and suffering, and the deprivation of his activities warrant substantial compensation. This is especially so given the known health benefits of moderate alcohol consumption.

The defendant's insurance carrier asked one of its investigators, David Randolf, to review and verify the plaintiff's alleged injuries. After an investigation, Randolf filed a report with the insurance carrier disputing the extent of the injuries claimed by the plaintiff. Randolf began his investigation by identifying the plaintiff by reference to a picture provided by the defendant's insurance company and by setting up a surveillance of the plaintiff's home on June 24, 2015. No unusual activity on the part of Mr. Brown was noted on the first day of the surveillance. On June 25, Mr. Randolf followed the plaintiff to the Nita Country Club. This was approximately two months after the plaintiff's alleged injury. At that time he observed Brown play two sets of tennis and then consume four or five beers. Randolf took several photographs and included them in his report. Two of the photographs follow this problem. Randolf's surveillance was then terminated.

At the time the photographs were taken, Brown was playing tennis with a business acquaintance, R. J. Oliver. Further investigation revealed that Oliver and Brown often played tennis together, but had not done so for the two months previous to June 25.

Randolf has located two witnesses who recall seeing Brown at the Country Club on June 25. Jeffrey Powers is a maintenance man at the Country Club. Monica Wilson is a bartender at the Country Club. Randolf interviewed both witnesses on June 29, 2015.

STATEMENT OF JEFFREY POWERS

My name is Jeffrey Powers. I am twenty-eight years old. I work as a clay court maintenance man at the Nita Country Club. I know a man named Ken Brown. He is one of the members of the Nita Country Club and always stops to say hello when I see him. I remember seeing Mr. Brown playing tennis during the past week. I was working on the court next to him at the time. I was working in court 9. Mr. Brown was playing in court 10. By looking at my work schedule for the past week I can see that I was working on court 9 on June 25, so that must be the day I saw him.

Signed: [*Signed*]

Jeffrey Powers

June 29, 2015

Witness: [*Signed*]

David Randolf

STATEMENT OF MONICA WILSON

My name is Monica Wilson. I am twenty-six years old and work as the patio bartender at the Nita Country Club during the spring and summer months. When it's too cold to open the patio bar, I work as the day bartender. I've had this job for two years. I know Ken Brown. Up until the early spring of last year, he was a regular. I would see him three or four times a week.

Mr. Brown was a confirmed beer drinker: Budweiser. On June 25, a few days ago, I saw Mr. Brown for the first time in a couple of months. He was his old self. He came up to the patio bar in his tennis clothes. During the next ninety minutes, he had a few beers. After looking at his tab, I see that he actually bought six beers that day, but my recollection is that he was also buying for his tennis partner.

Signed: [*Signed*]

Monica Wilson

June 29, 2015

Witness: [*Signed*]

David Randolf

The case is now at trial. The plaintiff has presented his case, and the defendants' midtrial motion for judgment as a matter of law has been denied. The defendant is now presenting its case.

For the defendant, introduce the photographs in evidence using the witness(es) of your choice.

For the plaintiff, oppose the offer.

—ID
— date

Powers: —est. date of pics
— ID

Wilson: — date
— ID
— beer (+ numbers)
— tennis clothes

Exhibit 1

Playing Tennis

Exhibit 2

Drinking Beer

PROBLEM 13

State v. Williams

(Photograph of Damaged Car)

For the basic facts of this case refer to Problem 10.

At the time of the arrest of Williams, the police took his 2014 Ford sedan into custody and impounded it for testing. Forensic testing of the car was negative for any evidence that might connect it with the hit-and-run incident. The police photographer, Mary Hansel, took a photograph of the scrapes on the right front of Williams' car before the car was returned to him. That photograph is part of this problem.

The case is now at trial. The State is presenting its case.

For the State, introduce the photograph of the Ford in evidence, using the witness(es) of your choice.

For the defendant, oppose the offer.

Exhibit 1

Photo of Ford

Problem 14

McArthur v. Rogers

(Photograph)

For the basic facts of the case refer to Problem 4.

The defendant, David Rogers, is defending this case on several grounds:

1. He claims that the plaintiff was negligent in the manner in which she ran on the snowy deck, and as a result was the cause of her own injuries;

2. He claims that he had not been present at the cabin for over a year before the injury to Ms. McArthur and therefore had no actual notice of the condition of the stairs; and

3. He claims that he had turned over the management of the property to PBA Management, which is a subsidiary of Paul B. Anthony Real Estate, and that responsibility for the upkeep and repair of the property belonged to the real estate agent as part of his agreement. The real estate agent denies that an agreement to repair existed with the defendant.

The summer before the injury to the plaintiff the cabin in question was offered for sale by PBA Management. In anticipation of putting the property on the market, Mr. Anthony held an open house for area real estate agents, as the property was to be listed in a multiple listings book. That open house was held on July 10, 2015.

On that same date, Mr. Anthony recalls that Mr. Rogers, the owner of the property, was present, and in fact was making some repairs to the steps leading up to the deck on the back of the cabin. Mr. Anthony was taking pictures that day to use in advertising, and to finish a roll snapped a picture of Mr. Rogers as he was in the process of repairing the stairs. That photograph accompanies this problem.

The case is now at trial. The plaintiff is presenting his case.

For the plaintiff, introduce the photograph of Mr. Rogers in evidence, using the witness(es) of your choice.

For the defendant, oppose the offer.

Exhibit 1

Rogers Making Repairs Photo

Problem 15

Gilton, et al. v. Nita Beverages, Inc.

(Accident Scene Photographs)

This is a wrongful death case arising out of an intersection collision. Richard Gilton was killed in the collision. His family has brought suit for damages under the Nita wrongful death statute.

The collision occurred at approximately 6:00 p.m. on the evening of January 15, 2016. Although it was dark at the time, the intersection was well lighted. The weather was clear and dry.

The plaintiffs' decedent, Richard Gilton, was northbound on Highway 501 in a 2015 Honda coupe. James Swanson, an employee of Nita Beverage, was westbound on Church Road. He drove a twenty-two-foot refrigerated beer truck owned and operated by the dedendant, Nita Beverages, Inc.

Gilton was traveling from Nita City to Benson, which is approximately thirty miles north of Nita City. Swanson's destination was Maria's Restaurant located on the service road on the west side of Highway 501. The right front of Gilton's car collided with the left front quarter-panel of the Nita Beverage truck. The force of the impact propelled Gilton through the windshield and onto the pavement. He was killed instantly. Swanson suffered a broken arm, several broken ribs, contusions and lacerations.

The plaintiffs claim that Gilton had the green light at the time of the collision or, in the alternative, that if he didn't have the green light the defendant's truck driver had the last clear chance to avoid the collision. The defendant claims that Swanson had the green light and that Gilton ran the light at a high rate of speed. There are witnesses to corroborate both versions. All witnesses agree that the light had just changed at the time of the collision, but they disagree on who had the green light when the collision occurred. The posted speed limit in the immediate vicinity of the intersection was 50 mph on Highway 501 and 30 mph on Church Road. The traffic signal facing the highway has a relatively long yellow light because, with a 50 mph speed limit, there is a need to allow enough time for the traffic to either clear the intersection or stop.

James Swanson stated that he was westbound on Church Road and stopped for the light at the intersection of Highway 501. He said he waited for the light to change and then proceeded into the intersection. He added that he did not see Gilton's car until just before the collision.

Officer Carol Boynton of the Nita City Police Department received the accident call and arrived at the scene a few minutes after the collision. She ascertained that Gilton was fatally injured and offered first-aid assistance to Swanson. An ambulance arrived, Gilton was pronounced dead, and Swanson was taken to Nita Memorial Hospital. Gilton's body was covered with a sheet, and Boynton stayed with it until another ambulance came to take it to the morgue.

Boynton interviewed the witnesses at the scene and completed a traffic accident report. Boynton is familiar with the intersection. It is within her normal patrol area, which she has been working since she became a police officer in 2012.

Anne Evans, a freelance photographer, heard about the accident on her police scanner radio. She went directly to the scene and took a photograph of Gilton's body lying on the pavement covered with a sheet. She has provided the photograph to the plaintiffs' attorneys. At the direction of the plaintiffs' counsel, she went to the scene of the accident on June 10, 2016, at approximately 9:00 p.m. and took photographs of the intersection. (Those photographs, as well as the one Evans took on the night of the collision and a diagram of the intersection, follow this problem.)

The intersection was in substantially the same condition in June 2016 as on January 15, 2016, except that a traffic sign had been removed from the triangle area at the southeast corner. The traffic sign faced south, and the top of the sign was seven feet above ground level. The sign itself was three feet high by four feet wide and was attached to two metal posts.

The case is now at trial. The plaintiff is presenting its case. The parties have stipulated to the use of the diagram that follows as illustrative of the scene of the accident.

Part A. Photograph of Gilton's Body

For the plaintiff, introduce the photograph of Gilton's body in evidence using the witness(es) of your choice.

For the defendant, oppose the offer.

Part B. Photographs of the Intersection

For the plaintiff, introduce the photographs of the intersection in evidence using the witness(es) of your choice.

For the defendant, oppose the offer.

Scale Drawing of Intersection

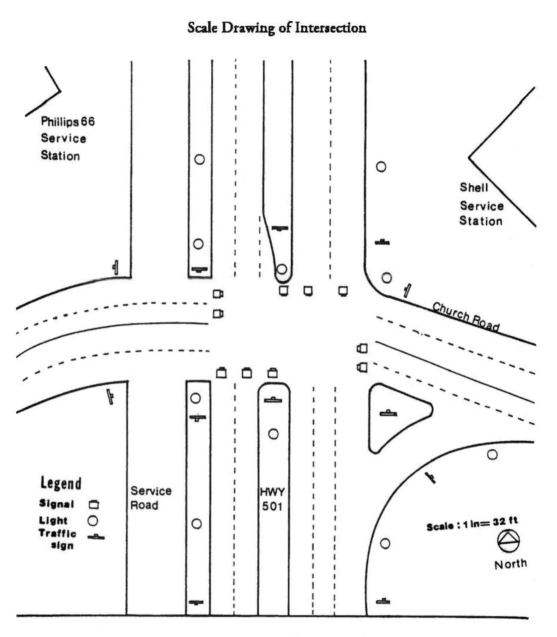

Legend

Signal ▢

Light ○

Traffic sign

Service Road

HWY 501

Phillips 66 Service Station

Shell Service Station

Church Road

Scale : 1 in= 32 ft

North

Scale Drawing of Intersection
HWY 501 AND CHURCH ROAD

Exhibit 2

Covered Body Photograph

Exhibit 3

Facing West on Church Road

Exhibit 4

Facing North on Highway 501 Bypass

PROBLEM 16

Nita Liquor Commission v. Cut-Rate Liquor

(Bag and Bottle)

For the basic facts of this case see Problem 1.

In addition, assume the following facts to be true:

When Bier placed Watkins under arrest on June 5, 2016, he took from Watkins the unopened bottle of Thunderbird wine with an intact tax seal, and the bag in which it was carried. The bag and bottle of wine were both tagged by Bier. The tags show the following information:

Date:	June 5, 2016
Time:	9:05 p.m. *20 min. after*
Place:	Cut-Rate Liquor—Seventh & Jackson
Investigator:	Bier
Case:	Cut-Rate Liquor and Dan Jones

These tags are on both the bag and the bottle.

The bottle and bag were then taken to the Nita City office of the Liquor Commission and placed in Bier's evidence locker. The bottle and bag remained in the locker until October 17 of 2016, when it was taken out by Bier so that it could be inspected by counsel for the Liquor Commission and counsel for Cut-Rate Liquor and Dan Jones. After inspection, it was returned to the evidence locker. The evidence was not removed from the locker until the day of trial. *stayed in locker*

The bag and bottle were brought to court on the day of trial by Investigator Bier. Bier has informed counsel for the Liquor Commission that the bag and bottle are unaltered from when they were taken from Watkins. The only exception is that the bag appeared new at the time of the arrest of Watkins and today it appears worn from the handling it has received since being taken into custody. *unaltered*

The case is now at trial. The plaintiff is presenting its case-in-chief.

For the plaintiff, introduce the bag and bottle in evidence, using the witness(es) of your choice.

For the defendant, oppose the offer.

PROBLEM 17

State v. Lawrence

(Stolen Purse)

For the basic facts of this case refer to Problem 3.

Further investigation in this case revealed that on the evening of July 1, 2016, the defendant, James Lawrence, was identified as being present at Dorothy's Bar & Grill, located in the 800 block of Main Street in Nita City. The person identifying Lawrence as being at the bar is Dorothy Byrne, its owner. The purse belonging to Ms. Fitzgerald was found in a mailbox located in that same block by postal carrier Janet Parker on July 5, 2016.

The case is now at trial. The State is presenting its case.

For the State, introduce Ms. Fitzgerald's purse in evidence using the witness(es) of your choice.

For the defendant, oppose the offer.

PROBLEM 18

State v. Carroll

(Computer Chip and Container)

For the basic facts of this case, refer to Problem 6.

When Special Agent O'Rourke placed George Moore under arrest, he took the metal box and computer chip from the lining of his raincoat and placed them in an evidence bag and sealed the bag. The bag was marked with a tag that stated the following:

Special Agent:	Paul O'Rourke
Date:	November 18, 2016
Time:	2:45 a.m.
Place:	Front Street, Nita City
Suspect:	George Moore
Contents:	Metal container and computer chip

O'Rourke took the bag to the Nita Bureau of Investigation headquarters where he booked Moore. The evidence bag was given to a laboratory technician named Eleanor Martin, who subjected the box and computer chip to fingerprint analysis on the morning of November 18, 2016. Analysis revealed that there were no discernable fingerprints on either the metal box or the computer chip and that the seized items had apparently been wiped clean.

O'Rourke then took the metal box and computer chip in the resealed evidence bag to the offices of Pear Electronics to identify the computer chip. The chip was taken from the evidence bag in O'Rourke's presence by Steven Ketaineck, the head of security at Pear Electronics. The chip was identified by Alice Franklin, Pear's head of product development, as being one of Pear's new platinum line of computer chips. The chip was then returned to the evidence bag by O'Rourke and resealed.

After identifying the defendant, Carroll, as the woman he had seen at the ATM on Front Street the night before from a photograph shown to him by Ketaineck, O'Rourke returned to NBI headquarters. The evidence bag was placed in O'Rourke's evidence locker on that date. It was removed on December 19, 2016, for inspection by counsel for Carroll and the State's Attorney. It was returned to the locker that day and has remained there until the day of trial when it was brought to court by O'Rourke.

The case is now at trial. The State is presenting its case.

For the State, introduce the box and computer chip in evidence, using the witness(es) of your choice.

For the defendant, oppose the offer.

Problem 19

Cipriano v. Byrne

(Baseball Bat and Beer Bottle)

Charles "Chip" Cipriano has sued Dorothy Byrne and Dorothy's Bar & Grill for injuries sustained in an alleged assault. The incident giving rise to this lawsuit occurred on April 14, 2016, at Dorothy's Bar & Grill on 810 Main Street in Nita City. Dorothy's Bar & Grill is owned and operated by Dorothy Byrne.

On April 14, 2016, the plaintiff, Charles Cipriano, was a customer at the bar. He had been there for a few hours when a short time after 9:30 p.m., Cipriano engaged in a heated conversation with another patron, Larry MacKenzie. A fight ensued; Dorothy Byrne and others attempted to break it up, and then Cipriano fell backwards onto the floor striking his head on a table. The Plaintiff suffered a concussion, minor lacerations, and contusions.

The following are the relevant portions of the depositions of Cipriano, Byrne, and White.

Deposition of Charles Cipriano

I went to Dorothy's Bar & Grill after I finished playing softball, which was about 7:30 p.m. About 9:00 p.m., I got into a conversation with another customer by the name of Larry MacKenzie about the upcoming baseball season and the prospects for the Nita Nats. Larry was getting obnoxious, so our discussion got kind of heated. Pretty soon, we were in a full-fledged argument. After a while, we were ready to duke it out, and we began fighting.

Then all of a sudden, the bartender, Dorothy Byrne, hit me with a baseball bat. She sort of stabbed me in the chest with the fat end of the bat, I fell backwards, and that was all I remember. I don't remember anything about having a beer bottle in my hand. All I remember is that Larry and I were fighting, we were mixing it up, and I got hit by the baseball bat.

The deposition was read and signed by Cipriano.

Deposition of Dorothy Byrne

I own and operate Dorothy's Bar & Grill. On the night of April 14, 2016, I was tending the bar. Sometime around 7:30 p.m., Chip Cipriano walked into the bar with his friend, Peter Sanger. Cipriano and Sanger had been talking together at the bar for an hour or so when another customer by the name of Larry MacKenzie came up to the bar and sat down next to Cipriano. Cipriano and MacKenzie were sitting together for a while having some sort of conversation. After a while though, they began arguing and getting obnoxious. They were getting pretty loud, so I told them to cool it. Still, they kept it up.

Suddenly, both of them stood up and moved away from the bar and knocked over several bar stools in the way. Cipriano and MacArthur started fistfighting. I hollered out to them to break it up, but they weren't listening. They kept on fighting. Out of the corner of my eye, I saw Cipriano grab a beer bottle by the neck of the bottle. I decided that this fight had gone far enough, and that I had to do something before somebody got seriously hurt or killed. I reached under the bar for the baseball bat that I keep there. I hollered to Cipriano, "That's enough. Drop it!," but Cipriano kept going toward MacKenzie with the beer bottle. I speared Cipriano in the chest with the hitting end of the bat to keep him away from MacKenzie. Cipriano lost his balance, fell backwards, hit his head on the table, and fell to the floor.

Cipriano was lying on the floor without moving. I went over to check on him, and he was unconscious. I called the police and the ambulance. I picked up the beer bottle that Cipriano had held in his hand, and I gave both the beer bottle and the bat to the police officers when they arrived.

Byrne read and signed her deposition.

DEPOSITION OF WILLIAM WHITE

On April 14, 2016, I responded to a call for assistance at Dorothy's Bar & Grill, located at 810 Main Street in Nita City. I received the call at about 9:35 p.m., and I arrived at Dorothy's Bar & Grill within three minutes. When I arrived at Dorothy's Bar & Grill, Mr. Cipriano was lying unconscious on the floor. The ambulance arrived, and the attendants took him to the hospital. I conducted an investigation of the incident. As part of my investigation, I talked to Dorothy Byrne about what had happened. She told me that Cipriano had grabbed a beer bottle and threatened another customer and that she had stopped him by spearing him with a baseball bat, whereupon Cipriano fell and hit his head. She gave me the beer bottle and bat.

I marked the beer bottle by putting my initials and the date on it. I took the beer bottle and the bat to headquarters, and I put them in the custodian's office there.

The District Attorney decided not to file any criminal charges against any of the people involved in this incident. Dorothy Byrne requested that the bat be returned to her, and we complied with her request. The beer bottle stayed in police custody.

White read and signed his deposition.

* * *

A baseball bat was produced by the defendant, Dorothy Byrne, pursuant to a request for production during discovery. The request for production was phrased as follows: "Please produce the baseball bat that was involved in the incident with the plaintiff in the defendant's place of business on the evening of April 14, 2014."

The beer bottle that Dorothy Byrne gave to the police officer was lost while in police custody.

The case is now at trial. The plaintiff is presenting his case.

Part A. Baseball Bat

For the plaintiff, introduce the baseball bat in evidence using the witness(es) of your choice.

For the defendant, oppose the offer.

Part B. Actual Beer Bottle

For the defendant, introduce the beer bottle in evidence using the witness(es) of your choice.

For the plaintiff, oppose the offer.

Part C. Similar Beer Bottle

For the defendant, introduce a similar bottle in evidence using the witness(es) of your choice.

For the plaintiff, oppose the offer.

PROBLEM 20

United States v. Potter and Dobbs

(Illegal Drugs)

After a prolonged surveillance, Special Agent Thomas Belote of the Drug Enforcement Administration arrested Gregory Potter for possession and sale of cocaine and Jane Dobbs for possession of cocaine. Belote's report follows:

8/20/2016 I observed suspect, John Potter, enter premises at Spanky's Bar and followed him inside. Observed him sit down next to Dobbs at bar. Dobbs passed something under bar to suspect, and in same exchange suspect returned a small plastic bag to Dobbs. Suspects exited premises, and I followed. Arrested suspects in parking lot. Informed them of their rights and searched them. Recovered from Dobbs a plastic bag containing white crystalline substance believed to be cocaine. Placed bag with substance in evidence bag and sealed it with date and initials. Returned to office and logged it into evidence locker.

9/3/2016 Mailed evidence bag with contents to DEA lab in Washington, D.C.; return receipt requested.

9/8/2016 Receipt received.

9/21/2016 Received evidence back. My seal broken. New seal intact. Initials on new seal RMN.

[Signed]

Thomas Belote, SA

The DEA chemist who tested the batch was Robert M. Norris. His report is as follows:

9/6/2016 Signed for drugs from the Nita Regional Office. Deposited in evidence locker. Seal intact.

9/16/2016 Removed item from evidence locker. Weighed contents 17.04 g. Visually appears to be cocaine. Removed 0.3 g for testing. Melts at 98 degrees C. Soluble in water, alcohol, and chloroform. Platinum-chloride produces feathery, pale yellow crystals; gold chloride produces long rod-like crystals with arms at right angles; and cobalt thiocyanate produces blue flaky precipitate. No reaction to Marquis's, Froehde's, or Mecke's reagents. Conclusion: cocaine of moderate purity (35–50 percent). Returned 16.54 g to Nita Regional Office.

[*Signed*]

Robert M. Norris, Chemist

* * *

The case is now at trial. The State is presenting its case.

For the State, introduce the alleged cocaine and the results of the chemical analysis in evidence using the witness(es) of your choice.

For the defendants, oppose the offer.

PROBLEM 21

Perkins v. Spring Lake Wineries of Nita, Inc.

(Wine Bottle)

The plaintiff, Edward Perkins, has sued the defendant, Spring Lake Wineries of Nita, Inc., for injuries sustained by him after consuming a quantity of wine at his wedding reception. The defendant is both the bottler and a vendor of the wine that was consumed. The plaintiff has alleged negligence, breach of implied warranties of merchantability and of fitness for a particular purpose, and infliction of emotional and mental distress.

Edward Perkins is a graduate of the MBA program at the University of Nita, and Wanda Kohler is a graduate of Swarthmore College, with a degree in music. They were married on July 26, 2016, at 3:00 p.m. in Nita City, Nita. A wedding reception and party followed shortly thereafter at the Nita City Country Club. Over 300 guests were in attendance.

It has been a century-old tradition in the Kohler family that the father of the bride buy a bottle of wine and present it to the groom at the wedding reception. After that, according to tradition, the groom is to uncork the bottle, make a toast to the bride's family, take a drink directly from the bottle, and then pour a glass for the bride who toasts the groom's family. The bride and groom then toast each other and the grand march begins. After the grand march, the bride and groom stand in a receiving line to greet the guests.

The defendant, Spring Lake Wineries of Nita, has its principal winery in Nita City, which also includes a retail outlet store for the sale of wine to the public. Jerome and Nancy Kohler, the parents of the bride, knew that Spring Lake wines had an excellent reputation in Nita City, and so on July 24, 2016, Mr. and Mrs. Kohler went to the retail outlet store at the defendant's winery in Nita City to purchase a very special bottle of wine for their daughter's wedding.

While at the defendant's retail outlet store on July 24, 2016, Mr. and Mrs. Kohler told the sales clerk that they wanted to purchase a very fine bottle of wine to be used in a toast at their daughter's upcoming wedding. The Kohlers told the sales clerk that the toast would be part of an old family tradition at the wedding, and thus they wanted to purchase a bottle of wine suitable for the occasion. On the sales clerk's recommendation, the Kohlers purchased a very expensive bottle of champagne. The bottle was opaque, and it looked very elegant and expensive. The sales clerk assured the Kohlers that it was an outstanding bottle of wine.

The date for their daughter's wedding was July 26, 2016, and Mr. and Mrs. Kohler wrote the following inscription on the label of the bottle of wine they had purchased at the defendant's winery—"Ed and Wanda, July 26, 2016, Love, Mom and Dad Kohler."

At the wedding reception on July 26, 2016, Jerome Kohler, pursuant to the Kohler family tradition, presented to the groom, Edward Perkins, the bottle of wine that he had purchased from the defendant. At the appropriate point in the reception, the groom uncorked the bottle and he took a drink directly from the bottle of wine. After drinking the wine, the groom began pouring a glass for his bride. All at once, Edward Perkins' face went ashen. He said, "My God, what did I just drink?" Edward saw debris that looked like insects and other foreign substances coming out of the bottle and into the wine glass. He felt nauseated and walked rapidly to the bathroom.

Jerome Kohler, the bride's father, immediately went to the groom's place at the head table to examine the bottle of wine he had purchased. Mr. Kohler picked up the bottle of wine that the groom had drunk from, examined it, corked it, and then took it back to his place at the head table.

While in the bathroom the groom, Edward Perkins, threw up and felt very ill. After spending fifteen to twenty minutes in the bathroom, a rather shaken-up and ill-looking groom returned to the reception. He spoke with his parents and in-laws for a few moments, and then the bride and groom left the reception.

After the bride and groom had left, Mr. Kohler picked up the bottle of wine from the table where he had left it and took it outside and put it in the trunk of his car. He then went back to the reception to make the most of a bad situation.

Because of the rapid departure of the bride and groom, the reception broke up thirty to forty-five minutes later, even before the band began playing. According to custom, many of the guests at a wedding reception will present gifts of money to the groom as they go through the receiving line after the grand march. Due to the early departure of the bride and groom, the grand march and receiving line were not conducted. The customary gifts of money were not received. Furthermore, the bride and groom were so upset by the incident that they were not able to enjoy the incidents of the nuptial night.

Upon arriving home, Jerome Kohler removed the wine bottle from his car and put it in a storage area in the basement of his home. When he hired counsel, he gave it to the attorney handling the case.

The case is now at trial. The plaintiff is presenting his case.

For the plaintiff, introduce the wine bottle in evidence using the witness(es) of your choice.

For the defendant, oppose the offer.

PROBLEM 22

Brown v. Byrd

(Accident Report)

For the basic facts of this case refer to Problem 2.

The accident between Brown and Byrd was investigated at the scene by Officer David Pierce of the Nita City Police Department. He filed a report (*see* Exhibit 1) on the accident.

In a brief deposition, Officer Pierce testified that he was called to the scene of this accident by the radio dispatcher and that he conducted the investigation as reflected in the report. He obtained the information contained in the report by interviewing the two drivers involved in the accident. The accident was, in his opinion, unavoidable. That, coupled with the fact that there were no injuries complained of, caused him not to issue any citations.

When asked why his report was not filed until the next day, Officer Pierce states that immediately after investigating this accident, that he was called to the scene of a twenty-car chain reaction pile-up on Interstate 76, where there were several serious injuries. The I-76 investigation required hours to complete and, as a result, he did not file the report in the accident in this case until the next day.

The case of Brown v. Byrd is at trial, and the plaintiff has presented its case-in-chief and rested. The defendant's midtrial motion for judgment as a matter of law has been denied.

Part A

For the defendant, introduce the report of Officer Pierce in evidence, using the witness(es) of your choice.

For the plaintiff, oppose the offer.

Part B

For the plaintiff, introduce plaintiff's diary on the issue of his pain and suffering.

For the defendant, oppose the offer.

Exhibit 1

NITA CITY POLICE DEPARTMENT
Accident Report

1. Investigating Officer: D. Pierce		2. Badge No: 2157
3. Date: April 20, 2015	4. Time: 3:40 p.m.	5. Place: Nita City
VEHICLE # 1		
6. Operator: Kenneth Brown	7. Address: 5 Scott Pl. N. C.	8. Vehicle Title #: G18M4443798
9. Year: 2013	10. Make: Honda	11. Model: Sedan
12. Lic. Plate: GSB 356	13. State: Nita	14. Insurance: State Farm
15. Pol. #: 00528–24–2234	16. Towed: Driveable	17. Damage: Rear bumper and trunk
VEHICLE # 2		
6. Operator: Robert Byrd	7. Address: 104 E. Main, N. C.	8. Vehicle Title #: IP644W5772
9. Year: 2015	10. Make: Volvo	11. Model: Sedan
12. Lic. Plate: KJM 044	13. State: Nita	14. Insurance: USAA
15. Pol. #: 3001–17750–1440	16. Towed: Driveable	17. Damage: Front fender
18. Principal Road: 12th Avenue	19. Speed Limit: 25	20. Intersecting Road: E. Main

21. Injuries: None - minor accident

22. Narrative: Interviewed both drivers. Vehicle #1 was traveling south on 12th Avenue. When he neared intersection of E. Main light was green. Light changed to yellow and #1 stopped short and was rear-ended by Vehicle #2. #2 appeared to be traveling within posted speed limit of 25 mph and to have his vehicle under control. #2 may have been following too close, but accident was made unavoidable by the sudden and unnecessary stop by #1. Note also that timing of yellow light was short as previously noted. In light of all of above—No Citations—Both vehicles driveable—No injuries

23. Investigating Officer Signature: [Signed]	Date: 4/21/2015

Exhibit 2

5/7

Pain in back and neck starts
after arrival in Chicago 4/20
Up all night with back and neck pain.
Also terrible headache — doesn't
respond to Tylenol or ibuprofen.
Saw internist next day. Told pain is
definitely from car wreck, though
didn't seem hit that hard. Stayed
home from work rest of week.
Returned to work but not able to
work full shift. Dr Gomes prescribes
rest and ibuprofen. Informed if
not better in couple of days try
heat and massage treatment, maybe
chiropractor. Pain still nagging in back,
headaches are not as frequent by 5/5
Made appointment with Dr McCullough
who has office in neighborhood,
recommended by Arnie down the
block. Treatment gives temporary
relief from pain. Treatment
schedule discussed. Pain not
quite as bad but enough to notice
today — unable to work fullday.

5/10

Stretching a little in morning helps
stiff back. Worked full day — pain
distracting at work — by 6:00 back
very painful. Called for McCullough
appointment.

5/11

Back still bothering me. — dull aching
pain — had to leave work early. Set up
regular treatments with Burmeister
Clinic for heat, massage, hot bath therapy.

5/15

Burmeister helps but still stiff
every morning — worked 6 hour days
this week.

5/20

Sharp pain today reaching for a
notebook at work — stays all day
until I get to Burmeister.

Exhibit 2 (con't.)

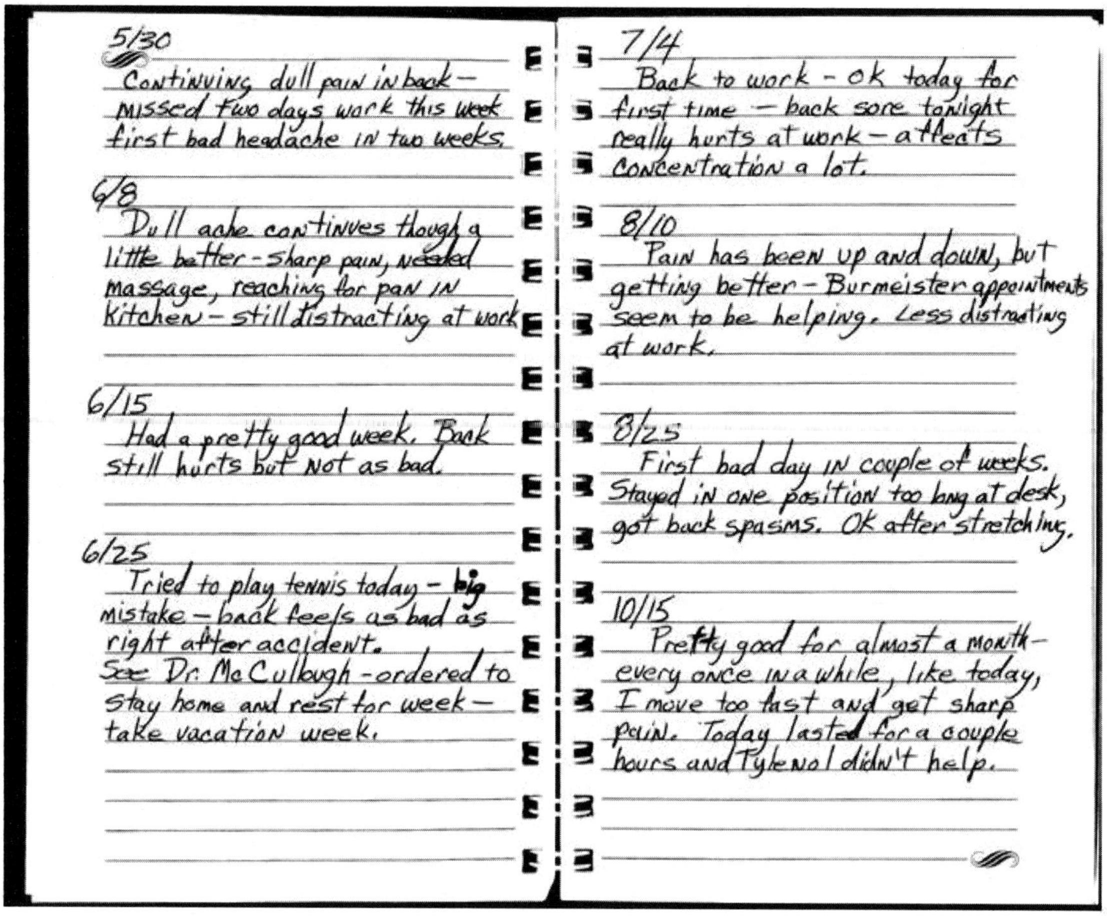

5/30
Continuing dull pain in back —
missed two days work this week,
first bad headache in two weeks.

6/8
Dull ache continues though a
little better — sharp pain, needed
massage, reaching for pan in
kitchen — still distracting at work.

6/15
Had a pretty good week. Back
still hurts but not as bad.

6/25
Tried to play tennis today — big
mistake — back feels as bad as
right after accident.
See Dr. McCullough — ordered to
stay home and rest for week —
take vacation week.

7/4
Back to work — ok today for
first time — back sore tonight
really hurts at work — affects
concentration a lot.

8/10
Pain has been up and down, but
getting better — Burmeister appointments
seem to be helping. Less distracting
at work.

8/25
First bad day in couple of weeks.
Stayed in one position too long at desk,
got back spasms. Ok after stretching.

10/15
Pretty good for almost a month —
every once in a while, like today,
I move too fast and get sharp
pain. Today lasted for a couple
hours and Tylenol didn't help.

Exhibit 2 (con't.)

10/17
Saw Dr. McCullough — he sees
good deal of improvement but
warns not to try too much.

11/20
Doc okays light tennis —
beginning with 20 minute
sessions.

PROBLEM 23

Cipriano v. Byrne

(Medical Record)

For the basic facts of this case refer to Problem 19.

In *Cipriano v. Byrne*, the case is now at trial, and the plaintiff has taken the stand and testified consistent with the facts in Problem 19, Part A. On the issue of damages the plaintiff's counsel would like to introduce the progress notes made by Dr. Barco marked as Exhibit 1 that follows this problem.

Part A

For the plaintiff, introduce the medical record into evidence using the witness(es) of your choice.

For the defendant, oppose the offer.

Part B

The defendant seeks to introduce the police report of Officer White marked as Exhibit 2 that follows this problem.

For the defendant, introduce the police report into evidence using the witness of your choice.

For the plaintiff, oppose the offer.

Exhibit 1

NITA GENERAL HOSPITAL
NITA CITY

Patient's Name	Cipriano, Charles	**Hospital No:**	04-297	**Room No:**	431T		
Admitted:	4/14/2016	**Date of Surgery**		**Discharged:**	4/15/2014		
Dictated:	4/14/2016	**Transcribed**	4/15/2016	**Insurance:**	Blue Cross		

PROGRESS NOTES

4/14   Patient admitted in emergency room at 10:00 p.m.

4/14   Subjective: Patient was unconscious when first brought in. Patient regained consciousness soon after he arrived. Patient complained of dizziness and pain in his head. Patient states he had consumed a couple of beers at a local bar (Dorothy's Bar & Grill), had been hit with a baseball bat by the bartender in an unprovoked attack, and fell and struck his head.

Objective: Patient has a small laceration on the crown of his head. There also appears to be a contusion and some swelling.

Empirin with codeine—5 mg every four hours.

4/14   X-ray report: Negative

4/14   Diagnosis: Patient appears to have suffered a mild concussion as the result of a fall. Minor laceration. Hold for observation.

4/15   2:00 p.m. Discharge—Barco

Certified as a true and correct copy of the original in the medical files of Nita General Hospital. Pursuant to N.G.S. 409, 1989, the original of all medical records must remain in the custody of the treating hospital.

[*Signed*]
William Sheffield
Director, Medical Records
Nita General Hospital

Exhibit 2

NITA CITY POLICE DEPARTMENT
Nita City, Nita

INVESTIGATIVE REPORT

1. Complaining Witness Response to a call from the premises	2. Address 810 Main Street, Nita City, NI
3. Phone 449-5689 (business)	4. Complained of Offense Bar fight
5. Date April 14, 2016	6. Time 9:35 p.m.

7. Narrative

Responded to a call for assistance at Dorothy's Bar & Grill located at 810 Main Street, Nita City, NI, at 9:35 p.m. on April 14, 2016.

When I arrived, Charles Cipriano was lying unconscious on the floor. The ambulance arrived and took him to the hospital. After talking with Dorothy Byrne and other witnesses at the bar, I did not file any charges. Byrne relayed that Cipriano had threatened another patron with a beer bottle in his hand. Byrne, in order to prevent the fight, hit Cipriano with a baseball bat.

It appeared to be a typical bar room fight, where each person was acting in their own self-defense. No charges were filed against any of the people involved.

8. Investigating Officer - Name and Signature
[Signed]
William White, Badge #8901

PROBLEM 24

Quinlan v. Kane Electronics

(Letters, Phone Log, and Form Contract)

For a basic statement of the facts of this case refer to Problem 9.

Assume there is no stipulation regarding the admissibility of exhibits. The case is now at trial, and the plaintiff is presenting her case-in-chief.

Part A

For the plaintiff, introduce Exhibit 1, the agreement letter between Quinlan and Kane Electronics, using the witness(es) of your choice.

For the defendant, oppose the offer.

Part B

For the plaintiff, introduce Exhibit 3, Quinlan's phone log of June 24, 2016, into evidence, using the witness(es) of your choice.

For the defendant, oppose the offer.

Part C

For the defendant, introduce Exhibit 4, the form contract, using the witness(es) of your choice.

For the plaintiff, oppose the offer.

Part D

For the defendant, introduce Exhibit 2, the draft letter, using the witness(es) of your choice.

For the plaintiff, oppose the offer.

Exhibit 1

ROBERTA QUINLAN

Business Broker

12 Meredith Lane
Nita City, NI 99992

June 12, 2016

Mr. Brian Kane
One Kane Plaza
P.O. Box 626
Nita City, NI 99992

Dear Brian:

It was a pleasure to visit with you this afternoon, and I write to confirm our understanding.

You, as the sole shareholder of Kane Electronics, desire to dispose of your stock holdings in the company by way of an exchange of shares of a corporation with a good investment future. If I arrange for such an exchange, which is acceptable to you, Kane Electronics will pay me a fee calculated at between 3–5 percent of the closing value to you, dependent upon my time and effort necessary on your behalf.

If I do not hear from you, I will assume that this arrangement is acceptable to you. I already have a prospect in mind and will be in touch with you in the near future.

Warm regards,

[*Signed*]

Roberta Quinlan

rq/s

COPY

Exhibit 2

ROBERTA QUINLAN

Business Broker

12 Meredith Lane
Nita City, NI 99992

Mr. Brian Kane
One Kane Plaza
P.O. Box 626
Nita City, NI 99992

Dear Brian:

It was a pleasure to visit with you this afternoon concerning the sale of Kane Electronics. As I told you, I am confident that I can find an appropriate purchaser of either the assets or the stock of the company, although I understand that you are also open to an exchange of your stock in Kane for stock in a company with a good investment future.

During our conversation, we agreed that I would use my best efforts and contacts (which are many) to find a suitable purchaser of Kane Electronics. Upon consummation of any sale, regardless of its nature or form, which results from my efforts, Kane Electronics will pay me an amount to be decided upon at a later date, but in no event less than 3 percent of the net closing value to the seller.

I will be in touch with you from time to time.

Warm regards,

[*Signed*]

Roberta Quinlan

rq/s

COPY

Exhibit 3

ROBERTA QUINLAN

Business Broker

Outgoing Phone Log

Date	Person Called	Telephone #	Business Purpose
6/24	Cliff Fuller NCW	287-440	Called re: potential interest in Kane Electronics. Says NCW looking to acquire companies like Kane. Thinks Kane may already be on their list of potential acquisitions. He will call Kane.
6/24	Brian Kane Kane Electronics	877-2893	Called to tell him to expect call from Cliff Fuller at NCW. Left message on voice mail.
6/24	Brian Kane Kane Electronics	877-2893	Called again. Secretary claims isn't in. I hope he isn't ducking me to try to get out of our agreement (don't be paranoid).

Exhibit 4

BROKER AGREEMENT

AGREEMENT made this ____ day of _____, by and between Roberta Quinlan, Business Broker, 12 Meredith Lane, Nita City, NI 99992, hereinafter "broker," and _____, hereinafter "customer."

In consideration of the mutual agreements hereinafter contained and other good and valuable consideration, the sufficiency and adequacy of which are hereby acknowledged, the parties hereto agree as follows:

1. The term of this contract is six months (180 days) from the date appearing above.

2. Customer hereby retains the Broker to locate a buyer or seller as appropriate for the requirements of the Customer.

3. Broker hereby undertakes to use best efforts to locate a buyer or seller as appropriate for the requirements of the Customer. Broker makes no guarantee or warranty of success with respect to any such efforts.

4. If the Broker locates a willing buyer or a willing seller as appropriate for the requirements of the Customer, the Broker has completed performance under this Agreement and is entitled to the fee described in paragraph 3.

5. Customer hereby agrees to pay to Broker a fee of ____% of the total selling price for the business, including the fair market value of any stock, stock options, warrants or other consideration of any kind, at the closing of the sale, in cash, by certified check, or by wire transfer.

6. This agreement shall inure to the benefit of, and shall be binding upon, the parties hereto and their successors and assigns. This Agreement shall be governed by the laws of the State of Nita. This Agreement may be executed in one or more counterparts, which, taken together, shall constitute the whole agreement, and there may be duplicate originals of this Agreement.

IN WITNESS WHEREOF, this Broker Agreement has been duly executed by the parties hereto as of the date first above written.

WITNESS:

_____

_____   _____
                                         Roberta Quinlan, Broker

                                         _____
                                         Customer

PROBLEM 25

NitaSport, Inc. v. Nita Slugger Corp.

(Letters and Phone Log)

For the basic facts of this problem, refer to Problem 8.

Assume there is no stipulation regarding the admissibility of exhibits. The case is now at trial, and the plaintiff is presenting its case-in-chief.

Part A

For the plaintiff, introduce Exhibits 1 and 2 into evidence, using the witness(es) of your choice.

For the defendant, oppose the offer.

Part B

For the plaintiff, introduce Exhibit 3 into evidence, using the witness(es) of your choice.

For the defendant, oppose the offer.

Part C

For the defendant, introduce defendant's phone log, Exhibit 4, into evidence using the witness(es) of your choice for the purpose of showing that Divine did not call with an order.

For the plaintiff, oppose the offer.

Exhibit 1

NITA SLUGGER CORPORATION

"The Bats of Champs"

Three Williams Plaza
Williamstown, NI 99992
Ph: 101-555-1717
Fax: 101-555-1700

January 4, 2016

Mr. Tom Devine, President
NitaSport, Inc.
1800 Riverside Drive
Nita City, NI 99992

Dear Tom:

I hope this letter finds you happy and well in the new year. As the new year begins, I am pleased to announce that NITA SLUGGER is introducing, for 2016, a new line of bats. The "Major League" model is one of our finest products in the long history of NITA SLUGGER.

We are pleased to offer the "Major League" bats to NitaSport at the introductory price of $1,928.00 per gross when you order a minimum of five gross of bats. We are confident that these bats will be an excellent seller for the upcoming season, and we encourage you to make your order early.

Tom, I hope that you can take advantage of this fine offer. I hope that we can speak about an order soon, or at the latest, at spring training for the NATS.

Sincerely,

[*Signed*]
Paula Blanchard
President

Exhibit 2

NitaSport, Inc.

1800 Riverside Drive
Nita City, NI 99992
Ph: 102-444-1000
Fax: 102-444-1019

January 25, 2016

Ms. Paula Blanchard, President
Nita Slugger Corporation
Three Williams Plaza
Williamstown, NI 99992

Dear Paula,

I am writing to accept your offer of January 6, 2016, to purchase a dozen gross of your new "Major League" line of bats at the price of $1,836.00 per gross for a total price of $22,032.00.

As we are currently going through an audit here at the home office, it will be several weeks before I will be able to get you the deposit check of $2,203.00. If this is a problem, please let me know.

Unfortunately, I won't be able to make it to spring training this year. I hope to see you next year.

Sincerely

[*Signed*]

Tom Devine

COPY

Exhibit 3

NitaSport, Inc.

Tom Devine

Outgoing Phone Log

Date: January 25, 2016

	Person Called	**Telephone #**	**Purpose**
1.	John Chambers Univ. of Nita Athletic Director	443-8001	Called re: supplying equipment for 2016 football season—Same deal as last year
2.	David Lange Nita Sports Films	441-2424	Obtained film for Chamber of Commerce Meeting on 2/2
3.	Paula Blanchard Nita Slugger	555-1717	Called to order 12 g. bats @ $1,836—left message
4.	Ray Roman Nita State Athletic Director	555-6000	Confirmed order of new uniforms for women's field hockey team—Ship by 8/1
5.	May Cravitz Lyman Hall H.S.	446-9423	Called re: 2016 equipment order for baseball team; she will get back to me with order by 2/1
6.	Tony Bello Nita NATS Ticket Office	441-NATS	Called to renew season tickets for 2016 season—same seats as last year 10% price increase
7.	Greg McDermott McDermott Dodge Service Dept.	443-5100	Repairs on van will be completed by 1/25 & delivered to Ridge Pike Store. Cost Estimate—$265

Exhibit 4

NITA SLUGGER CORPORATION

Incoming Phone Log of Paula Blanchard

Date: January 25, 2016

	Person Calling	Telephone Number	Purpose
1	Alex Roberts Nita Little League	498-8975	placed order for 26 gross of bats at 1,678 per gross
2	Patricia Smile Haircuts Plus	376-2345	Confirmation of hair appt.
3	Ron Roberts	230-7653	fix leak in roof of building
4	Greg Klein Nita bats	578-9902	confirmation of order for bats
5	Harry Pearlman South Nita Athletic Assoc.	782-6743	inquiring about new line of bats
6	Jenny Clark	670-8934	inquiring about sales position

PROBLEM 26

State v. Carroll

(Wiretap Transcript)

For the basic facts of this case refer to Problem 6.

Assume there is no stipulation regarding the admissibility of exhibits.

The wiretap of Moore was conducted on November 14, 2016, by Special Agent Richard Robertson. Robertson then called Special Agent O'Rourke, head of the investigation into the theft of computer chip technology in Nita's Silicon Valley. O'Rourke, who had known Moore for years and knew his voice, listened to the wiretap recording and identified Moore as the person who answered the phone at Moore's house at 8:00 p.m. on November 14, 2016.

The wiretap recording has been lost. The transcript, which is part of O'Rourke's report on the Carroll case, was prepared on November 14, 2016, at the conclusion of Special Agent Robertson's shift by Robertson's secretary, Harry Graves. Robertson compared the transcription to the tape for accuracy and passed the transcript on to O'Rourke.

The case is now at trial. The State is presenting its case-in-chief.

For the state, introduce Exhibit 1, the transcript of the wiretap, into evidence, using the witness(es) of your choice.

For the defendant, oppose the offer.

Exhibit 1

WIRETAP TRANSCRIPT
Subject: George Moore
Location: Moore residence, 38 Brighton Road, Nita City
Date: November 14, 2016
Time: 8:00 p.m.

Moore: Hello.

Unknown: George?

Moore: Yeah.

Unknown: Do you have a line on the Pear chip yet?

Moore: Yeah.

Unknown: When's it comin' in?

Moore: Two, three days max.

Unknown: Are you using the same drop?

Moore: What's it to you?

Unknown: We really need this chip, and I don't want
                you and your guy getting caught.

Moore: Front Street, near the Cove has worked for
                the last six months. It will work this time,
                too. You worry about the money; I'll worry
                about the chip

Unknown: You're the boss. I'll be in touch.

End of transmission.

Problem 27

McArthur v. Rogers

(Computer Printout)

For the basic facts of the case refer to Problem 4.

The plaintiff, Kathryn McArthur, as an element of her damages, must show her lost earnings for the period for which she was unable to work as a real estate agent. She seeks to introduce evidence of her earnings contained in the attached computer printouts. These reports have been generated by Marjorie Ulrich, the Office Manager at Reliance Real Estate where Ms. McArthur works. The deposition testimony of Ms. Ulrich is attached.

For the plaintiff, introduce the report into evidence, using the witness(es) of your choice.

For the defendant, oppose the offer.

DEPOSITION OF MARJORIE ULRICH

My name is Marjorie Ulrich. I am thirty-nine years old, divorced, and have three children. I have an associate's degree in business systems from Nita Community College, which I received in 2004. Aside from this degree, I have no formal training in accounting. I work at Reliance Real Estate, the same agency as Kathryn McArthur. I have worked there as the office manager for about ten years.

I have known Kathryn for about fifteen years. We attend the same church, and she helped me get the job as office manager at the agency by introducing me to the owner about ten years ago. She has been a good friend to me.

As the office manager, I am intimately familiar with the sales of each of our agents, who all work on a straight commission basis. I am charged with tracking their sales, calculating their commissions, and issuing their monthly checks. I do not attend all closing conferences, but I receive the closing documents from the realtors and ensure that the agency's fees are deposited in our account at Nita City Bank.

Exhibits 1, 2, 3, and 4 to this deposition are reports that I have prepared that show each of our agent's earnings for 2016, 2015, 2014, and 2013 on a monthly basis. I prepared the reports myself using a reliable, commercially available spreadsheet program named "Locust." I am self-taught on the system, but have been using it regularly for the past eight years. I consider myself to be very familiar with using the program. I keep reports similar to Exhibits 1 through 4 for our own records. To create the report, the program allows me to record an agent's earnings in commission from their sales on a monthly basis. I calculate these totals from the sales records that I maintain in my office. I keep a file for each salesperson for each year, with a copy of all the contracts on which they have earned a sales commission. Those files are available to be inspected, but our policy is that due to privacy considerations, you must subpoena them first. I try to enter the totals on the report each month, but do not always get around to doing it right away and sometimes may run a few months behind in entering the figures. The program then calculates a yearly total. I use the report at the end of each year to calculate year-end bonuses, so by the end of each year, the report is current.

No, Exhibits 1 through 4 are not identical to the reports I use in the office. But they are only different from the report that I usually use in that I have added the final column, which shows a monthly average for each agent for the years. Kathryn asked me to add a column to the reports that shows a monthly average. She did not tell me why she wanted me to do this, but asked me "as a favor." I used the Locust program to calculate the average by simply directing the program to divide the figure in the next to last column, the year total column, by twelve.

As the report shows, Kathryn's monthly commission average for 2015 was $18,860. Kathryn was one of our office's top performers in sales last year. Yes, the real estate business is cyclical in nature, which the exhibits show. Most sales come in the summer months. However, the agents are busy year-round generating business. Social connections and networking in the slow months can contribute to their obtaining listings and contacts that result in sales later in the year.

Yes, I am a very good friend of Kathryn, but I am an honest person and would not do anything to help her that would be dishonest.

Ms. Ulrich read and signed her deposition, making no corrections.

Exhibit 1

2016 Commissions per Agent (thousands $)

Sales Agent	Jan	Feb	Mar	Apr	May	June	July	Aug	Sept	Oct	Nov	Dec	Total 2016	Avg/Month
Bamber	4.1	5.3	5.5	6.2	7.3	7.1	8.3	10.5	9.2	7.1	5.1	4.3	80.3	6.6
Gumm	5.2	7.4	8.1	9.8	10.6	12.4	13.1	14.5	13.2	11.7	10.4	9.3	125.7	10.4
Kane	6.3	8.6	10.7	13.8	17.9	19.5	21.3	24.7	23.2	18.6	16.9	14.3	195.8	16.3
McArthur	0	0	8.7	11.5	16.7	20.7	26.4	28.9	24.4	17.5	15.4	14.2	184.4	15.3
Quinn*	0	0	0	5.9	6.2	8.7	11.6	12.4	9.3	8.1	7.9	5.6	75.7	6.3
Ruff	5.6	6.7	8.5	10.9	12.1	15.6	19.2	17.4	15.8	11.6	7.1	5.3	135.8	11.3

*Quinn started with the agency in March 2016.

Exhibit 2

2015 Commissions per Agent (thousands $)

Sales Agent	Jan	Feb	Mar	Apr	May	June	July	Aug	Sept	Oct	Nov	Dec	Total 2015	Avg/Month
Bamber	5.5	6.3	8.4	9.1	9.6	10.3	12.4	11.5	9.7	7.6	5.3	4.7	100.4	8.3
Gumm	7.1	8.4	9.5	11.6	13.8	16.4	19.5	17.1	13.6	9.5	7.4	6.3	140.2	11.6
Kane	13.8	15.3	17.9	19.4	20.6	22.3	24.9	20.5	17.6	13.3	10.7	9.2	200.5	17.1
McArthur	13.3	11.5	14.7	17.5	20.0	21.5	27.9	29.9	24.2	17.1	15.1	14.1	226.8	18.9
Parcell*	15.3	16.7	18.9	21.8	25.4	27.8	0	0	0	0	0	0	125.9	10.4
Ruff	6.9	8.2	9.7	13.4	15.8	16.5	19.7	17.2	12.6	10.3	8.6	6.7	145.6	12.1

*Parcell left the agency in July 2015.

Exhibit 3

2014 Commissions per Agent (thousands $)

Sales Agent	Jan	Feb	Mar	Apr	May	June	July	Aug	Sept	Oct	Nov	Dec	Total 2014	Avg/ Month
Bamber	0	0	4.4	5.7	6.1	7.2	9.3	8.4	5.8	5.3	4.1	3.5	59.8	4.9
Gumm	4.2	5.7	6.3	9.6	10.2	12.8	13.3	15.7	13.4	10.2	8.6	5.8	115.8	9.6
Kane	9.5	10.3	13.7	15.9	17.2	19.6	22.4	24.1	18.3	16.8	12.5	10.6	190.9	15.9
McArthur	11.3	9.5	12.7	15.5	18.0	19.5	25.9	27.9	22.2	15.1	13.1	12.1	202.8	16.9
Parcell	10.4	12.3	15.6	17.2	20.9	22.5	23.8	24.2	22.7	19.5	17.3	14.1	220.5	18.3
Ruff	5.2	7.4	8.6	10.8	11.5	14.9	16.4	15.7	13.3	11.2	8.8	6.5	130.3	10.8

*Bamber started with the agency in March 2014.

Exhibit 4

2013 Commissions per Agent (thousands $)

Sales Agent	Jan	Feb	Mar	Apr	May	June	July	Aug	Sept	Oct	Nov	Dec	Total 2013	Avg/Month
Coughlin*	10.9	13.7	16.6	17.5	19.7	22.9	23.5	25.8	0	0	0	0	150.6	12.5
Gumm	4.3	5.1	5.9	6.2	8.1	9.4	11.1	12.3	10.2	9.6	7.2	6.1	95.5	7.9
Kane	6.3	8.5	11.6	17.8	19.5	20.7	21.9	22.8	20.1	18.6	9.7	5.5	183.1	15.2
McArthur	9.4	7.4	10.8	13.4	16.1	17.4	24.0	25.8	20.3	13.0	11.2	10.0	178.8	14.8
Parcell	10.6	12.6	13.8	15.3	18.9	20.4	23.1	24.7	20.4	17.6	16.3	12.2	205.8	17.1
Ruff	5.1	6.4	7.1	8.3	9.5	11.9	13.6	14.5	12.7	11.6	10.3	9.4	120.4	10.0

*Coughlin leF the agency in August 2013.

SECTION III

IMPEACHMENT AND REHABILITATION

For substantive instructions on these subjects, please refer to any of NITA's texts on the art and science of trial advocacy.

Problem 28

Gentry v. Smith

(James Taylor) (Erica Klein)

On August 23, 2016, at about 4:00 p.m., a westbound Chevrolet, driven by Sam Smith, collided with a northbound Cadillac, driven by George Gentry, at the intersection of Jackson Avenue and Clark Street in Nita City. A diagram of the intersection follows this problem.

At the time of the collision, James Taylor was waiting for a northbound bus on Clark Street. The bus stop is just off the southeast corner of the intersection. Mr. Taylor gave his name to the police officer who came to the scene.

The next day, Larry Long, an investigator for Mr. Smith's insurance company, went to James Taylor's home to talk to him about the accident. At that time, Mr. Taylor gave the statement that follows this problem. The statement is in Long's handwriting, except for those places where Mr. Taylor wrote and initialed corrections.

Mr. Gentry has sued Mr. Smith for $10,000 in property damage and personal injuries, claiming that Smith went through the red light at a high rate of speed.

At trial, Mr. Taylor is called as a witness for Gentry. In summary, he testifies as follows:

> On August 23, 2016, at about 4:00 p.m., I was at the corner of Jackson Avenue and Clark Street, waiting for a northbound Clark Street bus. I happened to look toward the north when I saw a Chevrolet, traveling westbound on Jackson Avenue, go through a red light at a high rate of speed. The Chevrolet collided with a Cadillac that was going north on Clark Street. The Cadillac had the green light.

Smith's lawyer has received credible information that two weeks before the trial Taylor and his girlfriend were seen having dinner with Gentry's lawyer at LaBrach, the city's most expensive restaurant. Gentry's lawyer was seen paying for the dinner. Taylor, if asked, will admit this information is accurate.

Smith's lawyer also knows that on August 29, 2016, Taylor made a statement to Gentry's lawyer in the presence of a court reporter. That statement is entirely consistent with Taylor's trial testimony. Assume that the transcript has been prepared and is the same as Taylor's trial testimony.

Part A

For the defendant, conduct a cross-examination of Taylor, limited to those matters raised in this problem.

For the plaintiff, conduct any necessary redirect examination.

* * *

The defendant calls as a witness, Officer Klein, who investigated the accident. On direct examination, Officer Klein testifies as follows:

8	Q:	Did you interview the parties to the accident?
9	A:	Yes, I did.
10	Q:	What did Mr. Gentry tell you?
11	A:	He said he was distracted by spilling his coffee when it dislodged from his
12		cup holder and he grabbed for it as he went through the intersection. He
13		thought he had the yellow light, but he wasn't sure.
14	Q:	What did Mr. Smith have to say?
15	A:	He said that he had the green light. He was adamant about it.

Part B

For the plaintiff, conduct a cross-examination of Officer Klein, limited to an impeachment using her report (Exhibit 3).

For the defendant, conduct any necessary redirect examination.

Exhibit 1

Diagram—Intersection of Clark and Jackson

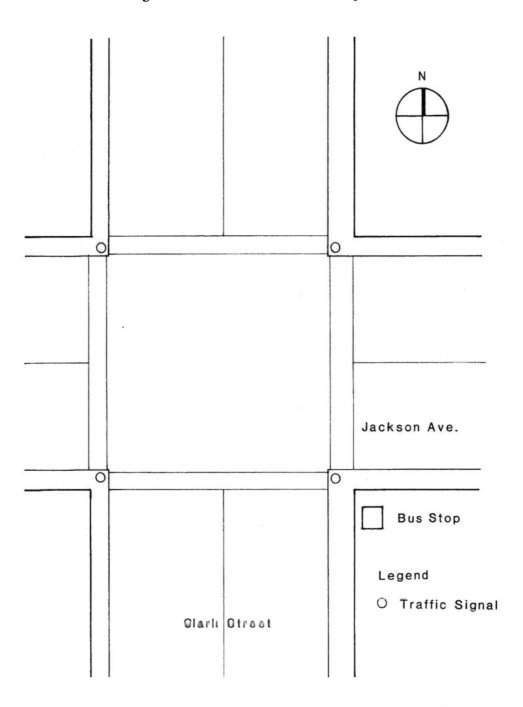

Exhibit 2

Statement of James Taylor

N. ~~97~~

My name is James ~~M.~~ Taylor. I am 24 years old and single. I work for General Electric as a ~~maintenance man.~~ *mechanic* JT

On August 23, at about 4 PM, I was at the corner of North and Clark, waiting for a bus to take me to the far north side. At that time, I was looking toward the south for my bus when I heard the screeching of breaks. I looked toward the corner, where I saw a westbound Chevrolet collide with a northbound Cadillac. At the time of the collision, the traffic light was green for the westbound traffic.

After the accident, I gave my name and address to the police officer.

Signed: *James Taylor*

Witness: Larry Long

Date: Aug. 24, 2016

Exhibit 3

NITA CITY POLICE DEPARTMENT
Accident Report

1. Investigating Officer: Erica Klein		2. Badge No: 7823
3. Date: August 23, 2016	4. Time: 4:00 p.m.	5. Place: Nita City
VEHICLE # 1		
6. Operator: Sam Smith	7. Address: 92 Clark Ave, N. C.	8. Vehicle Title #: H34L6653412
9. Year: 2012	10. Make: Chevrolet	11. Model: Sedan
12. Lic. Plate: LAJ-6593	13. State: Nita	14. Insurance: Nita Insurance Company
15. Pol. #: 00547-903-8876	16. Towed: Driveable	17. Damage: Front bumper
VEHICLE # 2		
6. Operator: George Gentry	7. Address: 89 Park Street, N. C.	8. Vehicle Title #: KL908W9882
9. Year: 2010	10. Make: Cadillac	11. Model: Sedan
12. Lic. Plate: MAG-9021	13. State: Nita	14. Insurance: Prudential Insurance Company
15. Pol. #: 9002-783-0931M	16. Towed: Driveable	17. Damage: Passenger door
18. Principal Road: Intersection Jackson and Clark	19. Speed Limit: 30 mph	20. Intersecting Road: Clark

21. Injuries:
No major injuries

22. Narrative:
Interviewed both drivers. Vehicle #1 was heading westbound on Jackson Avenue. Vehicle #2 was traveling northbound on Clark Street. The two collided. Driver of vehicle #2 relayed that as he approached the intersection he was a little bit distracted. He maintains, however, that the traffic light was yellow as he went through the intersection. Driver #1 proceeded through the westbound light. Stated he believed the light had just changed to green. No major injuries reported.

23. Investigating Officer Signature: [*Signed*]	Date: August 23, 2016

PROBLEM 29

Manning v. Carleton

(Melvin Carleton) (Doris Manning)

For the basic facts of this case refer to Problem 7.

The case of *Manning v. Carleton* is now at trial. The plaintiff has presented her case-in-chief, and the defendant's motion for judgment as a matter of law has been denied. The first witness for the defendant is the defendant, Melvin Carleton. Carleton has testified consistent with his deposition with the following exception:

1	Defense Attorney:	When did you first meet Ms. Manning?
2	Carleton:	When I moved into the Coventry Court Apartments
3		in September of 2015. I met both her and her young
4		son, Robby.
5	Q:	Was there anything in particular you noticed about Robby?
6	A:	Not at first. He seemed like a nice kid. But as time went on I noticed
7		that he was very quiet and withdrawn. I also noticed that he always
8		seemed to have a band-aid on his face or arms. He also had a black eye
9		three or four different times. His mother always had some excuse for it,
10		like he fell or he ran into a table or something like that.
11	Q:	Did you notice how Robby and the plaintiff interacted?
12	A:	Yes. He was very solicitous of her. Always looking for her approval. But
13		at the same time he seemed frightened of her. Whenever she called to
14		him, you could see him get real nervous and he would, quite frankly,
15		look frightened.

[handwritten annotations: "once?" near line 9; "INTRO DEPO." to the right of lines 9–11; "No other evidence?" below line 15]

* * *

At the time of the deposition of Mr. Carleton by plaintiff's counsel the following questions and answers were transcribed:

FROM THE DEPOSITION OF MELVIN CARLETON

Page 34, beginning at Line 4

4	Plaintiff's Counsel:	How frequently would you see Ms. Manning and
5		her son?
6	Carleton:	I noticed Ms. Manning and her son around the complex,
7		and usually spoke with her casually when we met.
8	Q:	In these meetings did you notice anything that would lead you to
9		believe that Ms. Manning was abusing her son?
10	A:	I didn't think much of it at the time, but from time to time when I saw
11		Robby he had a band-aid on his face, a bruise, or some relatively minor
12		facial injury.
13	Q:	Was there anything else that you believe was evidence of child abuse?
14	A:	I remember once Robby had a black eye, and when I kidded him about
15		it, Ms. Manning was quick to volunteer that Robby had run into the
16		corner of the kitchen table.
17	Q:	Was there any other evidence of child abuse?
18	A:	He also frequently had bruises and scrapes on his legs and arms. I don't
19		want to overstate his injuries because at the time I put them off to his
20		being an active boy who was a little careless, but I now believe there
21		were other, more serious problems.
22	Q:	Was there any other evidence of child abuse?
23	A:	Other than the night of May 6, no.
24	Q:	We'll get to May 6 in a while, sir. Have you told us every other indicator
25		of child abuse that you had from any source?
26	A:	Yes.

Doris Manning has testified consistent with the deposition with the following exception:

1 Plaintiff's Attorney: When did you first meet Melvin Carleton?

2 Manning: In September of 2015 when he moved into the Coventry

3   Court Apartments.

4 Q: Was there anything unusual about your relationship when you met?

5 A: No. He seemed like a nice enough guy. He was much younger than I

6   was. He told me that he was in school. It was a cordial first meeting.

7 Q: Did your son and Carleton have any contact?

8 A: It seemed as though Mr. Carleton was always trying to talk to my son.

9   He would always ask him questions and try to engage him in extra

10   lengthy conversations. I did not think anything of it at the time, but

11   now I guess that Mr. Carleton thought that something fishy was going

12   on and was trying to get it out of my son.

13 Q: Did your then-boyfriend, Bill, have any problems with Mr. Carleton?

14 A: No. He knew that Carleton was annoyed that he parked in his spot

15   once, but Bill thought since it was only once that it was no big deal. He

16   believed Carleton was making a big deal out of the minor issue. Other

17   than that, Bill believed that Mr. Carleton was a nice kid and had no

18   gripes with him.

* * *

At Manning's deposition she testified as follows:

6 Q: How did Melvin Carleton and Mr. Parrish get along?

7 A: Carleton really didn't like Bill, and I'd say the feeling was mutual.

8   Carleton was hostile towards Bill from the first time I introduced

9   them to each other. Bill's response was to ignore Carleton. Frankly, he

10   thought Carleton was sort of a geek and pretty weird. As a result, the

11   two hardly spoke at all.

12 Q: What was the source of their dislike?

13   A: The real problems between Carleton and Bill arose when Bill parked

14   his car in Carleton's space (Bill had bought me a stereo and was carrying

15   it upstairs so it was easiest to park in the space nearest the stairs) and

16   Carleton got really pissy about it. It was his space, and he did pay for

17   it as part of his rent, but the space for 2B was almost always available

18   because nobody lived in that apartment. The two of them had several

19   arguments about the parking space.

20   Q: Was that the end of it?

21   A: No, the problems got worse over the stereo. Bill and I like to play our

22   music on the loud side. When I could get a sitter, we'd go out dancing,

23   but because it was hard to find someone to watch Robby, most of the

24   time we'd play music and dance at my apartment. Yes, we did have an

25   alcoholic drink from time to time, but never more than one or two. I

26   would usually have work in the morning, and Bill would have to drive

27   home, so we never got what I would call drunk. More times than not,

28   when we were playing music and dancing, Carleton would call and

29   ask us to turn the music down. If it was late (after 10:00 p.m.) or on a

30   weekday, we'd usually turn the music down when he complained, but

31   on weekend nights (Friday and Saturday) I felt that I had just as much

32   right to enjoy and use my apartment as Carleton did, and I'd play the

33   music on the oud side and up until about 11:00 p.m. When Carleton

34   complained over the phone on the weekends (he never came in person,

35   although I caught him looking into my kitchen window from outside

36   his apartment several times), either Bill or I would tell him to lighten

37   up and not bother us.

Part A

For the plaintiff, conduct a cross-examination of Melvin Carleton, limited to those matters raised in this problem.

For the defendant, conduct any necessary redirect examination.

Part B

For the defendant, conduct a cross-examination of Doris Manning related to those matters raised in this problem.

For the plaintiff, conduct any necessary redirect examination.

PROBLEM 30

State v. Benjamin

(Mark Warden) (Alan Benjamin)

For the basic facts of this case refer to Problem 5.

The case is now at trial. The State calls Mark Warden in its case-in-chief. Warden has testified on direct examination consistent with his statement as it appears in Problem 5. Assume the following to be true:

1. Nita has a "three strikes" law that provides for life imprisonment without parole on conviction of the third felony for any defendant who does not provide "substantial cooperation" to law enforcement authorities. Warden is scheduled to be sentenced on his plea to one count of felony breaking and entering two weeks after the trial in *State v. Benjamin*. In Warden's case, the prosecution has filed a notice saying that it recommends that the "three strikes" law not apply to Warden because he provided substantial cooperation in Benjamin's case. Warden is aware of the prosecutor's recommendation.

2. Warden has two prior felony convictions in Nita. The first was on January 9, 2006, for filing a false statement with the unemployment office. Warden filed a statement that he was not working, but was caught by a fraud inspector working for cash for a local contractor. He pleaded guilty to obtaining money from a government agency by making a false statement and got a two-year sentence, all but sixty days of which were suspended, conditioned on successful completion of his sentence of probation. He was released from probation on January 10, 2008.

    On August 12, 2010, Warden was convicted of a felony for sale of cocaine. He sold the drug to an undercover officer. He was found guilty in a jury trial, this time getting a three-year sentence from which he was released in December of 2013.

3. In addition to the two felony convictions, Warden has two misdemeanor convictions. On March 3, 2014, he entered a guilty plea to a misdemeanor charge of larceny for shoplifting an inexpensive watch at a department store. He was sentenced to thirty days in the county jail. On July 17, 2015, he entered a guilty plea to misdemeanor assault arising out of a barroom fight. He was given a suspended sixty-day sentence for this conviction. Both carry a maximum sentence of six months.

4. Finally, although Warden has entered a guilty plea to one count of felony breaking and entering in his most recent case, he has admitted that he did, in fact, commit the six other larcenies, all involving theft of money and jewelry.

Alan Benjamin has testified on direct to the same facts as contained in his grand jury testimony with the exception of what follows:

Prosecution:	Did you ever meet Warden before late November or early December of 2016?
Benjamin:	I believe that he had come into my store a few times to sell me stuff.
Prosecution:	Did you buy anything from him previously?
Benjamin:	No. He seemed a little bit shady to me, and his stories about where he got the jewelry did not seem convincing, so I sent him on his way without making a purchase. You have to be careful in this business.
Prosecution:	Was there anything different about your business in November and December?
Benjamin:	Business was bad. People were just not coming to me to sell property. When people would come into the store to buy things, I did not have my usual inventory.
Prosecution:	Did you ask Warden any questions about where he got the jewelry that is in question today?
Benjamin:	I asked him where he got it, and he told me that he won it gambling.
Prosecution:	Did you ask him anything else?
Benjamin:	No. I believed him, so I bought the jewelry.
Prosecution:	Was there anything noticeable about him the day that he sold you the jewelry?
Benjamin:	He looked a little bit disheveled, and a little strung out.

Part A

For the defendant, conduct a cross-examination of Warden, limited to the matters raised in this problem.

For the State, conduct any necessary redirect examination.

Part B

Refer to the grand jury testimony of Benjamin in Problem 5.

For the State, conduct a cross-examination of Benjamin limited to the matters raised in this problem.

For the defendant, conduct any necessary redirect examination.

PROBLEM 31

State v. Carroll

(Paul O'Rourke) (Amanda Jones)

For the basic facts of this case refer to Problem 6.

The case is now at trial. The State called Special Agent O'Rourke as its first witness. A portion of the transcript of his testimony on direct examination follows:

1 Q: Directing your attention to 2:00 a.m. on November 18, 2016, what
2 did you see?

3 A: I had just gotten out of my surveillance vehicle and walked up Front
4 Street toward the ATM. At that time I saw the defendant, Ms. Carroll,
5 coming from the north toward ATM on the opposite side of the street.
6 As soon as I saw her, and before she saw me, I ducked back into the
7 shadows off the sidewalk opposite the ATM.

8 Q: How far from you was she?

9 A: Well, since I was directly across the street from her, I'd estimate a
10 distance of approximately forty feet.

11 Q: How did she appear at that time?

12 A: I saw a 5'5" white female, approximately 125 lbs. She had short brown
13 hair, almost like a man, was wearing glasses, and had several earrings
14 in each ear. She was wearing a tan trench coat, belted at the waist,
15 knee-high brown leather boots, and she was carrying a brown leather
16 shoulder bag on her right shoulder.

17 Q: What did she do at that point?

18 A: She walked up to the ATM e, which was well lit. I saw her look around
19 and reach into her shoulder bag. She removed a small silver box and
20 placed it in the envelope slot. She then left ATM, and headed south on
21 Front Street. I got a real good look at her.

22 Q: Special Agent O'Rourke, let me show you what has been marked as

23   Government's Exhibit 1 for identification. Do you recognize it?

24 A: Yes, that's the silver box with I saw Ms. Carroll place in the envelope

25   slot in the ATM on Front Street. It's the same box I later seized from

26   Moore and it's the one that had the Pear chip in it.

Assume that you have in your possession the report prepared by Special Agent O'Rourke, which follows this problem. It was received pursuant to a discovery request.

Jones's trial testimony is consistent with her statement with the following exceptions:

1   Defense Counsel: What time did you drop off Ms. Carroll?

2   Ms. Jones: Sometime around midnight, maybe a little later.

3   Q: Did you hear from her again that night?

4   A: Yes, it was a little after 1:00 a.m. I had just gotten home from

5   dropping off the sitter. Evelyn told me I had left my son's antibiotics

6   at her apartment—he had an earache. I asked her to leave them in her

7   mailbox and that I'd come and get them if my son needed them.

8   Q: Did you do so?

9   A: Yes, at about 1:30 a.m. my son started to cry and complained about his

10   ears, so we got in the car and drove over to Evelyn's.

11 Q: Did you see Evelyn's car at that time?

12 A: Yes, it was parked outside her apartment.

13 Q: Do you know where Front Street is in Nita City?

14 A: Yes.

15 Q: How long would it take to drive from Ms. Carroll's apartment to Front

16   Street?

17 A: At that time of night, about twenty minutes.

Part A

For the defendant, conduct a cross-examination of Special Agent O'Rourke limited to the matters raised in this problem.

For the State, conduct any necessary redirect examination.

Part B

For the State, conduct a cross-examination of Amanda Jones limited to the matters raised in this problem.

For the defendant, conduct any necessary redirect examination.

Exhibit 1

Front Street and Four Buildings

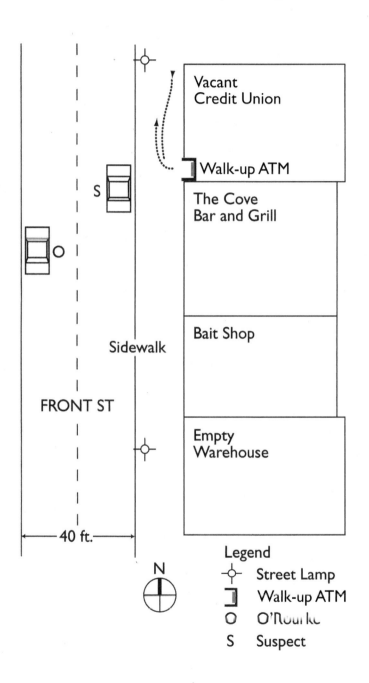

Exhibit 2

Memorandum Report

November 14, 2016: Pursuant to court approved interception of George Moore's home telephone (see transcript attached) learned that within the next three days a prototype of Pear Electronic's new "Platinum" chip would be passed from a Pear employee, identity unknown, to George Moore. Drop was to be made at an ATM outside the Cove Bar & Grill at 1201 Front Street in Nita City.

November 15, 2016: Set up surveillance with Special Agent Richard Robinson outside Cove Bar. Robinson took 8:00 a.m. to 8:00 p.m. shift. I was on surveillance from 8:00 p.m. to 8:00 a.m. Position taken up in unmarked vehicle some sixty feet from drop. Vehicle parked facing south on the west side of Front Street. Inspected the ATM for anything unusual. ATM found clean. No unusual activity observed on this shift.

November 16, 2016: Surveillance continues. No unusual activity observed.

November 17, 2016: Surveillance continues. No unusual activity on Robinson's shift. At 8:00 p.m., I resume surveillance after checking ATM, which is still clean. At 2:00 a.m. on 11/18 subject sighted. Subject approaches from north of the ATM, walks up, looks around furtively, places small container in envelope slot of the ATM, turns and proceeds north in direction of approach. Subject is female, 5'5", approximately 125 lbs., wearing tan trench coat.

Surveillance continues. At 2:10 a.m. Moore arrives in black, late model domestic sedan, parks in front of drop, the ATM. As Moore exits vestibule, he is apprehended and searched. Recovered a small metal container containing microchip with Pear logo. The item seized was in the lining of raincoat.

November 18, 2016: Attempted to interview Moore, but he insisted on counsel and refused to sign waiver. Proceeded to Pear Electronics. Spoke with head of security, Stephen Ketaineck. Informed he had a suspect. I was shown a photograph of subject. I made positive ID of woman who made drop. Located and arrested Carroll. After full explanation of her rights, she knowingly waived the same and submitted to an interview by this special agent. She denied taking anything from Pear and denied ever being at the ATM on Front Street. Suspect claims she was home with her sleeping child at time drop was made.

[*Signed*]
Paul O'Rourke, SA
Nov. 18, 2016

Exhibit 3

STATEMENT OF AMANDA JONES

My name is Amanda Jones. I am a thirty-five-year-old single mother of my son, Jimmy. I work for Pear Electronics, and I have for four years. I was under investigation for stealing confidential information and then giving it to a man by the name of George Moore. I do not know George Moore. No formal charges were ever made against me, so I assume they realized I had nothing to do with stealing anything from Pear.

Evelyn Carroll also works at Pear Electronics, and she has worked there for three years. She came to the company directly out of school where she got her associates degree in computer technology. To the best of my knowledge, she did not have any previous employment in the field of technology. Pear Electronics has been her one and only job in this field.

Evelyn and I are both single mothers and have developed a friendship throughout the time that she has been working at Pear Electronics. Because of family and work obligations, neither of us has a lot of spare time. However, the free time that we do have we tend to spend together. We spend our workdays together, and when we can, we share a babysitter and go out socially. We talk both about work and about personal situations that arise in our everyday lives. We are each other's confidants. I know that recently Evelyn has been concerned about her finances because her son's father was behind on his support payments.

Pear Electronics is a large company that employs over 300 employees. There are many female employees that work at Pear Electronics. I'm sure many of them had access to the chip that was stolen.

On the evening of November 17, 2016, Evelyn and I got a sitter and went out to a couple of clubs. Given Amanda's money situation, it was my treat, but as it turned out there were a couple of guys who bought us drinks, so it really didn't cost much. I brought my son Jimmy to her home where the sitter was and left him there. We then went out to a club and danced some. Evelyn had several drinks as I was the designated driver. I know she said she was very tired when I dropped her off and picked up my son at 11:30 p.m. No, I didn't see or talk to her after that until the next morning. I then drove the sitter home and was at my apartment at about 12:15 a.m. I did see Evelyn the next morning at work. We chatted about our evening out. She did not appear unusual in any way, although she seemed a little groggy. I kidded her about having too much to drink.

I heard from Evelyn the night of November 18, and she told me she had been arrested for stealing a computer chip. She told me they said she dropped the chip on Front Street at about 2:00 a.m. on November 18, 2016. That's impossible; she was home with her son. I'm sure she never stole anything. She's not that kind of person. You have just informed me that she was previously arrested and convicted for a misdemeanor of passing a bad check in 2011, but that doesn't change my opinion of her. I have no reason to think that she would do anything dishonest now.

Amanda Jones read and signed the deposition, making no corrections.

PROBLEM 32

Alexander v. McCormick Traction Co.

(Sydenham Alexander) (Ralph Cramden)

Sydenham "Syd" Alexander, the plaintiff, is suing the McCormick Traction Company, the defendant, for injuries he allegedly sustained when he fell while getting off one of the defendant's buses. The incident took place on July 29, 2016, at approximately 9:00 a.m.

Alexander gave a statement to an investigator for the defendant on August 18, 2016. In addition, he was deposed concerning this case on January 18, 2017. The case is now at trial, and Mr. Alexander is the first witness for the plaintiff. A copy of his statement to the bus company (Exhibit 1), a summary of his deposition (Exhibit 2), and a transcript of a portion of his direct testimony follow this problem. The bus driver, Ralph Cramden, gave a statement the day of the incident (Exhibit 3). His portion of his trial testimony also follows this problem.

Part A

For the defendant, conduct a cross-examination of Syd Alexander limited to the matters raised in this problem.

For the plaintiff, conduct any necessary redirect examination.

Part B

For the plaintiff, conduct a cross-examination of Ralph Cramden limited to the matters raised in this problem.

For the defendant, conduct any necessary redirect examination.

Exhibit 1

STATEMENT OF SYDENHAM ALEXANDER

My name is Syd Alexander. I live at 1516 Woodside Lane in Nita City. On July 29, 2016, I was a passenger on your company's bus. The bus picks me up near my house and drops me right across the street from my office.

When we got to my stop, I grabbed my briefcase with my right hand and started to get off the bus. The driver said something like, "Have a nice day," and when I turned to say goodbye to him, I slipped and fell, landing on my left knee. I had injured the knee when I was in high school playing football.

I was really in pain so they called an ambulance and took me to the hospital. It's still bothering me, though I'm able to get around using a cane.

That's everything I remember about the accident. I hope we can clear this up soon.

> [*Signed*]
>
> Sydenham Alexander

Witness: [*Signed*]

Julie Johnson

Subscribed and sworn before me this 18th day of August, 2016.

> [*Signed*]
>
> Harry Gibbons
> Notary Public

Exhibit 2

Summary of Plaintiff's Deposition

January 18, 2017

My name is Sydenham Alexander. Most people call me Syd. I'm twenty-six years old and live at 1516 Woodside Lane in Nita City. I work for Decker & Miller Real Estate Development Corporation, which has offices at Lafayette Plaza.

On July 29, 2016, I left my house at about 8:00 a.m., picked up the E-23 bus at the corner near my house at about 8:10 a.m. The bus took its usual route past City Hall and the Civic Center, through Cheeseman Park, and up Hilltop. We pulled up at Fifth and Main, by the Dart Drug opposite the movies, at 8:55 a.m. I'm sure of the time because I checked my watch to be sure I'd be on time for my 9:00 a.m. appointment.

I was sitting in the middle of the bus, so when I got up about five people were ahead of me. As I reached the three steps at the front of the bus, the person ahead of me was on the last step. I put my left hand on the railing and my right foot on the top step. I stepped down onto the next step with my other foot and onto the last with the one I used first. When that foot hit the third step, the rubber tread slipped back throwing me forward. My left foot landed between the bus and the curb, about two feet away, but my left toe caught the curb as I was thrown forward. I could hear my knee pop.

The pain was unbelievable. I was rushed to the hospital in an ambulance. They did all sorts of tests, wrapped the knee and let me go home. Even now, six months later, it still really hurts. I see the doctor once a month, and the physical therapist every week.

The plaintiff read and signed his deposition.

Transcript of Direct Testimony

The witness was sworn.

Examination by plaintiff's counsel.

1	Q:	Would you tell the judge and the jury your name and where you live?
2	A:	Sydenham Alexander. I go by Syd. 1516 Woodside Lane, Nita City.
3	Q:	How old are you?
4	A:	Twenty-six my last birthday.
5	Q:	How far did you go in school?
6	A:	I graduated from high school here in Nita City in 2007 and attended Nita
7		University, where I graduated with a degree in business administration
8		in 2013.
9	Q:	What do you do for a living?
10	A:	I work in real estate development for Decker & Miller Real Estate
11		Development Corporation located at Fifth and Main here in Nita City.
12	Q:	Directing your attention to July 29, 2016, what did you do that day?
13	A:	I got up at about 7:00 a.m., had breakfast, and went down to the corner
14		to catch my bus to work.
15	Q:	What bus is that?
16	A:	I take the 8:10 a.m. bus to work every day. It's the McCormick
17		Company bus that services Nita City. It leaves me off right across from
18		my office at about 8:55 a.m.
19	Q:	Do you remember anything about the bus ride on July 29, 2016?
20	A:	Yes. The bus was a little late, I guess because it was a new driver for
21		that route. I got on and recognized a former client of mine sitting in
22		the front of the bus. I usually sit closer to the middle of the bus, but it's
23		good to talk to former clients, just to keep good relations, so I sat down
24		and talked with her. There wasn't anything special about the ride until
25		we got to my stop.
26	Q:	What time did you arrive at your stop?

27 A: As I said, it was a little late. I remember looking at my watch; it was

28   9:00 a.m.

29 Q: What happened then?

30 A: Well, the bus pulled over to the side of the road at the bus stop. I

31   was the first one off the bus because I was in the front seat. There

32   were seven or eight other passengers getting off behind me. I know this

33   because they were the regulars on this particular bus. I had my briefcase

34   in my left hand and my right hand on the railing. When I reached the

35   bottom step with my right foot, I tripped over the raised portion of the

36   mat and landed on my bad knee on the edge of the curb.

37 Q: Excuse me, Syd, what knee is your bad knee?

38 A: My left. I hurt it playing softball about five years ago.

39 Q: How far was the bus from the curb?

40 A: Like I said, the bus driver was new and didn't get all the way over to the

41   curb. He was no less than a foot and a half from the curb. If he'd been

42   closer I would have landed on the curb and not hurt myself.

43 Defendant's Counsel: Objection as to the witness' conjecture as to the

44   cause of his alleged injury.

45 Court: Sustained.

46 Q: All right, Syd, tell the jury about your injury.

47 A. As I said, I landed on the edge of the curb and twisted my trick knee. I

48   was taken to the hospital and saw my doctor. I needed heat treatments

49   for the next ten months or so. My knee still isn't 100 percent, but I

50   don't want to have an operation.

The following statement was given by the bus driver directly after the accident in question.

Exhibit 3

STATEMENT OF RALPH CRAMDEN

July 29, 2016

My name is Ralph Cramden. I have been driving buses for McCormick Traction Company for nine years. I remember who I now know to be Sydenham Alexander getting injured getting off of my bus on July 29, 2016. Although I have been driving for this company for nine years, I had never driven the route that I was assigned to that day. The usual bus driver was sick, so I worked a double shift that day to fill in. It was good because I got paid overtime. I am sure that I said goodbye to Mr. Alexander when he exited the bus because I say "Goodbye" or "Have a nice day" to all of the commuters. I am not sure how he hurt himself. I saw him stumble, and the next thing that I knew he was lying on the ground right below the stairs of the bus. I was not sure what exactly happened, although I knew that he fell.

Ralph Cramden read and signed the statement.

* * *

At trial, the Defendant has called Ralph Cramden to testify. His testimony is consistent with his earlier statement with the exception of the following:

12	Defendant's Attorney:	Where do you work?
13	Ralph Cramden:	I work as a dispatcher for McCormick Traction
14		Company. I was promoted from my job as a driver
15		about a month ago. All the bus drivers now report
16		to me.
17	Q:	What was your job on July 29, 2016?
18	A:	I was working as a bus driver for McCormick. I was filling in on the
19		C-5 commuter route. It was my old route, so I know it very well.
20	Q:	Do you know how Mr. Alexander hurt himself on July 29, 2016?
21	A:	I told him to have a nice day, but I don't think he even heard me. He
22		was busy talking to other people getting off of the bus. He was not
23		paying attention at all and not looking where he was going. He seemed

24   like he was in a hurry. I was running a few minutes late that morning,

25   but that had nothing to do with Alexander hurting himself. He fell

26   on one of the steps. The next thing that I knew, he was lying on the

27   ground.

Problem 33

State v. Cunningham

(Richard Edwards)

Ralph Cunningham has been charged with murder in the first degree. The State alleges that in Nita City on November 15, 2016, Cunningham shot an on-duty police officer in the head, killing him instantly.

The case is now at trial, and Richard Edwards is a witness for the state. On direct examination, he testified that on the evening of November 15, 2016, at about 9:00 p.m., he and Cunningham walked up to a marked police car parked on the east side of LaSalle Street, just south of Division Street. Edwards added that pursuant to their plan, he opened the passenger door of the police car and Cunningham pulled a.38 revolver from his jacket pocket and shot the police officer in the head.

Investigation by defense counsel has revealed the following information:

1. Edwards was arrested for an armed robbery of a liquor store on November 29, 2016. He was apprehended running out of the store with a gun in his hand.

2. Edwards had given a statement to the police on November 29, 2016, and testified concerning the Cunningham case before the grand jury on December 2, 2016. His statement and a transcript of his grand jury testimony follow.

3. On December 15, 2016, the day his armed robbery charge was set for trial, Edwards agreed to become a witness for the State in the case against Cunningham. As a result of a plea negotiation between Edwards' attorney and the Assistant State's Attorney Robert Bench, Edwards made the following agreement with the State:

   a. Edwards will not be prosecuted for any crime related to the killing of the police officer, as long as he tells the truth.

   b. He will be allowed to plead guilty to the lesser included offense of robbery in the case involving the liquor store.

   c. The State will not recommend a sentence in the liquor store case.

In the state of Nita, murder in the first degree carries a penalty of life imprisonment without parole. Armed robbery carries a minimum penalty of five years imprisonment and a maximum penalty of twenty years. Robbery carries no minimum penalty and a maximum penalty of five years. Perjury carries a minimum penalty of one year imprisonment and a maximum penalty of ten years imprisonment.

The defense is considering two possible theories for use at trial:

1. Edwards was actually the person who committed the crime and is testifying against Cunningham. He learned from his questioning by the police that Cunningham was the person the police wanted to convict. Under this theory, Edwards' detailed knowledge of the crime is explained by the fact he actually committed it; or

2. Neither Edwards nor Cunningham committed the crime. Cunningham is testifying for the reasons outlined in (1), but got his information about the crime from the police.

For the defendant, conduct a cross-examination of Richard Edwards.

For the State, conduct any necessary redirect examination.

STATEMENT OF RICHARD EDWARDS

Taken on November 29, 2016, at Chicago Avenue Police Station

Questions asked by Officer Frank Kelly:

Q: What is your name?

A: Richard Edwards.

Q: How old are you?

A: Twenty-five.

Q: I am going to ask you some questions about the killing of a police officer on the corner of LaSalle and Division Streets on November 15 of this year.

A: I don't know anything about that.

Q: Were you anywhere near that corner on November 15 of this year at about nine o'clock?

A: No. I think I was at a movie on the south side with my girlfriend.

Q: Do you know Ralph Cunningham?

A: Never heard of him.

Q: Do you have any information at all about the killing of a police officer on that night?

A: I didn't even know a police officer was killed until you told me about it a few minutes ago.

Q: Do you have anything to add?

A: No. I have told you the absolute truth.

Q: Will you sign this statement after reading it?

A: Yes.

[*Signed*]   Witnessed by: [*Signed*]

Richard Edwards   Officer Frank Kelly

GRAND JURY OF DARROW COUNTY, DECEMBER TERM, 2016

TRANSCRIPT OF TESTIMONY TAKEN DECEMBER 2, 2016

PRESENT: Mr. Robert Bench, Assistant State's Attorney

Reported by Claus Flynn, Book #7254

WITNESS: Richard Edwards

* * *

RICHARD EDWARDS, having been first duly sworn was examined and testified as follows:

BY MR. BENCH:

1   Q: What is your name?

2   A: Richard Edwards.

3   Q: Do you realize you are now under oath?

4   A: Yes, sir.

5   Q: I call your attention to November 15, 2016, at around 9:00 p.m.

6   Where were you at that time?

7   A: I spent that entire evening on the south side of Nita City. I think I went

8   to a movie with my girlfriend.

9   Q: Were you anywhere near Division and LaSalle Streets on that date?

10   A: No, sir. I was nowhere near that neighborhood any time that day.

11   Q: When was the last time you saw Ralph Cunningham?

12   A: I told the police when they asked me that the last time, I've never heard

13   of him.

14   Q: Do you have any information about the killing of a police officer at

15   Division and LaSalle Streets on November 15, 2016, or any other day?

16   A: No. I don't know anything about it.

17   Q: Have you heard anything about the killing of a police officer on

18   November 15, 2016, around Division and LaSalle Streets?

19   A: The first I heard of that was when the policeman told me on the day

20   I was arrested.

21   Q: Is there anything you wish to add?

22   A: No. I have told you the honest-to-God truth.

23   Q: That will be all.

* * *

NO FURTHER PROCEEDINGS WERE TAKEN THAT DAY.

PROBLEM 34

Quinlan v. Kane Electronics

(Roberta Quinlan) (Brian Kane)

For the basic facts of this case see Problem 9.

Assume the following additional information was elicited from Quinlan during her deposition. Quinlan testified that when she returned to her home after the meeting with Brian Kane she prepared a draft of a letter to Kane before composing the final version. It was the final version she claims to have mailed to Kane. She produced not only a copy of the letter she claims to have sent Kane (Exhibit 2, reproduced as part of this problem), but also a copy of what she claims was the first draft of that letter.

The "draft" letter is also reproduced in this problem and is marked as Exhibit 3. Quinlan testified that after she read the draft, which was just a way to organize her notes concerning the meeting, she realized that it was not a clear statement of the agreement she had with Kane, so she wrote Exhibit 2, which, according to her, is a description of the agreement she had with Kane. Quinlan further testified that she destroyed her notes after she mailed out her letter to Kane.

The case is now at trial, and Quinlan has testified consistent with her deposition, which appears in Problem 9, as modified by the statement of this problem.

For the defendant, conduct the cross-examination of Ms. Quinlan limited to a comparison between Exhibit 3, the "draft," and Exhibit 2, the letter she claims to have sent to the defendant, Brian Kane. The theory of the cross-examination is that Quinlan was so unsure of the content of the conversation with Kane, as evidenced by the "draft" letter (Exhibit 3), that there could not have been an agreement reached at the time of their conversation.

For the plaintiff, conduct any necessary redirect examination.

Exhibit 2

ROBERTA QUINLAN

Business Broker

12 Meredith Lane
Nita City, NI 99992

June 13, 2016

Mr. Brian Kane
One Kane Plaza
P.O. Box 626
Nita City, NI 99992

Dear Brian:

It was a pleasure to visit with you this afternoon, and I write to confirm our understanding.

You, as the sole shareholder of Kane Electronics, desire to dispose of your stock holdings in the company by way of an exchange of shares of a corporation with a good investment future. If I arrange for such an exchange, which is acceptable to you, Kane Electronics will pay me a fee calculated at between 3–5 percent of the closing value to you, dependent upon my time and effort necessary on your behalf.

If I do not hear from you, I will assume that this arrangement is acceptable to you. I already have a prospect in mind and will be in touch with you in the near future.

Warm regards,

[*Signed*]

Roberta Quinlan

rq/s

COPY

Exhibit 3

ROBERTA QUINLAN

Business Broker

12 Meredith Lane
Nita City, NI 99992

Mr. Brian Kane

One Kane Plaza
P.O. Box 626
Nita City, NI 99992

Dear Brian:

It was a pleasure to visit with you this afternoon concerning the sale of Kane Electronics. As I told you, I am confident that I can find an appropriate purchaser of either the assets or the stock of the company, although I understand that you are also open to an exchange of your stock in Kane for stock in a company with a good investment future.

During our conversation, we agreed that I would use my best efforts and contacts (which are many) to find a suitable purchaser of Kane Electronics. Upon consummation of any sale, regardless of its nature or form, which results from my efforts, Kane Electronics will pay me an amount to be decided upon at a later date, but in no event less than 3 percent of the net closing value to the seller.

I will be in touch with you from time to time.

[*Signed*]

Roberta Quinlan

rq/s

COPY

PROBLEM 35

Scott v. Jamison

(Part A. Horrigan and Part B. Colson)

On July 18, 2016, the plaintiff, Harvey Scott, and the defendant, Susan Jamison, were involved in a car accident at the intersection of 17th Avenue and Pine Street in Nita City. The accident occurred at 3:50 p.m.

The plaintiff claims that as he was traveling north on 17th Avenue in his Toyota he made a right-hand turn onto Pine Street and was rear-ended by an eastbound Chevrolet driven by the defendant. The plaintiff claims that the light changed to green for the Pine Street traffic just as he turned. The defendant claims that she entered the intersection on a green light and that the plaintiff turned right on red directly into the path of her car.

Within minutes of the accident, Officer James White of the Nita City Police Department arrived on the scene and conducted an investigation. Officer White determined that in addition to the two parties there were two other witnesses to the accident: Robert Horrigan, a passenger in Scott's car; and Mary Colson, a pedestrian. After separating the parties and the witnesses, Officer White took statements from all four people. Scott and Jamison gave statements consistent with their respective positions in the lawsuit. Robert Horrigan and Mary Colson gave the following statements.

STATEMENT OF ROBERT HORRIGAN

My name is Robert Horrigan. I am thirty-four years old and live at 1205 Hemlock Court in Nita City. I am employed, together with Mr. Scott, as a warehouseman at the Flinders Aluminum Company in Nita City, where we work the 4:00 p.m. to midnight shift. I was a passenger in Mr. Scott's car at the time of the accident that just happened at about 3:50 p.m. We were on our way to work at the time of the accident. I have known Mr. Scott for five years, and in addition to working with him, we are social friends. He is my regular ride to work.

Just before the accident we were traveling north on 17th Avenue and intended to turn right on Pine Street. Flinders is located on River Road, just off Pine, about two miles from 17th. As we approached Pine Street on 17th, the light was red for the 17th Street traffic. As we got to the intersection, Mr. Scott slowed down. I looked at my watch to check the time, and we started to turn onto Pine Street. Just after we entered the turn we were hit from behind by the Chevrolet. I can't tell how fast the Chevrolet was going, but we were hit pretty hard. Fortunately, I had on my seat belt. Since I wasn't looking at the traffic light as we made the turn I can't be sure if the light had changed to green for us. That's all I know about the accident.

[*Signed*]
Witness: Officer James White

[*Signed*]
Robert Horrigan
Date: July 18, 2016

STATEMENT OF MARY COLSON

My name is Mary Colson. I am thirty years old and live at 1746 Pine Street in Nita City. I work as a claims adjuster for homeowner's policy claims for the Nita Fire and Casualty Company in Nita City. I'm a witness to a car accident that just happened a few minutes ago.

At the time of the accident I was walking east on Pine Street near the intersection of 17th and Pine. I had left work early because I felt a migraine headache coming on. I had just started to cross 17th Street from the southwest corner when the accident happened. I really don't know how fast the cars were going or who had the green light because I wasn't paying much attention to what was going on. After the accident happened I called the police on my cell phone. Because I work as a volunteer on the Nita Rescue Squad, I then went to see if anyone was seriously injured in the accident.

That's all that I know about the accident.

[*Signed*]

Witness: Officer James White

[*Signed*]

Mary Colson

Date: July 18, 2016

Part A. Robert Horrigan

The case is now at trial, and Robert Horrigan was called as a witness for the Plaintiff. On direct examination he testified, in part, as follows.

14	Plaintiff's Lawyer:	What happened as you got to the intersection of 17th
15		and Pine?
16	Horrigan:	As we approached the intersection traveling north on
17		17th, the light was red for the 17th Avenue traffic,
18		and Mr. Scott slowed down. The light then changed
19		to green for our lane of traffic, and we started into
20		the intersection. It was right then that the Chevy rear-
21		ended us. I saw the Chevy out of the corner of my eye
22		just before it hit. I'd estimate that the Chevy was going
10		about 40 mph. Pine Street has a 30 mph speed limit.

[End of trial testimony excerpt.]

At his deposition in December of 2016, Mr. Horrigan testified consistent with his trial testimony, but added his opinion that he "was sure that the light had changed to green and that Mr. Scott was not turning right on red because he did not come to a full stop before turning." Defendant's lawyer also learned during Horrigan's deposition that Horrigan met with the plaintiff's lawyer shortly after the accident and had discussed the accident with her. That meeting took place in October of 2016. During the discussion with the plaintiff's lawyer, Horrigan gave the same version of the accident to which he testified at trial. Several months later in February 2017, Horrigan was involved in a work-related accident and hired plaintiff's lawyer to represent him in his workers compensation claim. That litigation is ongoing.

Horrigan has completed his direct examination.

For the defendant, conduct the cross-examination of Mr. Horrigan.

For the plaintiff, conduct any necessary redirect examination.

Part B. Mary Colson

The plaintiff has completed his case-in-chief and has rested.

During the defendant's case-in-chief Mary Colson was called as a witness. She testified in part as follows on direct examination:

22	Defendant's Lawyer:	Did you see the accident between the eastbound
23		Chevrolet and the Toyota?
24	Mary Colson:	Yes, I did.
25	Defendant's Lawyer:	What happened?
26	Mary Colson:	Well, as I said, I was walking home from work
27		and had just started to cross 17th Avenue from
28		the southwest corner of the intersection toward
29		the southeast corner. At that point I noticed a
30		Chevrolet traveling east on Pine Street. The Toyota
31		that was headed north on 17th Avenue turned right
32		on red in front of the Chevrolet and the Chevrolet
33		couldn't avoid hitting the Toyota. The Chevrolet
34		had the green light. It wasn't going very fast, maybe
35		20 mph.

[End of trial testimony excerpt.]

At her deposition on December 12, 2016, Ms. Colson testified consistent with her trial testimony. As the testimony developed at the deposition, plaintiff's lawyer discovered that on September 20, 2016, Ms. Colson was interviewed by an investigator for the defendant's insurance company. Ms. Colson testified, "It was during this meeting that I realized that the Chevrolet must have had the green light, because I had started into the intersection myself. 17th and Pine is a dangerous intersection in my neighborhood that I cross twice daily, and I always cross only with the light. In fact, my neighborhood civic association has lobbied the city council to not allow right turns on red to make the intersection safe for pedestrian traffic, but to no avail as of yet. At any rate, if the light was green for me then it must have been green for the Chevrolet."

Colson has completed her direct testimony.

For the plaintiff, conduct the cross-examination of Ms. Colson.

For the defendant, conduct any necessary redirect examination.

Exhibit 1

Diagram

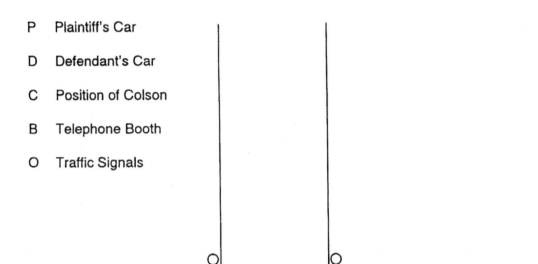

P   Plaintiff's Car

D   Defendant's Car

C   Position of Colson

B   Telephone Booth

O   Traffic Signals

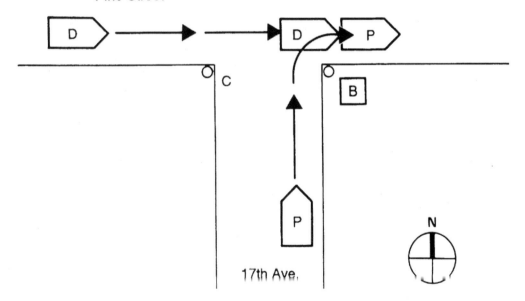

SECTION IV

ADVERSE EXAMINATION

For substantive instructions on this subject, please refer to any of NITA's texts on the art and science of trial advocacy.

PROBLEM 36

The Group v. Personality Posters, Inc.

(David Bentley)

THE GROUP is a rock band that during the past year has achieved a great deal of success. THE GROUP recently completed its maiden concert tour of the United States and has taken the country by storm.

The defendant, Personality Posters, Inc., has been producing and marketing a poster of THE GROUP in concert. The poster has not been authorized by THE GROUP or anyone connected with the band. THE GROUP has filed a petition for a temporary restraining order against Personality Posters, Inc., to preclude the further production and distribution of the posters.

Plaintiff's counsel has hired an investigator, Harold Bender, who has obtained the following information from Jane Fitzgerald who, until recently, was the secretary to the President of Personality Posters, Inc., David Bentley.

David Bentley recognized the star quality of THE GROUP and decided to quickly market a poster to be sold outside places where THE GROUP is performing in concert and in record stores. The poster of THE GROUP was produced from a photograph taken by David Bentley during its tour-opening concert in Nita City during M-7.[2] The poster depicts THE GROUP in concert with the inscription "THE GROUP" in large letters at the bottom of the poster.

Mr. Bentley's first run of the posters was in a quantity of 20,000. This "first run" was quickly sold out at concerts by THE GROUP in Philadelphia, Los Angeles, San Francisco, Fresno, Houston, and New Orleans during the month of M-5. During M-3, a second run of posters in a quantity of 50,000 was produced and distributed to record stores throughout the United States. In M-1, approximately 30,000 of the posters produced in the second run have been sold, and the orders have been coming in at a remarkable pace. A third run of 100,000 posters was requested in late M-1.

The retail price for the poster was $3.00 per poster on the first two runs, and the retail price for the posters on the third run is scheduled to be increased to $6.00 per poster. Mr. Bentley has personally handled all aspects of the production and marketing of the poster.

Ms. Jane Fitzgerald has furnished the above information on a confidential basis, and she will not be available as a witness in the proceedings for a temporary restraining order. THE GROUP's tour is continuing and will run in New York City, Buffalo, Pittsburgh, Cleveland, and

---

2. M-0 denotes the current month in which this problem is being used; M-1 denotes the next preceding month (please use the actual month); M-2 denotes the second preceding month (please use the actual month), etc.

Chicago during the next five weeks. In this proceeding, THE GROUP is seeking a temporary restraining order to prohibit future marketing of the poster by the defendant.

The name of the band, "THE GROUP," is a registered trademark. The trademark "THE GROUP" has been registered jointly to the members of the band. The trademark registration symbol, (, does not appear next to the words "THE GROUP" on the posters of the band that are being produced by the defendant, Personality Posters, Inc.

The statute governing the Plaintiff's petition for a temporary restraining order is 9 Nita Consolidated Statutes, 202, et seq: Section 203 provides:

> The court, after hearing, may issue an appropriate order exercising its full equitable jurisdiction. Plaintiff has the burden of establishing by clear and convincing evidence that there is no adequate remedy at law by demonstrating:
>
> a.   money damages will be difficult or impossible to compute;
>
> b.   defendant is, or was, engaged in a course of conduct that would necessitate numerous lawsuits for damages; and
>
> c.   defendant will continue to violate plaintiff's protected rights.
>
> Unless the Court is satisfied that subsections (a), (b), and (c) have been met, it shall not issue a temporary restraining order.

The documents that follow this problem were produced by the defendant, David Bentley, in response to a subpoena duces tecum.

Assume that the case is ready to proceed at the hearing on plaintiff's petition for a temporary restraining order.

For the plaintiff, examine Mr. Bentley on whatever topics you think appropriate.

For the defendant, conduct a cross-examination of Mr. Bentley.

For the plaintiff, conduct any necessary follow-up examination.

Personality Posters, Inc.
Suite 1200
217 East Weston Drive
Chicago, Illinois 60606
000-000-0000

D-10*

Mr. Richard Crosby
151 42nd Street
Great Lakes Concert Distributions, Inc.
New York, New York 10017

Dear Dick:

Under separate cover 100,000 posters of THE GROUP are being sent to your New York office for distribution at Madison Square Garden and the other concert sites.

As previously agreed, the retail price for each poster sold is $6.00. These posters will be delivered on a consignment basis if $100,000 will be placed in escrow with our agent, Dennis Snyder, CPA, Nita City. Thereafter, all accounting for sales is to be certified by said agent.

An additional lot can be ready in five weeks.

Yours truly,

[Signed]
David Bentley
President

DB/lk

COPY

*D-10 denotes ten days before the hearing on the petition for a temporary restraining order.

LEDGER

Account No.: 443176

Sheet No.: 201

NAME: Great Lakes Concert Distributions, Inc.

Terms: On Consignment (escrow agent-D. Snyder)

ADDRESS: 51 42nd Street
New York, N.Y. 10017

Rating: ***
Credit Limit: 1,000,000

DATE	ITEMS	PAYABLES	RECEIPTS Rec'd from D. Snyder
M-6	THE GROUP—Posters		
	20,000 on consignment		
	at $3.00		
M-4			$39,000
M-3	THE GROUP—Posters		
	50,000 on consignment		
	at $3.00		
M-2			$112,000
D-8	THE GROUP—Posters		
	100,000 on consignment		
	at $6.00		

Section V

Expert Witnesses

For substantive instructions on this subject, please refer to any of NITA's texts on the art and science of trial advocacy.

PROBLEM 37

McArthur v. Rogers

(Anthony Meyer) (Kristen Lovell)

For the basic facts of the case refer to Problem 4.

After falling, Ms. McArthur was taken to the hospital at the University of Nita, where she was treated by Dr. Meyer. Following this problem are portions of her medical records, x-rays, and three medical illustrations.[3] Also attached is a glossary of the medical terms used in this problem.

The medical records attached are:

1. A discharge summary prepared after Ms. McArthur was released from the hospital by her treating physician, Dr. Meyer, based on the care she provided as reflected in her other records at the hospital;

2. Two x-ray reports. One is for each of the attached x-rays, showing when the films were taken and how they were interpreted by the radiologist who reviewed them; and

3. An outpatient record showing what happened each time Ms. McArthur returned to the hospital for a follow-up appointment.

The attached medical illustrations show what Ms. McArthur's femur would have looked like before it was broken, what it looked like after the break but before treatment, and what it looked like after treatment.

As a part of the plaintiff's case-in-chief, Dr. Meyer will be called. In a report to plaintiff's counsel, which has been provided to the defendant, Dr. Meyer stated:

1. The injuries Ms. McArthur sustained are consistent with the fall she describes;

2. Ms. McArthur is familiar with all aspects of her treatment and can testify as to what she did and what was done by other health care professionals;

3. She was a generally cooperative patient, but she was not good about attending physical therapy. This is not uncommon because PT is difficult and painful, but Dr. Meyer always tells her patients that the harder they work in PT, the faster their recovery. Generally, PT effort only affects the rate of recovery not its extent; and

4. McArthur's medical bills are reasonable and all related to her fall.

The defendant has received a report from its expert, Dr. Lovell, who reviewed the file, which follows this problem. Her opinion is that the injury is consistent with the fall described

---

3. NITA thanks Bradley Smith, a medical illustrator with Bio Image, Inc., in Durham, NC, for preparing the medical illustrations that accompany this problem.

and that Meyer did an excellent job. In the letter to defense counsel, which has been provided to the plaintiff, she makes several observations about the case:

1. After the first few minutes of physical examination and x-rays in the emergency room, Ms. McArthur was sedated;

2. Once the rod is inserted, the femur is stronger than it was before;

3. In this kind of case, the patient typically makes a full recovery without any permanent disability. The patient's recovery time, however, depends largely on their effort in physical therapy; and

4. Ms. McArthur's recovery time was longer than would be expected perhaps because she was not good about coming to physical therapy sessions.

The case is now at trial. The plaintiff calls Dr. Meyer in her case-in-chief.

Part A

For the plaintiff, conduct a direct examination of Dr. Meyer assuming that her expertise has been stipulated.

For the defendant, conduct a cross-examination of Dr. Meyer.

Part B

For the defendant, conduct a direct examination of Dr. Lovell assuming that her expertise has been stipulated.

For the plaintiff, conduct a cross-examination of Dr. Lovell.

GLOSSARY

ambulating	moving around
AP	anterior posterior (front to back), an x-ray view
bite	the grab felt when a screw digs into the material into which it is entering
comminuted	a fracture in which the bone is broken into more than two pieces with extensive injury to surrounding soft tissues, usually caused by crushing force
contamination	(wound contamination) foreign material present at wound site
cortical	having to do with the core or center
distal	situated away from the median line of the body; the part of the bone that is furthest from the center of the body
emergent	emergency, hurried
femoral shaft	the straight portion of the femur between the ends
femur	(thigh bone) a long bone between the hip and the knee
fixation	setting broken bones
fracture	a breakage of a bone
IM nailing	abbreviation for intramedullary nailing, in insertion of a rod in the central core of a bone to repair a fracture
incision	the surgical cutting of soft tissue
intramedullary	the central core of a bone
mid-diaphysis	the shaft or central part of a long bone
nailing	the insertion of a rod in a bone to repair a fracture
nonweight bearing	ambulation in which weight is borne by one leg and not the other; usually a walker or crutches are involved
oblique	on an angle to the long axis of a bone
open	(as in open intramedullary nailing) a surgical procedure involving an incision; (as in open fracture) a fracture in which the bone breaks through the skin
partial weight bearing	ambulation in which full weight is borne by one leg and only partial weight is borne by the other; usually a cane or crutches are involved

permanent disability   the condition that results when a disease or injury leaves the body forever unable to function in the way that it did before the disease or injury; a disability that resolves over time is a temporary disability; if the disability is incomplete, it is a permanent (or temporary) partial disability

physical therapy   exercises designed to strengthen muscles and speed recovery from a disease or injury

prognosis   assessment of the future course and outcome of a patient's injury based on knowledge of the course of the injury in other patients together with the general health, age, and sex of the patient

proximal   situated close to the median line of the body; the part of the bone that is closest to the center of the body

PT   abbreviation for physical therapy

screws   used here as in ordinary meaning, a device for attaching two items together; see bite

transverse   situated at right angles to the long axis of the bone

University of Nita Hospital

Nita City, Nita

DISCHARGE SUMMARY

Patient Name: Kathryn McArthur
Patient Number: 043-38-1882

Admitted: 12/28/2015
Discharged: 1/2/2016
Dictated: 1/4/2016
Typed: 1/7/2016

Attending: A. Meyer, MD
Referring: Blue Cross/Blue Shield HMO
                   6350 Quadrangle Drive
                   Nita City, Nita 27514

Final Diagnosis: Left femur fracture

HISTORY OF PRESENT ILLNESS: Patient is a forty-one-year-old white female who was brought to the Emergency Room via ambulance after sustaining injuries in a fall at a ski cabin. She reported to ambulance personnel that a rotten handrail on stairs collapsed when she tried to grab it as she was falling and, as a result, she fell off top of stairs landing on her leg or hip.

On arrival at emergency room, patient was alert and oriented but in pain. A 10 × 8 centimeter open wound with gross contamination was present on the left thigh, which appeared to be an exit wound for the fractured shaft of the femur. The shaft, however, was no longer protruding at examination. X-rays were negative except for left femur showing transverse with slight oblique comminuted fracture. The patient was admitted to the hospital by the Trauma Surgery Service, sedated, and taken to the operating room for emergent intramedullary fixation of her left femur fracture.

PAST MEDICAL HISTORY: Medications, allergies: None.

PHYSICAL EXAMINATION: Nonremarkable except obvious displaced femur fracture.

LABORATORY DATA: Normal values on all tests.

HOSPITAL COURSE: The patient was admitted to the Orthopedic Surgery Ward post operatively from her intramedullary rodding of her left femur. Surgery by Dr. Meyer with Dr. Brown assisting. Diagnosis: left open femur fracture. Procedures performed: 1) incision and drainage, left femur fracture; 2) open intramedullary nailing of left femur fracture. Estimated blood loss: 1,000 cc. Operative findings: grade III fracture and 10 × 8 centimeter open wound with gross contamination present. Large bony fragment about 6-cm long and about 50 percent of the bone's diameter was found detached from femur. Fragment had lost blood supply and was discarded.

Procedure: classic intramedullary nailing. Bones separated at point of fracture and insertion of 10- × 36-cm nail was attempted in distal portion of the bone. Rod would not fit, so 13-mm reamer was used on both portions of bone. After reaming out bones, original nail was inserted. Nail was too short when inserted into proximal end of bone. 10 × 40 nail was tried with success. After insertion of nail in both ends of bone, pins were used at both ends to locate holes in nail. Pins were then removed and drill used to create holes for two screws into nail and its distal and proximal ends. Screws were placed and good bite was obtained. The patient was closed in the usual fashion. The patient recovered well from this surgery. By discharge at 01/02/2016, patient was ambulating nonweight bearing with crutches. Patient's prognosis is good for full recovery with physical therapy.

Dictated By:
Timothy Brown, MD

[*Signed*]
A. Meyer, MD
Attending: Department of Orthopedic Surgery

Transcribed By: bj

University of Nita Hospital

Nita City, Nita

X-Ray Report

Patient Name:	Kathryn McArthur
Patient Number:	043–38–1882
Order No.:	373096
Date:	12/28/2015
Order:	Portable AP Left Femur
Findings:	

There is a short oblique fracture of the mid-diaphysis of the left femur with 1 cm of overriding, 1–2 mm of lateral displacement, and normal alignment in this single frontal projection. The proximal and distal ends of the femur are not included on this film.

Images interpreted by:

Jordan B. Renner, MD

Preliminary interpretation by:

Joanne Clark, MD

Exhibit 1

X-Ray

Kathryn McArthur
043–38–1882
12/28/2013
Order 373096

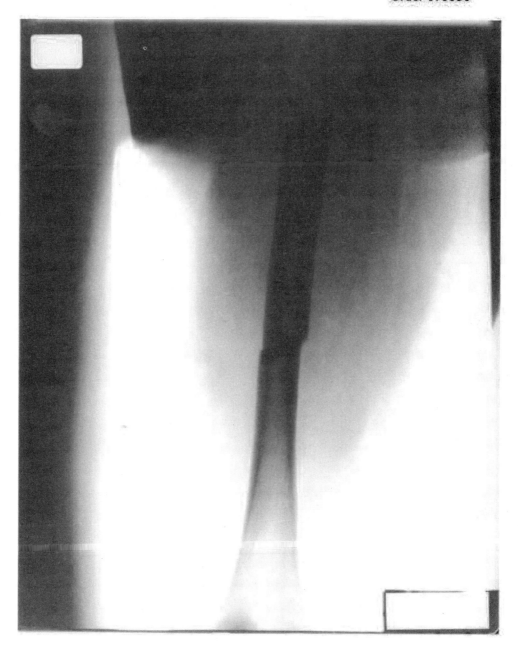

University of Nita Hospital

Nita City, Nita

X-Ray Report

Patient Name:	Kathryn McArthur
Patient Number:	043–38–1882
Order No.:	373142
Date:	12/29/2015
Order:	Portable AP Left Femur
Findings:	

An interlocking intramedullary rod traverses the transverse midfemoral shaft fracture. A large cortical fragment is missing just above the fracture site.

Images interpreted by:

Carol Bayless, MD

Preliminary interpretation by:

Lawrence Samuels, MD

Exhibit 2

X-Ray

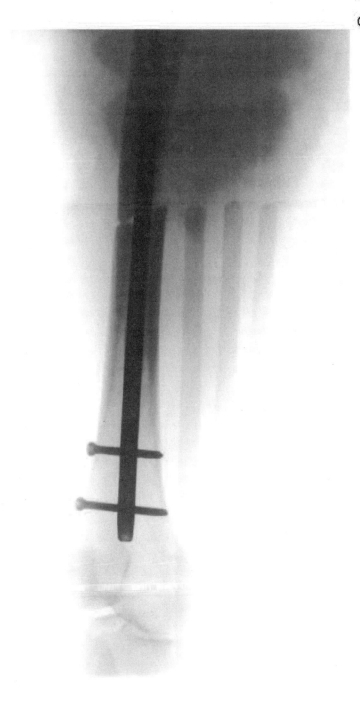

043–38–1882
12/29/2013
Order 373142

University of Nita Hospital

Nita City, Nita

OUTPATIENT RECORDS

Patient Name: Kathryn McArthur

Patient Number: 043–38–1882

Date of visit: 1/14/2016

Doctor: A. Meyer

Patient returns for first follow-up visit following IM nailing after fall from ski cabin deck. No complaints. Ambulating well on crutches, nonweight bearing. X-rays are satisfactory and show fracture healing well. Wound healing well. Patient cleared to begin physical therapy and for partial weight bearing after initial PT session including instruction on mobility techniques. I would like to see her again in one month to see new films. She may return sooner if she has any problems.

Date of visit: 2/18/2016

Doctor: A. Meyer

Patient returns for second follow-up visit following IM nailing after fall from ski cabin deck. No complaints. Ambulating adequately on crutches, partial weight bearing; however, I would have expected her to have been doing better. X-rays show continued healing. Wound fully healed with satisfactory scar. Patient cleared to go to full weight bearing with cane. I review her PT record with her and counsel her not to miss appointments. She has missed four of sixteen since last visit with me. Final follow-up visit in two months unless problems develop. No x-rays needed then unless she reports problems.

Date of visit: 5/2/2016

Doctor: A. Meyer

Patient returns for final follow-up visit. Has made adequate progress despite missing a third of her PT sessions. Full range of motion. No complaints. No x-rays taken or reviewed. Patient discharged. She understands that she can return if she starts having any problems. I anticipate no permanent disability from this injury. IM nail can be removed later if problems, but probably will remain without need for removal.

Exhibit 3

Diagram of Normal Bone

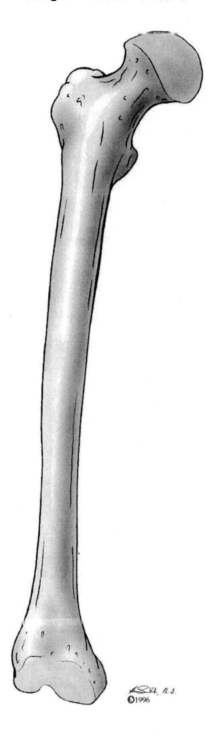

©1996

Exhibit 4

Diagram of Bone before Surgery

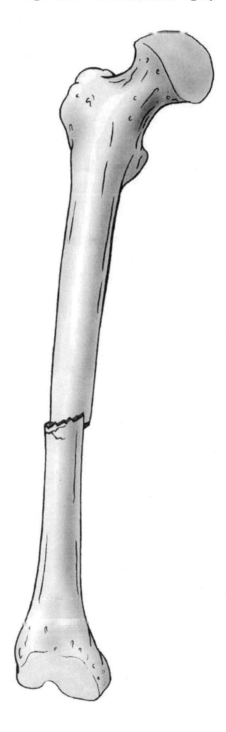

Exhibit 5

Diagram of Bone after Surgery

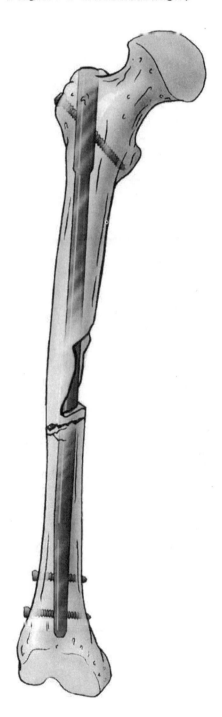

The following is a letter from the independent medical examiner hired by the Defendant to evaluate the injuries of Kathryn McArthur.

Dr. Kristen Lovell
290 Main Street
Nita City, Nita 90012
498–8732

March 4, 2016

Frank Gandly
3910 Frank Avenue
South Nita, NI 90054

At your request I examined Ms. Kathryn McArthur at my office on March 1, 2016. The following is a report of my examination of her left femur. In preparation for this independent medical examination, I have reviewed Ms. McArthur's medical records and x-rays and her deposition.

Identification. Kathryn McArthur is a forty-two-year-old married woman with two children. She is a real estate broker in Nita City. Ms. McArthur lives at 35 Stenton Avenue in Nita City, Nita. She was injured when she fell on December 28, 2015, at a rented ski cabin in Bear Valley, Nita.

Statement of the Presenting Problems. Ms. McArthur sustained a short oblique fracture of the mid-diaphysis of the left femur with 1 cm of overriding, 1–2 mm of lateral displacement. After the first few minutes of examination she was sedated. IM nail inserted during surgery. Problem was corrected with surgery. Alignment was normal in the single frontal projection. After surgery, McArthur began physical therapy. Although she was less than diligent in her rehabilitation therapy, which lengthened her recovery time, there were no complications in the healing of her fracture. The pain she experienced was normal for a fracture of this sort, normally controlled by over-the-counter medication. The surgery for reducing the fracture was successful, and not a painful process as it is done under general anesthetic.

Past History. Plaintiff did not have any major physical problems prior to this incident.

Examination. My examination after the surgery and physical therapy reveals that Ms. McArthur has healed quite nicely

Prognosis. She is not restricted in any physical activity. In fact, her femur with the rod inserted is stronger than it was before the surgery. It is my opinion that she can continue to ski. She is able to work full time. The IM does not and probably will not need to be removed.

She did not complain of any pain or discomfort. It is my opinion that the injury has had no lasting effect on the patient.

If you have any questions, please feel free to contact me at the above telephone number.

Respectfully submitted,

[*Signed*]

Dr. Kristen Lovell

Problem 38

Nita Sports and Exposition Authority v. Parsons

(James Matson and Janet Stevens)

Background

The Nita Sports and Exposition Authority, known as NSEA, is a duly created agency of the State of Nita. It was formed to find a suitable site, acquire it by purchase or condemnation, and build a stadium for the Nita Nationals, known as the Nita Nats. The Nats are Nita's only professional baseball team, and it was the wisdom of the Nita Legislature that losing the team to another state would be a blow to both the pride and the economy of Nita generally, and Nita City, in particular.

After considerable searching and analysis, NSEA decided that the best location for the new stadium was an area euphemistically known as the Lealands, after the word "lea" meaning a grassy land or park. Actually, the Lealands are an old swampy area, long ago used as dumping grounds for Nita City's waste, which was pulled across the Nita River on barges to this disposal site. Once the dump was filled and closed, natural grass grew rampant on the site, leading to its name.

One of the major reasons this site was selected for the Nats' stadium is that Nita City already owns the land and will provide it free of charge for the stadium. However, there are some adjacent properties that must be acquired to complete the tract necessary for the stadium, parking, and related facilities, including practice fields. One of those tracts is the property at issue in this case known as Lot 9, Block 107, and also known as 358 Paterson Plank Road, Nita City. It was part of a taking by NSEA on February 15, 2016. The owner of record is Marian Parsons.

The property taken is level in contour and at street grade. At the time of the taking, the property was improved with four separate structures. The first structure was a dwelling containing 816 square feet of ground floor, with a porch of 123 square feet. This structure had been used by the owner, Marian Parsons, as her residence and to house a nonprofit religious organization known as the Royal Priesthood. The second building was a garage and loft enclosing 2,135 square feet, which was used by Parsons' former husband, Wayne, many years ago for truck repairs, but it has been abandoned for a long time. At the time of the taking, this structure was vacant and was not being used for any purpose. The third building was a garage enclosing 1,040 square feet. This also was used previously for commercial purposes by the owner's former husband and has not been used for many years. At the time of the taking, this structure had been abandoned. The fourth structure was a tool shed enclosing 240 square feet. At the time of the taking, it also was not being used.

This taking was done under Chapter 40 of the Nita statutes entitled "Eminent Domain." The relevant provisions of the statutes are:

40A-3 [Purposes Permitted] Establishing, enlarging, or improving parks, playgrounds, and other recreational facilities.

40A-4 [Procedure] The power to acquire property by condemnation shall not depend on any prior effort to acquire the same property by gift or purchase, nor shall the power to negotiate for the gift or purchase of property be impaired by initiation of condemnation proceedings. A potential condemnor who seeks to acquire property by gift or purchase shall give the owner written notice of the provisions of NS 40A-6. [*The parties have stipulated that proper notice was given.*]

40A-12 [Rules] Where the procedure for conducting an action under this Chapter is not expressly provided for in this Chapter or by the statutes governing civil procedure, or where the civil procedure statutes are inapplicable, the judge before whom such proceeding may be pending shall have the power to make all the necessary orders and rules of procedure necessary to carry into effect the object and intent of this Chapter. The practice in each case shall conform as near as may be to the practice in other civil actions.

40A-41 [Institution of action and deposit] A public condemnor shall institute a civil action to condemn property by filing in the superior court of any county in which the land is located a complaint containing a declaration of taking declaring that property therein is thereby taken for the use of the condemnor. The complaint shall include a statement of the authority under which and the public use for which the property is taken; a description of the entire tract or tracts of land affected and of the portion taken; the names and addresses of those persons who the condemnor is informed and believes may be, or claim to be, owners of the property; and a statement of the sum of money estimated by the condemnor to be just compensation for the taking. The filing of the complaint shall be accompanied by the deposit to the use of the owner of the sum of money estimated by the condemnor to be just compensation for the taking. [*The parties have stipulated that these procedures were properly followed by NSEA and that the answer filed by the defendant was proper.*]

40A-48 [Report of Commissioners or Deposit as Evidence] The report of commissioners shall not be competent as evidence upon the trial of the issue of compensation in the superior court, nor shall evidence of the deposit by the condemnor into the court be competent upon the trial of the issue of compensation.

40A-64 [Measure of Damages] The measure of compensation for a taking of property is its fair market value.

40A-65 [Effect of Condemnation on Damages] The value of the property taken does not include an increase or decrease in value before the date of valuation that is caused by the proposed improvement or project for which the property is taken; the reasonable likelihood that the property would be acquired for that improvement or project; or the condemnation proceeding in which the property is taken.

The complaint was filed by NSEA, who provided a deposit of $96,001.00. After the pleadings were completed, the only issue remaining was damages for the taking of the described property. The defendant did not contest the right of NSEA to use eminent domain for a taking of this property. Commissioners were duly appointed by the Clerk of Court, and they set a value on the land of $96,000.00. As was her right, the defendant, within the time permitted, demanded a de novo jury trial on damages.

Expert Witnesses

In this case, there are two expert witnesses: Janet W. Stevens, retained by NSEA, and James W. Matson, retained by Ms. Parsons. Both have previously been accepted as expert witnesses in the courts of Nita, both state and federal. Portions of their depositions follow their reports.

APPRAISAL
by Janet Stevens

358 PATERSON PLANK ROAD
NITA CITY, NITA

Location

The street address of the subject property is 358 Paterson Plank Road, Nita City, Nita. It is situated on the south side of that artery, approximately 3,450 feet west of the intersection of Paterson Plank Road and Route 20. The property is identified as Lot 9, Block 107 on the Tax Assessment Map for the Borough of Nita City, County of Darrow, Nita.

Appraisal Premise

The purpose of the appraisal in this case is to arrive at an estimate of the market value of the subject property. The phrase "market value" as used herein means:

> The most probable price in terms of money that a property should bring in competitive and open market under all conditions requisite to a fair sale, the buyer and seller, each acting prudently, knowledgeably, and assuming the price is not affected by undue stimulus.

Area and Neighborhood

Certain parcels surrounding the subject have been rezoned for industrial/commercial use, and a significant portion of the immediate area has been developed for such use. Development has been halted in recent years because of the dedication of this area for development by the Nita Sports and Exposition Authority.

Zoning

The subject property is zoned for residential use.

Tax Rate and Assessed Value

Real property in Darrow County is assessed at a rate of $2.13 per $100 of assessed value. The 2015 assessment for the subject property is

Land	$56,000
Improvements	$34,200
Total	$90,200

Title

Holder of record title: Marian Parsons

Description of Property

The subject property is a narrow rectangular parcel of approximately .637 acres, having a frontage on Paterson Plank Road of 75 feet and an approximate depth of 375 feet. The property is level on grade with the street. All public utilities are available to the subject. The property is improved with four separate structures. The first structure is a dwelling containing 816 square feet of ground floor area, with a porch of 132 square feet. The second building is a garage and loft containing 2,135 square feet. The third building is a garage containing 1,040 square feet. The fourth is a shed containing 240 square feet. As of the date of this appraisal, only the dwelling structure is being used for any purpose, each of the other three having been previously abandoned.

Highest and Best Use

The highest and best use of a property is the use, from among reasonably probable and legal alternative uses, that supports the highest present value as of the date of the appraisal. Zoning restrictions on the subject property indicate that its highest and best use is residential use.

Appraisal Approach

Reproduction (Cost) Approach

The cost approach is not useful in the case of the subject property. There is no circumstance under which it would be economically prudent to reproduce any of the appraised buildings.

Income Approach

The income approach is not useful in the case of the subject property. There are currently no leases in effect on the subject property. Further, the deteriorated condition of the improvements makes it impossible to arrive at a supportable estimate of income and expenses if these improvements were to be leased.

Comparable Sales Approach

I have relied on the comparable sales or market data approach in arriving at an estimate of value for the subject property. In so doing, I have compared to the subject property recent sales of comparable residential properties in the immediate vicinity. They are, however, not within the area dedicated for the Sports and Exposition project.

Properties in that area have not sold in the past five years because of the prospect of the Sports and Exposition development. The residential properties used are in an adjacent neighborhood.

Comparable Sales Data

Comparable #1

Location: 19 East Main Street, Nita City, Nita

Sale Price: $75,000

Date: February 1, 2015

Zoning: R-1

Remarks: Property improved with two-story residence of 1,200 square feet, with garage. Land area approximately 1.334 acres. Improvements are in fair to good condition. Improvements are thirty-four years old.

Comparable #2

Location: 201 Clinton Street, Nita City, Nita

Sale Price: $36,000

Date: January 15, 2014

Zoning: R-1

Remarks: Property improved by one-story residence of approximately 800 square feet. Land area of.75 acres. Improvements in fair condition. Improvements are sixty years old.

Comparable #3

Location: 330 Columbus Road, Nita City, Nita

Sale Price: $56,000

Date: April 7, 2014

Zoning: R-1

Remarks: Property improved with one-story residence of approximately 1,000 square feet. Land area of .75 acres. Improvements in good to excellent condition. Neighborhood suffering some deterioration. Improvements are fifty-eight years old.

Comparable #4

Location: 414 Apolo Drive, Nita City, Nita

Sale Price: $45,500

Date: October 3, 2014

Zoning: R-1

Remarks: Property improved with one-story residence of approximately 1,500 square feet, with two small outbuildings. Land area of one acre. Residence in good condition; outbuildings unused, deteriorating. Improvements are sixty-two years old.

The foregoing sales represent the most recent sales of comparable properties within the subject area. All occurred within the past three years. The indicated range of values is relatively wide, but may be narrowed by selecting the most similar of the comparable sales and by making appropriate adjustments for differences among the properties. Comparables 2, 3, and 4 are more closely related to the subject property in quality, style, and location. The overall condition of the improvements located on the subject property is most closely related to Comparable 2. Residential property values in this area have risen only marginally within the last several years, so the comparable sales shown above remain good indications of the market value of similar properties. Taking these comparable sales into account and adjusting for size, time, and location, it is our opinion that the market value of the subject property is $96,000.

Addendum

In connection with the foregoing appraisal, I have also been asked to provide an estimate of the value of the subject property if it were currently zoned for industrial/commercial use. Because none of the existing structures provides utility for any foreseeable commercial or industrial use, the property must be appraised as if vacant, deducting from the estimated land value the cost of demolition of the existing structures.

Comparable	1	2	3
Location	Paterson Plank Rd., East Nita City, Nita	890 Paterson Plank Rd., East Nita City, Nita	S/S Commerce Rd., East Nita City, Nita
Sale Price	$300,000	$760,000	$350,000
Date	10/17/2005	9/12/2013	7/17/2013
Remarks	Two acre tract, 223' frontage on Paterson Plank Road ($75,000/ acre)	2.97 acres; frontage on Paterson Plank Road ($128,000/ acre)	1.439 acres; 236' frontage on Commerce Road ($121,800/acre)

The foregoing sales, when adjusted for time, location, topography, and the size of the parcels involved, indicate a value for the subject property—if zoned for industrial/commercial use—of $230,000 per acre. Deducting the cost of demolition of the existing improvements produces an estimated of value of $134,000.

CERTIFICATION

STATE OF NITA   )

)   SS

COUNTY OF DARROW   )

The undersigned, being duly sworn on her oath, deposes and says that she has personally inspected the property.

That she has no present or contemplated interest in same.

That the opinion of value of the real property as of the date hereof is $96,000.

[*Signed*]

Janet W. Stevens, M.A.I.

Sworn and subscribed to before me this 17th day of March 2016

[*Signed*]

Joan M. Granger

Exhibit 1

Exhibit 2

Exhibit 3

DEPOSITION OF JANET W. STEVENS

My name is Janet W. Stevens, and I work for Janet W. Stevens & Co., which is a real estate advisory firm consulting on the feasibility, valuation, evaluation, and investment aspects of real estate. Our company has over 100 full time employees, ten of whom are MAI appraisers. MAI stands for Member, American Institute (of Real Estate Appraisers), and is the highest certification available for real estate appraisers. To achieve the designation, an appraiser must pass rigorous education requirements; pass a final comprehensive examination; submit specialized experience that must meet strict criteria; receive credit for a demonstration appraisal report; adhere to strict continuing education requirements to ensure up-to-date knowledge of the evolving real estate field; and conduct his or her professional activities in accordance with the Appraisal Institute's Code of Professional Ethics, which enforces the Code of Professional Ethics through a peer review process.

My company is headquartered in Nita, but we work nationwide. We provide services for all types of property, including retail, office, residential, industrial, golf courses, and retirement communities. Among the services we provide are valuation studies and appraisals for loans, purchase or sale transactions, and investment analysis; counseling in real estate for feasibility and design; feasibility and investment analysis for specifically designed market and project studies as needed by our clients; and market research covering all areas of the marketplace in support of or independent of our valuation studies.

Our research staff has computer access to all available databases, including Marshall & Swift, Datatimes, and other data sources. We continuously update and expand our database to keep up with the demand for sales histories on properties, which are required to meet the Standards of Professional Practice of the Appraisal Institute.

As publisher of the online *Greater Nita Scrapbook*, our company has immediate access to print and digital data regarding current national and regional real estate trends and a historical record of real estate activity announced in ten area newspapers and multiple online reporting services covering business, real estate, banking, and government activity.

I have my undergraduate degree from Princeton and my MBA from Duke. I have personally been involved in real estate for over twenty years, specializing in real estate valuation and consulting for the past fifteen years. I am a member of the American Institute of Real Estate Appraisers (MAI). I have been involved at international, national, and local levels of the National Association of Realtors and its affiliates, serving on numerous committees and boards, including a position as Advisory Director to the School of Architecture at the University of Nita. I have completed the following course work:

- Basic Appraisal Principles

- Basic Appraisal Procedures

- Real Estate Finance, Statistics, Valuation Modeling

- General Appraiser Market Analysis and Highest and Best Use
- General Appraiser Sales Comparison Approach
- General Appraiser Site Valuation & Cost Approach
- General Appraiser Income Approach/Part I
- General Appraiser Income Approach/Part II
- Report Writing and Valuation Analysis
- Advanced Income Capitalization
- Advanced Market Analysis and Highest and Best Use or equivalent
- Advanced Sales Comparison and Cost Approaches
- Advanced Applications

I have also completed over twenty seminars and workshops on specific areas of appraising. I also have taught classes in real estate for the University of Nita and Nita City Junior College. I am currently approved by the Nita Real Estate Commission as an instructor in real estate.

In Nita, I have done most of my work on the side of the condemnor, though in other jurisdictions my practice is more balanced. There's no particular reason for that other than an accident—I did my first case for the State of Nita shortly after getting my certificate, and they have been hiring me ever since. Once they started hiring me, all the other governmental entities and utilities started hiring me, too. Since I am usually hired before the property owner even knows their property is going to be taken, by the time lawyers for property owners or property owners call me, I am usually conflicted out because I have worked on the case for the condemnor.

I suspect my rates for appraisals are the same as everyone else's or lower, because otherwise government entities would not use me. I know I probably charge more for testifying than most appraisers because I price my time based on my overall earnings and what I lose by not being available to manage my business and do other projects. My prep time is billed at $400 per hour, as is my travel time portal to portal. My deposition time is billed at $500 per hour with a $2,000 minimum, and my trial time is billed at $600 per hour with a $4,800 minimum.

As for this job, everything I considered is in my report. No, I did not consider initially any use other than residential and, in truth, even that was a stretch. The buildings are decrepit, and I really can't imagine who would want to live in any of them. In truth, this is basically raw land after the cost of taking down the buildings, but I was instructed to value it for residential, and that is what I did.

After I completed the draft of my report and shared it with counsel for NSEA, I was instructed to do a valuation of the property as if it was zoned for industrial/commercial use, which it is not. I should also point out that no application for rezoning was ever filed. Yes, I understand that people have known for years that this property was probably going to be taken for the new stadium, but there was nothing that would have kept the owner for applying for rezoning if she thought that would maximize the value of her property. While I did look at the valuation as though it was zoned for industrial/commercial use, I do not believe that such valuation is accurate or fair. I only did it because I was told to do so. I believe the reason for the request was because the owner's appraiser, Mr. Matson, was using that zoning for valuation.

I did not keep track of exactly how long I spent at the property and in the vicinity, but I doubt it was more than thirty minutes. With the tall grass, walking around was dangerous because of snakes. I only looked inside the building and did not wander around in them because it was apparent from the outside that they were uninhabitable, so since I had been instructed to treat them as habitable, it did not make any sense to spend any time documenting the interiors in detail. I viewed the comparable properties using Google Satellite and Google Street View. For my purposes, that was more than sufficient.

I have read this deposition and made any necessary corrections. I swear that what I have testified to is the truth.

[*Signed*]

Janet W. Stevens

APPRAISAL

by James W. Matson

DESCRIPTION, ANALYSIS, AND CONCLUSIONS

Location

The subject property is located on the south side of Paterson Plank Road, approximately 3,450 feet west of Route 20, Nita City, Nita. It is further identified as Lot #9 in Block #107 as shown on the Tax Assessment Map for the Borough of Nita City, Nita County, Nita, and, as Parcel #T2H by the Nita Sports and Exposition Authority.

Purpose, Value, and Property Rights

The purpose of this appraisal is to estimate the fair market value of the fee simple of the property herein described. Fair market value may be defined as "the highest price estimated in terms of money that a property will bring if offered for sale on the open market for a reasonable length of time, with both buyer and seller being fully aware of all the uses to which it can be adapted and neither party acting under duress or compulsion."

Neighborhood Data

The immediate area is approximately 50 percent developed with industrial- and commercial-type structures. The progress of other development in the area has been halted for a period of years with the oncoming development of the Nita Meadowlands Commission, wherein they had dedicated this area for development of the Nita Sports and Exposition Authority's facilities.

Utilities

All municipal utilities are available to the site.

Zoning

The zoning of the Borough of Nita City provided for residential use. Surrounding tracts have been rezoned for industrial use. The Nita Meadowlands Commission has indicated this area to be zoned as sports complex use. However, for the purposes of this report it was treated as though it were Industrial A.

Taxes and Assessments

Land	$56,000
Improvements	$34,100
Total	**$90,100**

2015 Tax Rate $2.13 per $100

Title Data

Owner of Record: Marian Parsons

Highest and Best Use

Highest and best use is defined as the most economically profitable use to which a piece of land may be put over a given period of time. It also is known as the legal use that will yield the land the highest present value. In my opinion, the highest and best use would be for industrial and/or commercial development. I am also aware that at the time of the taking the owner was in the process of seeking rezoning of the property for this use.

Description of Property

The subject property is a rectangular plot having 75-foot frontage on Paterson Plank Road with a depth of approximately 375 feet, containing .637 acres. The property is level in contour and at street grade. The property at the time of the taking was improved with four separate structures. The first structure was a dwelling enclosing 816 square feet of ground floor area and a porch attached thereto of 132 square feet. The second building was a garage and loft enclosing 2,135 square feet. The third building was a garage enclosing 1,040 square feet. The fourth was a shed enclosing 240 square feet.

Appraisal Approach

In this instance, I made an effort to use the market data approach, but found no particular properties sold within the general area that had four separate structures.

The income approach was attempted, but there were no leases in effect at the time and the structures were such that it would have been difficult to place economic rent and expenses thereto.

Accordingly, I have employed the reproduction cost approach, wherein I have ascertained comparable land sales and added to the land value the cost to reproduce the structures new, less depreciation.

Comparable Vacant Land Sales

Sale #1

Book:	#5705	Page #13
Block:	#151	Lot: Part #37A
Grantor:	Morris Kanton	
Grantee:	Albert Frazier	
Date of Sale:	10/17/2005	
Sale Price:	$300,000	
Location:	Paterson Plank Rd., East Nita City, Nita	
Remarks:	This tract contains 2 acres and reflects $150,000 per acre; 223' frontage on Paterson Plank Road.	

Sale #2

Book:	#5425	Page: #307
Block:	#105A	Lot: #4A & #5A
Grantor:	Charles Spickler	
Grantee:	Top Notch Metal Realty Co.	
Date of Sale:	9/11/2015	
Sale Price:	$760,000	
Location:	890 Paterson Plank Rd., Nita City, Nita	
Remarks:	This tract contains 2.97 acres with frontage on Paterson Plank Rd.; the indicated price per acre is $255,892.	

Sale #3

Book:	#5801	Page: #48
Block:	#151	Lot: #67N
Grantor:	James V. Conan, Sr., et al.	
Grantee:	Marcel Linden	
Date of Sale:	7/17/2015	
Sale Price:	$350,000	
Location:	S/S Commerce Rd., East Nita City, Nita	
Remarks:	Frontage 236'; 1.437 acres or 62,596 sq. ft.; reflects $243,563 per acre.	

An analysis and study of the foregoing sales, with adjustments being made for time, plottage, topography, and location, results in an indicated value of the subject property to be $200,000 per acre.

Reproduction Cost Approach

Under the reproduction cost approach, I have ascertained the land value and have added to that land value the cost to reproduce the structures new less depreciation.

Land Value

.637 acres @ $200,000/acre	$127,400

Improvements

Dwelling: 816 sq. ft. @ $25/sq. ft.	$40,800
Porch: 132 sq. ft. @ $5/sq. ft.	1,320
Garage & Loft: 2,135 sq. ft @ $10/sq. ft.	42,700
Garage: 1,040 sq. ft @ $7.50/sq. ft.	15,600
Shed: 240 sq. ft. @ $5/sq. ft.	2,400
Total	$102,820
Depreciated 40 percent	41,092
Depreciated Value	61,692
TOTAL INDICATED BY THE REPRODUCTION COST APPROACH	$189,092
SAY	$189,000

CERTIFICATION

STATE OF NITA)
)   SS
COUNTY OF NITA)

The undersigned, being duly sworn on his oath, deposes and says that he has personally inspected the property.

That he has no present or contemplated interest in same.

That the opinion of value of the real property as of February 22, 2016, is $189,000, which may be allocated as follows:

Land	$127,400
Improvements	$ 61,600
Total	**$189,000**

[*Signed*]

JAMES W. MATSON, M.A.I.-S.R.P.A.

SWORN and subscribed to before me this 17th day of March 2016

[*Signed*]

JOAN M. GRANGER

Exhibit A

Exhibit C

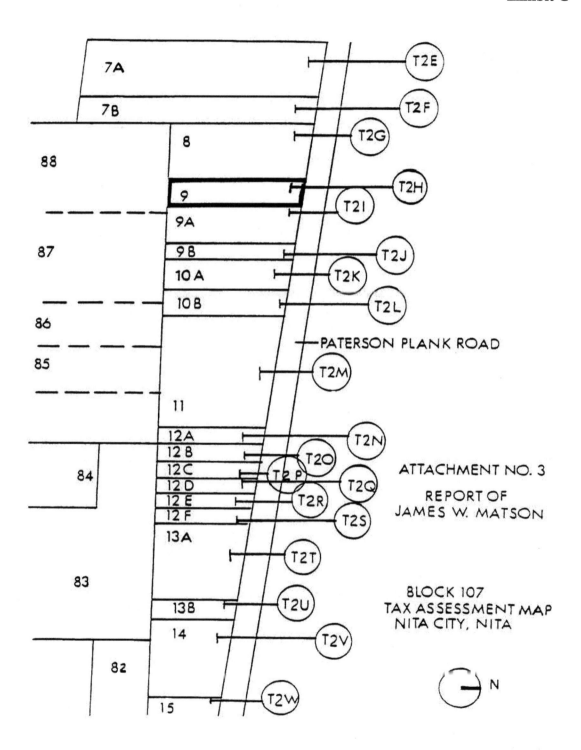

7A

7B

8

88

9

9A

87   9B

10 A

10 B

86

85

11

84   12A

12 B

12 C

12 D

12 E

12 F

13A

83

13B

14

82

15

T2E

T2F

T2G

T2H

T2I

T2J

T2K

T2L

PATERSON PLANK ROAD

T2M

T2N

T2O

T2P

T2Q

T2R

T2S

T2T

T2U

T2V

T2W

ATTACHMENT NO. 3

REPORT OF
JAMES W. MATSON

BLOCK 107
TAX ASSESSMENT MAP
NITA CITY, NITA

N

DEPOSITION OF JAMES W. MATSON

My name is James W. Matson, but everyone calls me Jimmy. I have lived in Nita City all my life. I have my college degree from Nita City Community College. I got that by going to night school while I was working construction in the daytime. Once I got my degree, I apprenticed in a real estate broker's office, ultimately got my salesman's license, did that for four years, and then became a real estate broker. That was in 1989. I still have an active broker's license and buy and sell real estate for my own account and for others. I have been an MAI real estate appraiser in Nita City since 1992. I also have the SRPA designation, which requires substantially more practical experience than the MAI designation. I received that a few years after I got my MAI designation.

After a while, I realized that all the money made in real estate was in being able to value it and paying less than it was worth, so I decided to become an appraiser so I could make good decisions for myself and my clients. I took the same courses that Ms. Stevens took, since those are the required courses to be an MAI appraiser. It took me about seven years to get all the courses, but that was because I was working full time while I was taking the courses. Yes, it is true that the first sample appraisal I turned in did not pass and I had to do another one. My first wife ran off with someone and left me with two young kids, so my attention was elsewhere at the time. The next one I turned in was fine. The same thing happened with my first MAI qualification exam. I did not pass the first time, but passed the second time. That's kind of been the story of my life. I don't always get it right the first time, but I always do in the end. My second wife is great, and we have been married for more than twenty years.

I am a big believer in professional service. I am a Past President of the Central Nita County Board of Realtors and a Past Director of the Nita Association of Real Estate Boards. I am also a member of the National Association of Real Estate Boards.

I work for both condemnors and property owners, about 50 percent each. Over the years I have worked for nearly every company in Nita and lots of Fortune 100 companies, but I have also worked for Joe Smith and Mary Smith, just regular folks whose property is being taken.

On February 14, 2014, Ms. Parson's attorney hired me to do an appraisal of her property for condemnation purposes. Yes, I acknowledge that the property has a peculiarly narrow shape. It is rectangular with dimensions of 75×375 feet, more or less, and consists of .637 acres. I also acknowledge that the property as it sits was zoned residential when I did my appraisal. I did not believe that residential was its highest and best use. Since it was located in an area that was transitioning from residential to industrial and/or commercial use, I believed that its high and best use was industrial/commercial.

Yes, I really did go to the site four times and probably spent over eight hours on the property or in the immediate neighborhood. I also went to each comparable property in person. I don't believe that you can do a competent appraisal without really getting to know the ground, buildings, and area. I also believe that you have to visit each comparable property in person, and I did that. Of course I went in the buildings. I was in every room in every building, and no, I did not see any snakes or anything like that on the property. People who know that area know that the rats have eliminated all the snakes.

My rates are pretty standard for appraisals. We all work for banks and other providers, and the marketplace is very competitive. My charge for forensic work is $225 per hour for actual time preparing or giving testimony, whether it's in a deposition or trial. No, I don't know what portal to portal means. What I know is how many hours I have actually worked on a project, and that's what I bill for. No, I don't bill for my travel time at the same rate. I bill for time travelling at one half my hourly rate.

My company is just me and a part-time typist. I like it that way. I have had other people working for me in the past, but no one really had the entrepreneurial spirit—they just were happy to get a check. I tried commissions and other incentive pay arrangements, but they just did not work, so it's just me now, and I am happier that way. I limit my buying and selling of real estate and appraising to just the Nita City area. I do the required amount of continuing education for all my certificates, but generally no more than that because with sales, broker's and appraiser certificates, that's already nearly a week's worth of time. Teaching is not something I do. I just don't have the time.

I have read this deposition and made any necessary corrections. I swear that what I have testified to is the truth.

[*Signed*]

James W. Matson

Deposition of Marian Parsons

My name is Marian Parsons, and I live in the Midpines Mobile Court in Trailer 34, which I rent from the owner of the trailer park. I used to live in my house on Paterson Plank Road. I had to move out because I could not afford to keep the place up and cover the utilities in the winter. It also was dangerous out there. Since most people who lived out there had moved out and most of the businesses only ran in the day time, at night there was no telling who would come around. So when this trailer near one of my coworkers came available, I grabbed it. I feel much safer now, but I really miss my house.

I am forty-three now. I grew up in the Paterson Plank Road house, raised by my mom and dad. I was an only child. My father built that house from scratch and all the outbuildings, too. He was really good with his hands. His real job was running a truck repair business. He could fix or build anything.

Dad died when I was about sixteen. Cigarettes got him, which is why I have never smoked them. After he died, my mom, who until then was doing all the paperwork for the repair company, went to work as the manager at the Truck Stop Café, about a mile from the house. She got lots of customers to come because all the truckers knew my dad and wanted to look out for her. I started working there too when I was in high school. I did finish high school, but I never went further than that in school.

After I was done with high school, one of the guys who came in to the Café was talking one day about being tired of being on the road as a trucker and wanting to start a repair shop. I told my mother about him, and she met with him. His name was J. J. Parsons (Joshua Joseph. My mother decided she liked him, and she leased him the space my father used to use for his repair business. J.J. and I started hanging out. He was about ten years older than I was, really good looking, and knew about life. Not long afterwards I was pregnant with Wayne, and J.J. and I got married. That's when Mom died and left us the house. We did pretty well for a while, but then J.J. started drinking and gambling—and the women were not too far behind. Finally, I threw him out in 2004 when Wayne was fourteen. I had had finally had enough when I found out he was looking into borrowing money against the house to pay a gambling debt.

I don't know what the Royal Priesthood has to do with any of this. There were a group of us that were pretty dissatisfied with organized religion, had some things in our lives that were not going well (my marriage, being my particular problem), and we decided that we needed to "worship" together. We were not an organized religion, did not have a holy book, had no commandments, or anything like that. We would get together privately, light some candles, burn some incense and do some drugs, mainly marijuana, though we had some mushrooms a couple of times. We did that for a few years, but eventually people drifted away and we stopped. I have not done any drugs in years.

You are showing me Exhibits 1 through 3 and, yes, they do look like the Paterson Plank property has looked since I moved out, but it sure looks like someone went out of the way to find the worst things to photograph. The photos with Mr. Matson's report really are more like what the property looks like. The house needs some work, but it's a great old house, really good bones underneath everything. I think anyone would want to live there if all the neighbors had not moved out because of the stadium.

Of course, my plan after I moved out was to get the property rezoned and sell it off for a factory or some such thing. I knew the writing was on the wall and that was never going to be a residential neighborhood again. Yes, I am the one who provided Exhibit P-1 to my lawyers. It's a letter I received in response to a phone message I left for a lawyer who did zoning work. We never met because the lawyer died about a month after he sent the letter. His office called and told me someone else would be in touch with me, but they never were. No, I didn't send the retainer he requested or sign the letter. Yes, I had $2,000 in the bank, but it is also true that I did not have $5,000 and certainly did not have $10,000.

It is true that I did tell Wayne I would not sell the house or change the zoning. It's true that I said that, but it is not true that that was how I felt. I was going to get the house rezoned and sold. I just did not want Wayne or my ex to know about it. I have refused to send Wayne money, and I do have my reasons. My ex never paid a penny of the child support he was supposed to pay me for the three years before Wayne left for the Marines. He could have, he just didn't after I won the custody fight. I do believe that you reap what you sow, and I would feel a lot different if he had done anything for Wayne or me other than take our money.

Yes, I am looking at Exhibit P-2, and it does appear to be in my handwriting. Where did you get this? Yes, it does sound like me. No, I have no idea when it was written, but it was obviously before I moved out. I remember Kelli as one of the people in the Royal Priesthood group. She had an awful husband, and more than anyone else in the group, she needed our "worship" sessions. I assume she was really worried when the neighborhood deteriorated that I would sell the place or tear down the house, and I wrote her the note to reassure her. Of course I wrote that long before the neighborhood emptied out completely and I knew about the stadium.

I hired my lawyers in this case right after I got the papers offering me only $96,001.00, which is an insult for my family's property and my family home. I love that place, and if the government was building a park like they should be instead of a stadium for some rich baseball team owner, my property would be worth plenty, and I would fix up my house and move back there. One thing I have learned from all of this is that when the government wants your property, there is no way they are not going to get it and all you can do is keep them from getting it cheap. My goal is to make the government pay dearly for taking my house.

HAND & GLOVER
CERTIFIED REAL ESTATE LAW SPECIALISTS IN NITA
1100 NITA BANK TOWER
NITA CITY, NI 22300
(354) 555-1800

LEONARD W. HAND
lhand@hglaw.nita

July 14, 2015

Ms. Marian Parsons
34 Midpine Mobile Court
Nita City, Nita 22322

Re: Possible Rezoning of 358 Patterson Plank Road

Dear Ms. Parsons,

Thank you for your voicemail at my office over the weekend. I understand that you are interested in contemplating a rezoning of the above property, which you own. I am writing in response to your call because you indicated that currently you do not have a working telephone number.

I looked briefly at the property online and realized that it is probably a property that the Nita Sports and Exposition Authority might be interested in acquiring for the new Nita Nationals stadium. Under the circumstances, you are wise to consider upzoning this property to increase its value before any taking. We are glad to help you with that process.

In your call you asked about fees. I charge on an hourly basis, $325 per hour for zoning work. I have no way to estimate the exact cost of rezoning for this property because there is no way to know in advance whether adjacent owners or the Nita City Planning Office will oppose it. Depending on that and other factors, I would estimate that the fees involved (exclusive of surveyor's costs) will be between $5,000 and $10,000, probably nearer to the lower figure because other properties in the area have been successfully rezoned. Since we have not worked together in the past, we will require a $2,000 deposit to get started.

I look forward to representing you in this process. To get started, please return a signed copy of this letter along with your check for $2,000. Once I have that, I will begin work on your rezoning application.

Sincerely,

[*Signed*]

Leonard W. Hand

LWH/vy

Enclosure: Letter copy for signature and return envelope

Exhibit P-2

Dear Kelli,

I know you are worried with everyone moving out of the neighborhood that I will sell the old homestead or let someone make a factory out of it. There is no way we are going to stop having our Royal Priesthood meeting here. My Dad built this place and I would sooner spit on his grave than sell it or let someone tear it down. Until I take my last dying breath the Priesthood meetings are going to be here and the house is going to stay just like it is.

Faithfully yours,

Marian

DEPOSITION OF WAYNE PARSONS

When my mother and father got divorced, I was fourteen and had to live with my mother until I joined the Marines at seventeen, which was about six years ago in 2011. I would have rather lived with my father, and I knew he wanted me, but my mother won custody and I had no choice. She was totally into this Royal Priesthood thing, and there were all these religious wackos around. The Royal Priesthood was based on some book my mother read or heard about, and there were about ten or twenty of them, mostly women; they would have meetings on Sundays and one other day of the week to pray. I never did exactly understand who they were praying to or what they were praying about, but there were lots of candles, incense, and wailing and crying. I put up with it until I could leave, and then I joined the Marines. Back then the Marines would take you without a diploma or a GED.

The place was a dump even back then, and it got worse over the years. I helped my mother move out about three years ago after I had busted out of the Marines. I got caught huffing some ether while I was working as a corpsman's assistant. When I helped her move out, the place was not fit for habitation. Yes, I have looked at Exhibits 1 through 3 and at Exhibits A and B. All of them are photos of what the property has looked like for the past couple of years. I know because I sometimes go out there with buddies to have parties. As between the exhibits with numbers and the ones with letters, the ones with numbers paint a more accurate picture. The place is pretty run down. There is debris everywhere, and what look like flowers outside the main house are just blooming weeds. I have seen lots of rats both on the property and in the buildings.

My mother was very attached to the property and hated to leave, but she just could not afford to keep it up, and the neighborhood was getting more and more deserted as people were leaving because they had heard the property was going to be taken for the stadium. I know my mother tried to rent the place to supplement her salary from working as a waitress, but no one would rent it because of its condition or location, or at least that's what she told me. I can understand why no one wanted it.

Several times I tried to get my mother to sell it because she needed the money, and I could have used a bit of help, too. When she wouldn't sell it, I tried to get her to see if she could get the zoning upped to something where it would be worth more for some use other than living there. She wasn't interested. One time when I really needed some money I tried to get her to talk to a real estate guy I knew who knew all about zoning changes and knew people on the Board of whatever that takes care of zoning. She absolutely refused. "It's my house, it's where you grew up," was all she said.

In the last year my mother and I have had a falling out. Dad had a stroke and cannot work, and I have moved to Georgia to take care of him. Taking care of him is pretty much a full time job. He does get disability, but that feeds him and puts a roof over his head and the visiting nurse thing really does not do much more. I am the one who cooks for him, helps him bathe, get in and out of his wheelchair, drives him around, and takes care of his place. That doesn't leave me time to work, and we are barely getting by. I asked Mom if she would help out a bit, and she told me that there was no way that one penny from the house was going to pay for anything that helped my father after what he did to her and that what was happening to him was God's punishment for how he had treated her. I know my father probably messed around on her, but from the way she is acting it must have been something worse than that.

No, I did not contact anyone connected with the stadium. One day out of the blue they called me and asked if I was Marion Parson's son and could they interview me about the property. I said yes and told them what I have told you about the property. I think we spent a lot of time on the zoning thing. I am not sure why that matters now, but I am positive that my mother never tried or planned to try to have it rezoned.

No, I have not been promised anything for my testimony if I come to trial. They did agree to pay me my travel expenses and pay the cost of bringing in a person to stay with my father for as long as I was gone. I did ask them for season tickets to the Nats for when I move up there again, and they said they couldn't agree to do that because it would look bad. They did say to give them a call the first time I was up there after the stadium is finished. By "they," I mean the man from NSEA who came to see me after the telephone interview. No, I don't know his name. Since then, all my meetings have been with lawyers. I have had two meetings, one last night over dinner at the Outback down the road, and one this morning at this lawyer's office before the rest of you folks came for my deposition.

I have read this deposition and made any necessary corrections. I swear that what I have testified to is the truth.

[*Signed*]

Wayne Parsons

PROBLEM 39

Jerry's Wiring, Inc. v. Smith Construction Company

(Accountants)

Introduction

This problem involves the presentation of expert accountant testimony on the amount owed to an electrical subcontractor (Jerry's Wiring, Inc.) as a result of cost overruns it incurred due to delays in a construction project. Assume that the expert accountants are called to testify after other witnesses have testified concerning the causes for the various delays, and that some of those witnesses have also given opinion testimony as to who is to blame for the various delays that produced the cost overruns. The general nature of that conflicting testimony is described below in the problem's narrative.

The expert witnesses in this case were not present on the scene during construction. The information used by the accountants to form their opinions consists of the results of Crowe & Co.'s investigation, interviews with persons who were on the scene, and the records of both parties made available to both sides through discovery. (Crowe & Co. is an independent engineering consulting firm hired by the plaintiff's accounting firm, Sanford & Co.) The task of the accounting experts who will testify in this case was to gather all relevant information concerning the project, analyze that information using generally accepted accounting principles, and reach a conclusion based on those principles as to the proper amount of Jerry's Wiring's claim against the Smith Construction Company. Plaintiff's accountant reached the conclusion that Jerry's Wiring is entitled to $2,427,000. Defendant's accountant has concluded that Jerry's Wiring is only entitled to $354,000. The lawyers' task is first to understand how two respectable and expert accountants could reach such different conclusions based on the same data, and then to use that understanding to present a clear and convincing explanation of his or her client's position through well-organized and understandable direct and cross-examination.

Background

In February 2016, Smith Construction Company finally completed a $30 million wastewater treatment plant in the southwestern section of Nita City, Nita. The initial contract called for the job to be completed in 500 days, but the project was actually completed nearly 1,000 days behind schedule and had incurred numerous cost overruns. The largest cost overrun involved the electrical work for the project that had been subcontracted to Jerry's Wiring, Inc. The initial subcontract was for a fixed price of $1,775,000. That subcontract was also to have been completed within 500 days, but was not completed until the job was finished. Exhibit 1 contains extracts of the key provisions of the contract between Jerry's Wiring, Inc., and Smith Construction Company.

During the course of the work, there were seven (7) formal change orders issued to the electrical subcontractor (Jerry's Wiring) by Smith Construction Company. These change orders required work not contemplated in the initial contract, including the use of significant additional materials, and caused the job to take longer than originally expected. Jerry's Wiring prepared billings for each of these change orders and, by the time of the litigation, all of the billings had been paid by the general contractor. The total amount billed and paid for these seven (7) formal change orders was $200,000. Unfortunately, Jerry's Wiring did not estimate these costs as accurately as it should have.

In addition to delays caused by the formal change orders, there were continual problems with groundwater, which caused the subcontractor to stop his work frequently and expend extra money when the job could not be completed in an efficient manner. Although the subcontract required the general contractor to provide adequate working conditions for the subcontractor, in some cases the subcontractor actually had to hire another contractor to pump water out of the underground manholes where electrical work needed to be done. This was clearly the responsibility of the general contractor.

The general contractor encountered many problems on this particular job. These problems included delays caused by the general contractor's failure to develop an adequate schedule for work to be done by subcontractors, the general contractor's failure to receive necessary supplies on time, and strikes that shut down the construction site for 100 days during the last 1,000 days of the project. Ultimately, the job extended 1,000 days beyond the original targeted completion date, for a total of 1,500 days to complete the contract.

Every time a problem of groundwater was encountered, Jerry's job superintendent brought this to the attention of the general contractor and asked that the water be pumped out. Unfortunately, often this was not done on a timely basis. Jerry's executives also brought to the attention of Smith's management the fact that there were cost overruns attributable to the delays. In response, Smith's management indicated that it would deal with these additional costs in accordance with the terms provided in the subcontract. All of the communications concerning the incidents that caused the delays were oral, and Jerry's Wiring never submitted a bill for these cost overruns until the project was completed. Jerry's Wiring ended up incurring substantial costs beyond the original contract amount of $1.9 million, and billed Smith Construction Company for those cost overruns (*see* Exhibit 3.)

It should be noted that Jerry's Wiring itself made several mistakes during the performance of the work on the job, which caused extra work on its part. Such mistakes included installing wiring incorrectly in several locations that had to be ripped out and redone. Jerry's claim has been reduced by an estimate for the costs of the extra work due to its mistakes.

The electrical subcontractor (Jerry's Wiring) also encountered other difficulties during the job that were not the fault of the general contractor. These difficulties were seven (7) strikes by different labor unions and an unusual number of days in which the weather caused difficulties in the performance of the work. Jerry's job superintendent has told the plaintiff's accountants that the strikes and bad weather ran concurrently with delays caused by Smith Construction Company and did not, by themselves, serve to extend the job any further. Although the accountants for both sides have been able to determine exactly when the strikes occurred, Jerry's job superintendent did not keep careful records concerning the various causes for delays. However, Jerry's job superintendent claims to have a good memory of the events.

Accounting Problems and Issues

The books and records of Jerry's Wiring that relate to this job have been made available to all of the accounting experts who have been retained in this case. These books and records leave much to be desired from an accounting standpoint. All costs on this contract were charged to a single job code[4] for the first eighteen months. The labor cost records do not reflect the use of detailed activity codes[5] to reflect the specific activities actually performed during this period. Thus, there are no accounting records that specify exactly what given employees were doing on any given day for the first 500 days. For this first 500 days, Jerry's Wiring kept only minimum documentation in the form of the job superintendent's daily log, which indicated where people were working and generally what they were doing.

The work during the last 1,000 days of the job was fairly well documented. During this time period Jerry's job superintendent did a much better job of determining what his people were doing once the contract had overrun, and the detailed activity codes were used in the labor cost records.

Jerry's Wiring also did not keep records of actual project overhead (costs associated with maintaining the project) incurred during the job. Instead, accounting records reflect only estimated overhead based on an allocation of 12 percent of direct labor dollars. Jerry's controller knew that actual overhead was higher than 12 percent, especially during the latter stages of the project, but did not change the percentage to be more realistic. Accordingly, the preparation of Jerry's claim by Jerry's accountant included making a proper overhead calculation and applying an actual overhead rate to the labor incurred on the job (*see* the approach used by the plaintiff's expert as described in his deposition, Exhibit 4.)

Both sides have hired expert accounting witnesses to help them in this case. The credentials of the experts will be similar. Both experts gave depositions prior to the trial.

A summary of the deposition of the plaintiff's expert, a partner in the accounting firm of Sanford & Co., is attached hereto as Exhibit 4. During the deposition, Exhibit 3 was produced.

A summary of the deposition of the defendant's expert, a partner in the accounting firm of Madden & Co., is attached hereto as Exhibit 6. During the deposition, Exhibit 5 was produced.

Exhibits 1–6 have been made available to the experts for both parties. Furthermore, both sides are aware of the facts in this narrative of the case. However, both sides have been effective

---

4. A job code is an identification number assigned to a particular job
5 An activity code is a number assigned to a particular task.

in limiting discovery of their expert's work product. Consequently the information contained in the exhibits is all that each side knows about the other's work.

Both experts are partners in large public accounting firms. Neither accountant has any specific experience in dealing with electrical subcontracts for wastewater treatment plants, but both have dealt with commercial construction cost claims. As with most accounting experts, the partners themselves did not perform the analyses that support their conclusions as set forth in the exhibits. Instead, the detailed work was performed by staff accountants, seniors, and managers under the supervision and direction of the partners. The partners are familiar with and have approved the approach used and the conclusions reached.

The persons playing the roles of the experts will have to use their experience and training in determining what they would have done in preparing their analysis of the claim in this case. However, care should be taken to make sure that all facts and conclusions are consistent with the documents that have been produced during discovery (Exhibits 1 through 6).

The experts have also reviewed Exhibits 1 and 2. Exhibit 1 is a summary of the key provisions of the subcontract. Exhibit 2 is a summary of the original bid worksheets that Jerry's had prepared when they first bid the job. Defendant's counsel found these worksheets very interesting because they show a lower overhead rate than reflected in the claim and much lower labor and material costs.

Pursuant to a stipulation of the parties, all of the exhibits are admissible and may be used during direct or cross-examination.

In pretrial proceedings, the court ruled that the burden of proof in this case is as follows:

1. Plaintiff, Jerry's Wiring, has the burden of proof on damages. Thus, the plaintiff must prove by a preponderance of evidence the amount of damages it incurred due to the change orders and delays in the project.

2. Defendant, Smith Construction, has the burden of proof on whether the plaintiff failed to properly mitigate its damages. If the jury finds that the plaintiff could have reasonably avoided some of the damages incurred in the cost overrun on the project, then such damages must be deleted from the final award of damages to the plaintiff.

The case is now at trial.

Part A. Plaintiff's Expert

The plaintiff calls the accountant from Sanford & Co. as its expert witness.

For the plaintiff, conduct a direct examination of the accountant from Sanford & Co.

For the defendant, conduct a cross-examination of the accountant from Sanford & Co.

For the plaintiff, conduct any necessary redirect examination.

Part B. Defendant's Expert

The plaintiff has rested. The defendant's midtrial motion for judgment as a matter of law has been denied.

For the defendant, conduct a direct examination of the accountant from Madden & Co.

For the plaintiff, conduct a cross-examination of the accountant from Madden & Co.

For the defendant, conduct any necessary redirect examination.

SUMMARY OF KEY PROVISIONS OF
THE SUBCONTRACT BETWEEN
JERRY'S WIRING, INC. AND SMITH CONSTRUCTION COMPANY[6]

The Subcontractor, Jerry's Wiring, Inc., will supply all material and labor to complete the specified work and agrees to all provisions and conditions stated in the contract documents between the Owner, City of Atlanta, and General Contractor, Smith Construction Company. In addition to the stated provisions and conditions, the Subcontractor and General Contractor agree to the following:

[*only certain excerpts are shown*]

Duration

The duration of this job shall be 500 days from date of execution of this agreement.

1. Change Orders: The General Contractor shall have the unilateral right of change. The Subcontractor shall make no change in his scope of work as described herein, and by attachment hereto, without prior written consent of the General Contractor. In the event that a change causes additional labor and/or materials to be expended or deleted, then the contract price shall be accordingly amended thereby, and should said change cause the work to extend in time beyond the original contract duration, then the Subcontractor's duration of work shall be amended on a day-for-day basis and all associated direct and/or indirect costs shall be paid for by the General Contractor.

Site Conditions

The Contractor shall provide adequate working conditions at the job site on an unrestricted basis so as to allow the Subcontractor to complete his work in accordance with the schedules appended hereto.

---

6. This Subcontract was dated August 17, 2013.

Exhibit 2

SUMMARY OF ORIGINAL BID WORKSHEETS
FOR ELECTRICAL SUBCONTRACT*

Direct Labor	$ 880,000
Fringe Benefits at 15%	132,000
Total Labor Cost	$1,012,000
Overhead at 12% of Total Labor Cost	121,000
Material Cost	450,000
Other Direct Costs	50,000
Indirect Costs	57,000
Profit at 5%	85,000
Total Bid	$1,775,000

* The bid worksheets were prepared in July 2013.

Exhibit 3

PLAINTIFF'S SUMMARY OF ADDITIONAL COSTS CLAIMED
(Prepared 7/20/2016 by Sanford & Co.)

Labor (including fringe benefits)		**1,527,000**
Actual labor incurred	$2,579,000	
Less initial estimate	(1,012,000)	
Labor overrun	1,567,000	
Less labor for extra work due to plaintiff's mistakes	(40,000)	
Amount claimed	**1,527,000**	
Overhead		**$305,000**
Jerry's overhead is calculated at 20% of labor costs		
20% of labor overrun	$313,000	
Less 20% of labor for extra work due to plaintiff's mistakes	(8,000)	
Amount claimed	**$305,000**	
Materials		**$400,000**
Actual materials	$900,000	
Less initial estimate	(450,000)	
Materials overrun	450,000	
Less cost of materials used in extra work due to plaintiff's mistakes	(50,000)	
Amount claimed	**$400,000**	
Other Direct Costs		**$120,000**
These are the costs for renting a warehouse near the job site for an extra 1,000 days ($85,000) and the additional costs of hiring subcontractors to pump ground water from the job side ($35,000).		
Indirect Costs		**$150,000**
Costs of maintaining an office and project management at the job site for an extra 1,000 days.		
Total of Above Charges		**$2,502,000**

Lost Profits   **$125,000**

    Jerry's past experience has shown that normal pretax profits
on similar jobs are 5% of the contract amount. The amount
shown is 5% of the costs overruns set forth above.

Total Costs   **$2,627,000**

    Less change orders already paid per changes in design
specifications made by owner   (200,000)

                                          Total Amount Claimed   **$2,427,000**

DEPOSITION SUMMARY OF PLAINTIFF'S EXPERT

Deposition was taken in the office of Defense counsel on August 17, 2016.

- Went through credentials.

- Employed by attorney for Jerry's Wiring. The attorney has used the expert before, but the expert had no previous connection with Jerry's Wiring.

- Expert has dealt with several different construction contract claims before. Never one involving wastewater treatment plant or one where groundwater was an issue.

- Expert is familiar with the contract between the subcontractor and general contractor and also between the general contractor and owner.

- Expert was employed by attorney for Jerry's Wiring in April of 2014 after the subcontract with Smith Construction had been completed. The attorney concluded that Jerry's Wiring accounting personnel needed help in preparing the claim and in determining their costs on this job.

- Expert was asked by plaintiff's attorney to:

    1. determine the total costs incurred on the job by the plaintiff;

    2. determine if all costs incurred by the plaintiff with respect to the change orders had been included in the billings already made for such changed work;

    3. determine the costs associated with certain mistakes made by the plaintiff, which caused the plaintiff to incur extra labor, overhead, and materials;

    4. prepare a claim showing the expert's best estimate of costs that should be claimed from defendant; and

    5. provide expert testimony on the claim and its preparation.

- Expert reviewed books and records of Jerry's Wiring and performed certain tests to determine that each and every cost related to the Nita City job was included in the Sanford & Co. analysis. There were approximately $20,000 of charges included in Jerry's Wiring records that were charged to the Nita City job, but were miscoded and belonged to other jobs. The expert properly excluded such costs from his analysis. The expert believes such miscoded costs were normal and were just isolated errors.

- Expert is satisfied that all of the $2,579,000 for labor was actually incurred and did in fact relate to the Atlanta job.

- Expert determined the different items for "extra work due to plaintiff mistakes" by estimating the costs. The estimates were made based on Crowe & Co.'s analysis of the time and materials used in performing certain tasks that had to be redone because of plaintiff's mistakes, such as improper installation of wires, the use of improper insulating materials, etc. (Crowe & Co. is an independent engineering consulting firm hired by plaintiff's accounting firm, Sanford & Co.) The tasks that had to be redone were identified through 1) discussion with plaintiff's personnel; 2) review of all correspondence for the job; and 3) review of all payroll records and logs of how plaintiff's personnel spent their time. The labor times and materials from the Crowe study were costed out by Sanford & Co. based on actual costs paid for such items by Jerry's Wiring.

- Expert admits that approach to costing extra work due to plaintiff's mistakes is less than perfect due to poor labor cost records by activity code early in the job. However, expert doubts that estimates are off by more than $10,000 or $20,000.

- Overhead was recalculated for the Nita City job since amounts in Jerry's Wiring records did not reflect "actual" overhead, but rather "estimated" overhead. Overhead was totaled for all jobs on a year-by-year basis. The total overhead was compared to total labor dollars in each year. Since all other jobs were similar to the Nita City job, the 20 percent figure was felt to be reasonable by the expert.

- Other direct costs and indirect costs were determined by identifying all such costs actually incurred and taking 67 percent of such costs since the job was 1,000 days longer than the 500 days originally planned.

- Lost profits are calculated as shown in the claim.

- Expert believes that this claim is the best estimate of the costs actually incurred by plaintiff due to defendant's changes or nonperformance of contract provisions.

- Expert notes that it is amazing how fast charges for delay and disruptions can mount—mainly because Jerry's Wiring made such a substantial commitment of labor and materials to this project. These labor and material resources had to be maintained during periods of delay and could not always be diverted to other productive activity.

Exhibit 5

DEFENDANT'S EXPERT'S ANALYSIS OF PLAINTIFF'S CLAIM

(Prepared 9/6/2016 by Madden & Co.)

	Plaintiff's Claim*	Analysis by Madden & Co.
Labor	$1,527,000	$450,000
Overhead	305,000	54,000
Materials	400,000	50,000
Other Direct Costs	120,000	—
Indirect Costs	150,000	—
Lost Profits	125,000	—
Total Costs	2,627,000	554,000
Less—Change Orders Already Paid	(200,000)	(200,000)
Amount Claimed	$2,427,000	$354,000

*See Exhibit 3.

Exhibit 6

PAGE 1 OF 2

Deposition Summary of Defendant's Expert

Deposition was taken in the office of Plaintiff's counsel on October 17, 2016.

- Went through credentials.

- Employed by attorney for Smith Construction Co. Had performed similar work for both Smith Construction Co. and their attorneys in other disputes with subcontractors. No specific experience with electrical claims on wastewater treatment plants or problems with groundwater.

- Expert is familiar with all contracts relating to this claim.

- Expert was asked to assist attorneys as follows:

    1. Help in preparing deposition questions for plaintiff and plaintiff's expert.

    2. Review of plaintiff's documents to determine the costs incurred on the job for labor and material and the propriety of plaintiff's claim for other costs such as overhead and lost profits.

    3. Analyze plaintiff's claim and relate the items being claimed to actual support.

    4. Prepare an alternate claim showing the expert's best estimate of costs actually incurred by plaintiff due to defendant's change orders and untimely performance of contract provisions.

    5. Provide expert testimony on the alternate claim and the approach used to develop it.

    6. Prepare support for a subsequent claim to be filed against Nita City, if plaintiff is successful on any of this claim.

- Initial subcontract was for a fixed price of $1,775,000. Examination of bid documents suggests that the labor efficiency assumed in this bid is approximately 10 percent greater than Jerry's Wiring had ever actually achieved. Clearly, the initial job was substantially underbid, and this claim is to try to recover some of the plaintiff's own mistakes in underbidding.

- There were seven (7) change orders, but all of them have been paid. It is quite unreasonable that after Smith Construction has paid all seven change orders for $200,000 the plaintiff should come up with this wild claim of $2.4 million more on a $1,775,000 contract.

- Plaintiff's labor records are practically meaningless for the first eighteen months of this contract. Even if the plaintiff actually incurred these costs, it is quite likely that much of the costs were due to the plaintiff operating in an unfamiliar city, dealing with an unusually bad winter (certainly the weather is not the general contractor's fault), and encountering seven strikes. Plaintiff's claim that these difficulties did not cause the job to extend at all and that all delays were Smith Construction Company's fault is quite hard to believe. Furthermore, plaintiff can offer no documentation to substantiate its claim that the delays were caused by Smith Construction Company.

- Some of the water-related delays can probably be attributed to the general contractor, Smith Construction Company. However, there must be some limit to the responsibility of the general contractor; the subcontractor has a clear duty to mitigate its damages, and there is evidence that it did not do so. For example, on one specific task, the initial estimate was forty-one hours of work, but actual time charged to this task was 420 hours, allegedly due to water delays. This means that Jerry let his men sit around and watch a hole filled with water instead of getting on with the task of pumping out the hole or laying his men off until the problem was corrected.

- If the court finds that the plaintiff is owed some money for delay and disruption, most of the cost should be borne by the owner (Nita City) since it was the owner who ordered the changes that ended up extending the job. Smith will then be forced to sue the city to recover these costs.

- To prepare the Alternate Claim shown on Exhibit 5, expert reviewed plaintiff's own labor records and material charge slips and accumulated all charges identified as "Extra" at Smith's request or that were in any way identified as due to changed work. In this way, the expert arrived at the $450,000 labor figure and the $50,000 material figure.

- Overhead on Exhibit 5 is calculated based on 12 percent since this is what plaintiff bid (*see* Exhibit 2.)

- We did not include in the Alternate Claim, Exhibit 5, any amounts for Other Direct Costs, Indirect Costs, or Lost Profits as claimed by plaintiff. Defendant's attorneys advised us that such items could not be claimed under the subcontract. Expert, who is not an attorney, read the subcontract noting no provision for reimbursement of such extra items.

Problem 40

Jenkins v. Manchester

(Saul Winer and Alexander Christenson)

The plaintiff, Ralph Jenkins, was employed at the manufacturing plant of F.N.B. Products, Inc., in Nita City, Nita. Jenkins was a machine operator, whose duties included operating a press brake.

The function of a press brake is to bend ("brake") a piece of stock (usually pieces of thin steel or aluminum). This procedure involves placing the stock on a die in the die space of the press brake and activating the press by means of a foot pedal. A long narrow ram then strikes the stock and thereby bends it to the angle prescribed by the contour of the die. The operator then must remove the stock from the press and place it in a stock box, which is periodically emptied by other employees.

The machine, as originally manufactured, contained no guards or point-of-operation safety devices designed to prevent injury to the hands of an operator. The machine was designed, manufactured, and sold in 2004 by Scheiter Machine Company of Horseshoe Bend, Arkansas. At that time, Scheiter and two other companies were the only companies that manufactured press brakes. None of the companies manufactured press brakes with guards or point-of-operation safety devices. Pedal guards and tongs (for use by the operator in inserting and removing stock) were available in 2004 from Scheiter as optional equipment. Since 2007, two sets of tongs have been attached by chains to all press brakes sold by Scheiter. Pedal guards (the function of which is to prevent inadvertent depression of the pedal) became available in 2007 and still are only optional equipment.

On February 8, 2011, the plaintiff was operating the Scheiter press brake and was assigned to bend to a 90 degree angle pieces of aluminum stock, which were approximately four feet long, one foot wide, and 1/32 of an inch thick. No tongs or similar devices were available for his use, nor was a pedal guard attached or available. As happened occasionally, one of the pieces of stock slipped toward the rear of the die space after being bent by the ram. The plaintiff placed his hands under the ram in order to retrieve the stock. When he did so, he inadvertently depressed the foot pedal causing the ram to strike his hands and resulting in the loss of two fingers (index and middle) of his left and three fingers (index, middle, and ring) to the first knuckle of his right hand. Efforts to reattach the severed fingers failed.

The plaintiff was hospitalized for eight days and off work for four months following the accident. He then returned to work at F.N.B. Products in his former capacity as a machine operator. He still works for F.N.B. Products, and he is able to perform all the duties of his job.

In November 2012, the plaintiff was referred by a friend to an attorney, Norman Manchester, who maintained a storefront office in downtown Nita City. The only contact between Jenkins and Manchester occurred on November 12, 2012.

In March 2014, the plaintiff commenced this action against Manchester, alleging legal malpractice—specifically complaining of:

1.   Manchester's failure to properly investigate bringing a cause of action against the manufacturer of the brake press;

2.   Manchester's failure to commence an action against the manufacturer of the brake press during the statutory period; and

3.   Manchester's failure to refer the case to an attorney specializing in products liability cases.

The defendant has denied that the plaintiff in any way has been damaged by his failing to bring a cause of action against the manufacturer of the brake press or to refer it to a lawyer who specializes in products liability cases. Manchester maintains that he only advised Jenkins on his rights regarding workers' compensation and never represented Jenkins at all with regard to the potential products liability action against the manufacturer of the brake press. The depositions of the plaintiff and defendant follow this problem.

In order to prevail in his case against Manchester, Jenkins must show 1) that Manchester was negligent in his representation of Jenkins regarding the potential products liability lawsuit, and 2) that he would have prevailed, if the product liability suit had been brought.

The law in Nita at all times relevant to Plaintiff's injury and his claim against Mr. Manchester is:

1.   In personal injury cases, contributory negligence by an injured person is an absolute bar to the recovery of damages for any claims that are based upon a negligence cause of action;

2.   In products liability cases, misuse of a product by an injured person is an absolute bar to the recovery of damages for any claims against the manufacturer of a product;

3.   The statute of limitations in Nita is three years for negligence actions and two years for products liability actions;

4.   Workers' compensation is the sole remedy that an employee has against an employer for injuries sustained in the workplace; and

5.   Any award an employee receives from a cause of action arising out of an injury in the workplace is subject to subrogation by the workers' compensation provider.

The plaintiff has retained Saul Winer (see attached biographical data) as an expert. The defendant has retained Alexander Christenson (see attached biographical data) as an expert.

The case is now at trial.

Part A. Plaintiff's Expert

For the plaintiff, conduct a direct examination of Mr. Winer.

For the defendant, conduct a cross-examination of Mr. Winer.

For the plaintiff, conduct any necessary redirect examination.

Part B. Defendant's Expert

The plaintiff has rested. The defendant's midtrial motion for judgment as a matter of law has been denied.

For the defendant, conduct a direct examination of Mr. Christenson.

For the plaintiff, conduct a cross-examination of Mr. Christenson.

For the defendant, conduct any necessary redirect examination.

LAROS, RUSSELL, GOLDSTEIN, BECKER, WILSON & WINER
2470 BUHL BUILDING
NEW YORK, NEW YORK 10027

August 5, 2016

Lawrence Dubey, Esq.
1212 Cadillac Tower
Nita City, Nita 46556

Re: Jenkins v. Manchester

Dear Larry:

I have received all pleadings and depositions in this matter and will be happy to testify on behalf of the plaintiff.

It is my opinion that attorney Manchester committed malpractice by failing to take the third-party case; by failing to refer it to, or at least consult with, an attorney who specializes in personal injury or products liability matters; by failing to further investigate the facts of the case, especially those concerning the maintenance and operation of the equipment in question; and by failing to inform your client that he could seek out another legal opinion.

In addition, contrary to what Mr. Manchester informed Mr. Jenkins, contributory negligence is not a defense in Nita to a products liability case. I assume that Mr. Manchester was referring to the recognized defense in products liability cases known as "products misuse." I have insufficient facts at this time to form an opinion as to whether products misuse would be a bar in this case. At the time he rendered his opinion to your client, Manchester, as well, had insufficient information to provide such an opinion.

My opinion is fortified by my own experience in handling a press brake case in Nita against Scheiter Manufacturing Company in 2006. The factual setting was almost identical to yours. The thrust of our claim was Scheiter's failure to equip the press brake with tongs or with a pedal guard. My client lost the upper half of three fingers of his left hand. We settled the case before trial for $53,000. Obviously the case would have been worth more had liability been stronger.

Please let me know as soon as you have a trial date so I can arrange my schedule. As you know, about 90 percent of my practice has been in New York over the past five or six years, but I always look forward to returning to Nita City.

My fee will be $5,000 for testifying at trial. Enclosed please find my bill for $1,000 for my work to date.

Looking forward to working with you.

Very truly yours,

[*Signed*]

Saul Winer

BIOGRAPHICAL DATA

Saul Winer

Education

BA, University of Michigan, 1992
MA, Harvard University, 1994
JD, University of Nita Law School, 1997

Practice

Justice Department, Washington, D.C., 1997 to 2000.
Joined firm of Laros & Russell, currently Laros, Russell, Goldstein, Becker, Wilson, & Winer, in 2000, and has worked there to date.

Nature of Practice

The firm of Laros, Russell, Goldstein, Becker, Wilson, & Winer specializes in civil and criminal litigation, including workers' compensation representation with offices in Nita City and New York City. It is comprised of twenty partners and eighty associates. Mr. Winer limits his practice to plaintiff's personal injury work, including products liability and medical malpractice. The great majority (at least 90 percent) of his cases are referrals from other attorneys.

Affiliations

New York Bar Association
New York City Bar Association
Nita Bar Association
Nita City Bar Association
American Bar Association
Nita Trial Lawyers Association (Executive Board)
American College of Trial Lawyers
American Civil Liberties Union (Executive Board)
International Society of Barristers

CHRISTENSON & BARNARD

Attorneys at Law
1280 Eleven Mile Road
Nita City, Nita 46556

August 5, 2016

Reginald Davis, Esq.
1234 Guardian Building
Nita City, Nita 46556

Re: *Jenkins vs. Manchester*

Dear Mr. Davis:

At your request I have reviewed copies of all pleadings and discovery in the referenced matter.

It is my opinion that your client Mr. Manchester was correct in not pursuing any third-party action in connection with the injuries sustained by Mr. Jenkins on February 8, 2011. Mr. Jenkins was clearly at fault in the accident. The machine was working properly and was not defective. The acceptance or rejection of any personal injury case is clearly a matter of judgment. I believe that the judgment exercised in this case by Mr. Manchester was absolutely correct.

Since there was no case to be pursued, Mr. Manchester can hardly be faulted for failing to inform Jenkins that he could seek advice from other counsel. It was sufficient for him to inform Jenkins of the two-year statute of limitations on products liability cases.

It seems that, on the one hand, we attorneys are criticized for being overly litigious and causing lengthy docket delay while, on the other hand, we can be charged with professional malpractice for failing to put a hopeless case to court.

I will be happy to testify in accordance with the opinions set forth herein.

Sincerely,

[*Signed*]

Alexander Christenson

BIOGRAPHICAL DATA

Alexander Christenson

Education

BA, University of Nita, 1994
JD, University of Nita School of Law, 1997

Practice

Staff Attorney, Nita Bell Telephone Company, 1997–2002
Private Practice, Christenson & Barnard, 2002 to present

Nature of Practice

General neighborhood practice in Nita City, Nita. The firm of Christenson & Barnard has since its inception consisted only of Alexander Christenson and Albert Barnard, both of whom worked as staff attorneys for Nita Bell before setting up their own firm. They handle a general practice including probate, personal injury, workers' compensation, divorce, real estate, and general small business matters.

Affiliations

State Bar of Nita
Nita County Bar Association
American Bar Association
Noon Optimist Club of Nita City
Kiwanis
Knights of Columbus
Junior Achievement

DEPOSITION

June 17, 2016

RALPH JENKINS, the Plaintiff herein, having first been duly sworn to testify the truth and nothing but the truth, was examined and testified as follows:

* * *

EXAMINATION (by Mr. Davis)

1	Q:	Please state your name and address.
2	A:	Ralph Jenkins, 1438 Drury Circle, Nita City, Nita.
3	Q:	How old are you?
4	A:	I am thirty-five.
5	Q:	What is your wife's name?
6	A:	Sally.
7	Q:	What are the names and ages of your children?
8	A:	Tommy, eight; Linda, four; and Liza, eighteen months.
9	Q:	Where are you employed?
10	A:	I'm a machine operator at F.N.B. Products.
11	Q:	What is your salary?
12	A:	$14.50 an hour.
13	Q:	How long have you been a machine operator?
14	A:	I started right out of high school in, let's see, 2000. I was a general
15		laborer for a couple years, and then I was moved up to machine
16		operator.
17	Q:	How did the accident of February 8, 2011, happen?
18	A:	Well, I was breaking pieces of aluminum like I always did. One of the
19		pieces jumped up after the ram hit it and wound up toward the press.
20		I reached in to get it, I and must have accidentally hit the pedal. I'm
21		not sure. Anyway, the ram came down on my hands and took off five
22		fingers.

23   Q: How often did a piece of stock jump after the ram hit it so that you'd

24   have to place your hands under the ram to retrieve it?

25   A: Oh, if I'd used the press all day, maybe once or twice.

26   Q: Did it ever cause you any particular concern prior to the time of your

27   accident?

28   A: No.

29   Q: Did you ever accidentally hit the foot pedal before your accident?

30   A: Not as I can recall.

31   Q: Do you ever use tongs to put stock into the press or to remove it?

32   A: Weren't any in the plant that I knew of.

33   Q: Did you ever ask for any?

34   A: Never saw any reason to.

35   Q: Did the press brake ever trip without your hitting the pedal?

36   A: Not that I remember.

37   Q: Would you remember something like that?

38   A: I suppose.

39   Q: Who paid your hospital and doctor bills for the treatment you had

40   after this accident?

41   A: The workers' compensation company. The bills were a lot, about

42         $26,000 because they tried to reattach two of my fingers, but they

43   weren't successful.

44   Q: Did they always make payments directly to you?

45   A: Yes, but the medical bills were paid directly to the hospital.

46   Q: How much and for how many weeks?

47   A: $184 per week for, I'm not sure, I think about sixteen weeks.

48   Q: As you understand it, was that the proper amount for the proper

49   number of weeks?

50   A: Yes.

51   Q: When did you first meet my client, Norman Manchester?

52	A:	In November, about nine months after I was hurt. A friend of mine
53		suggested I go see him to make sure I had gotten all the comp I was
54		entitled to and to see if I could sue anybody for my injuries. My friend
55		had read in the newspaper how somebody who got hurt on the job was
56		able to get some money from somebody other than his employer if he
57		had to work on dangerous machinery, and he said I should check it
58		out. I didn't see any harm. Especially because the worker's comp I got
59		didn't seem fair given I had lost my fingers.
60	Q:	Did you only speak to him on that one occasion?
61	A:	Yes.
62	Q:	Was that in his office?
63	A:	Yes.
64	Q:	What happened at the meeting?
65	A:	Well, I told him about my accident and that I wanted to make sure
66		I got all that was due me. He told me the workers' comp company
67		should pay all medical bills and that they should pay so much a week
68		for so many weeks. He looked in a book, and he told me it was $184
69		for sixteen or so weeks and longer if I couldn't work. I asked him if I
70		could I sue somebody because the machine wasn't safe. He said, no,
71		because it was my fault that I hit the pedal. I said, "What about all
72		the people you read about in the papers who go to court and get so
73		much money?" He said this just wasn't one of those cases. I figured he
74		ought to know, so that was the end of it. He told me to call him if the
75		workers' comp company gave me any problem. On the way out, the
76		secretary told me that would be $20, and I paid her.
77	Q:	Did Mr. Manchester ever mention a statute of limitations or a time
78		after which it would be too late to sue?
79	A:	Yeah, he said something about you have to sue in three years after you
80		get hurt, but because he told me that I couldn't sue anyone, I didn't

81   think much of it at the time. It was only when I was at Mr. Dubey's

82   office for a car wreck I was in, and he asked me about my fingers

83   and whether I sued the maker of the machine, that I figured out that

84   Manchester was wrong and that I should have been able to sue the

85   brake press machine manufacturer, but that by then it was too late.

86   Q: When did you have the conversation with Mr. Dubey?

87   A: That was in March of 2014, right after my car wreck. He represented

88   me in that case, too.

89   Q: Going back to your conversation with Mr. Manchester, did he say you

90   couldn't sue or that he advised you not to sue?

91   A: He just said there wasn't any case.

92   Q: Did you ever see or talk to another lawyer about your injury to your

93   fingers?

94   A: Not until it came up with Mr. Dubey. When Manchester told me

95   I didn't have a case, I believed him. He was the lawyer, not me. I trusted

96   him. That was my big mistake.

DEPOSITION

June 17, 2016

NORMAN MANCHESTER, the defendant herein, having first been sworn to testify the truth, the whole truth and nothing but the truth, was examined and testified as follows:

* * *

EXAMINATION (by Mr. Dubey)

1   Q: Please state your name and office address.

2   A: Norman Manchester, 234 Main Street, Nita City.

3   Q: Are you an attorney licensed to practice law in the state of Nita?

4   A: Yes.

5   Q: Where and when did you go to college and law school?

6   A: I went to Alma College from 2001 to 2006. Then I worked in Nita City

7   as an insurance salesman for about a year, and I went to law school in

8   2006 at the Columbus Law School.* I graduated in June 2009.

9   Q: When did you first receive your license to practice law?

10   A: January 2011.

11   Q: What did you do between June 2009 and January 2011?

12   A: Well, I took the bar exam during the summer of 2009, but I failed it.

13   I took it again in the winter of 2010 and failed it again. I didn't get any

14   Nita law at Columbus since it's out of state. Then I took the exam in

15   the summer of 2010 and passed and was sworn in to the bar right after

16   New Year's in 2011. I've been practicing on my own ever since.

17   Q: How did you earn a living from June 2009 until January 2011?

18   A: I sold life insurance.

19   Q: Have you ever had partners or associates in the practice of law?

20   A: Just my secretary.

21   Q: Is she a lawyer?

---

*Columbus Law School is a mythical institution.

22	A:	No.
23	Q:	Describe the nature of your practice.
24	A:	It's a general practice. I handle personal injury cases, workers' comp,
25		writing wills, divorces, real estate, some small business stuff, and a
26		couple of adoptions. It's a real general neighborhood kind of practice.
27	Q:	You say you handle personal injury cases. Have you ever handled a
28		medical malpractice case?
29	A:	I've had a couple of cases, but nothing that ever panned out.
30	Q:	What do you mean?
31	A:	You know, couldn't find an expert.
32	Q:	Have you ever referred a medical malpractice case to another lawyer
33		who specialized in medical malpractice or even consulted with such a
34		lawyer?
35	A:	No.
36	Q:	Have you ever put a medical malpractice case into court?
37	A:	No, they weren't good enough.
38	Q:	How many of these potential cases have you had?
39	A:	Two or three.
40	Q:	What happened to them?
41	A:	I told the people there was no case.
42	Q:	Have you ever handled a products liability case?
43	A:	Three or four.
44	Q:	Which is it, three or four?
45	A:	Well, I had a bug in a bottle of Pepsi case that I settled.
46	Q:	For how much?
47	A:	$75.
48	Q:	What else?
49	A:	I had a brake failure case, but it didn't pan out.
50	Q:	Why not?

51	A:	Well, the car had about 14,000 miles on it so there wasn't a case, and
52		there hadn't been any recall on that model car.
53	Q:	So what did you do with the case?
54	A:	Nothing, told the people there was no case.
55	Q:	What were the injuries in that case?
56	A:	Just a fractured thigh bone.
57	Q:	What other products cases?
58	A:	The only one I can think of is Jenkins.
59	Q:	Have you ever referred a products case to an attorney who specializes in
60		products cases, or have you ever consulted with such an attorney?
61	A:	No.
62	Q:	Do you know the names of any attorneys who specialize in products
63		cases?
64	A:	Rick Goodman in West Nita City.
65	Q:	Any others?
66	A:	Not that I can think of. Oh, Bill Dole, also.
67	Q:	Who?
68	A:	Bill Dole.
69	Q:	How many times did you speak to my client, Mr. Jenkins?
70	A:	Just one time.
71	Q:	Tell me about it.
72	A:	Well, he told me that he lost some fingers when he accidentally hit
73		the pedal on a press while his hands were under the whatchamacallit,
74		the ram. He wanted to make sure he was getting all the comp he was
75		entitled to. So I looked it up, and he was. That's about all there was to
76		it. I told him I couldn't help him.
77	Q:	Did he ask you about the possibility of suing somebody?
78	A:	I really don't remember, but the accident was clearly his fault, so a
79		third-party case would have been unsuccessful.

80	Q:	What do you mean?
81	A:	Well, he was contributorily negligent.
82	Q:	Is contributory negligence a defense to a products case in Nita?
83	A:	Of course.
84	Q:	Is that why you didn't encourage Mr. Jenkins to file a lawsuit?
85	A:	That, plus there was nothing wrong with the press. It worked like it
86		was supposed to. When he kicked the pedal, the ram came down. No
87		double tripping or anything like that.
88	Q:	Have you ever inspected the machine on which Mr. Jenkins was
89		injured?
90	A:	No, no need to.
91	Q:	Have you ever spoken to an engineer or other such expert with respect
92		to Mr. Jenkins's case?
93	A:	No.
94	Q:	Did you inform Mr. Jenkins that there was a statute of limitations
95		applicable to a third-party action?
96	A:	I told him that the statute of limitation was three years. I'm positive that
97		I told him about that. I went to a seminar on Professional Responsibility
98		to get my Nita CLE credits, and they told us to always inform potential
99		clients of the statute of limitations when you turn down a case, just in
100		case they want to get a second opinion. I do remember that I told him
101		that I didn't think there was a case.
102	Q:	Did you inform Mr. Jenkins that he could get a second opinion or that
103		he should get a second opinion?
104	A:	I might have, but I doubt it. As I said, he didn't have a case, so I doubt
105		I would have suggested that he waste his time and money.
106	Q:	Just to be sure, sir. You told Mr. Jenkins he had three years from the
107		date of injury to sue if he wanted to.
108	A:	That's right.

109 Q: How long did your meeting with him last?

110 A: About twenty or thirty minutes.

111 Q: Did you charge him?

112 A: I don't remember, but if he says so, I can't argue with it.

113 Q: Did you ever hear from or speak to Mr. Jenkins after this meeting?

114 A: No.

115 Q: Did you ever open a file on Mr. Jenkins?

116 A: Not that I can recall.

117 Q: Did you communicate with Mr. Jenkins in any way after this one
118   twenty- or thirty-minute meeting?

119 A: No.

120 Q: Nothing further.

LEARNED TREATISE

On December 1, 2013, an article entitled "Litigation Ethics" appeared in the *Nita Bar Journal*, vol. 68, no. 1. It was written by Arthur Prosserberg. The judge in the Jenkins case has agreed that the article qualifies as a learned treatise and may be used at trial to the extent allowed by the rules of evidence.

Professor Prosserberg has been a member of the New York and Massachusetts bars since 1985. For the past twenty-eight years he has been a professor of law at the Harvard Law School, where he teaches courses in Ethics, Jurisprudence, and the Litigation Process. His articles concerning matters of ethics and the legal profession have appeared from time to time in legal periodicals and journals. His book, *Ethical Conduct and the American Lawyer*, has been a standard law school text since its publication in 2005.

Excerpts from the article:

> One of the first questions a lawyer must decide is whether to accept a case. The overriding principle appears in the ethics code of every state in the Union and provides that a lawyer shall not handle a legal matter that he knows or should know that he is not competent to handle, without associating with him a lawyer who is competent to handle it.

> On occasion a client will present a factual situation with which the lawyer is not familiar. For example, a lawyer who specializes in commercial transactions would not be expected to accept a murder case without at least questioning his own ability to handle such a matter.

> This is an age of specialization. That situation has come about because of the subject matter and procedural complexities of the different fields. In short, a lawyer cannot be expected to know the legal intricacies of every area of law. When confronted with a fact situation, he should pause before giving advice, unless he feels comfortable with his knowledge of the subject.

> A lawyer is not obligated to accept every case that comes into his office. He may feel he is not competent to handle the case. There might be something about the case or the client that so troubles him that he feels he cannot effectively represent that client. Or he simply might feel the client does not have a case.

> It would be improper for a lawyer to accept a case when he honestly believes there is no merit to it. Unnecessary litigation is perhaps the number one reason for the public disquiet about the legal profession. The public's lack of confidence in lawyers can be traced directly to the needless proliferation of lawsuits during the past ten years. Bar associations and other bodies charged with the task of enforcing ethical considerations have been too slow to police those in

their ranks who thoughtlessly and carelessly file lawsuits that have neither merit nor substance.

On the other hand, when a potential client comes to a lawyer's office, the lawyer must exercise careful consideration before he decides whether to accept or reject the case. In most cases, that would entail investigation of the pertinent facts and the applicable law. No one seeking legal assistance should be summarily dismissed. At times, that might mean consultation with a lawyer who specializes in that particular area. Such consultation is mandatory when the attorney knows, or reasonably should know, he is not competent to handle the matter.

There can be no litmus paper test for competency. That determination depends upon the lawyer's education, training, and experience. In the long run, it will depend upon the lawyer's good judgment and sense of propriety.

When a lawyer declines to accept a case, he should offer the rejected client a full explanation of his reasons for doing so. The lawyer should suggest alternatives, if there be any. In other words, even when declining a case, a lawyer owes a duty of due care to one who seeks advice. The potential client cannot be dismissed lightly. He must be fully informed. At a minimum, when declining a case, the client should be informed of any applicable statute of limitations.

Members of the legal profession must aim for and establish high standards of conduct. The "usual way of doing things" in a specific legal community is not necessarily the right way. Of course, a lawyer owes a high duty to any client, potential or real. But his highest obligation is to the legal profession and to the administration of justice.

PROBLEM 41

State v. Hamilton

(Dr. Arthur W. Randall)

The defendant, Richard Hamilton, has been charged with assault with a deadly weapon and attempted murder for the shooting of a Nita City police officer on July 28, 2015. It is alleged that the defendant, dressed in combat boots, white pants, white shirt, and a white hooded cape approached a parked police car, pulled out a shotgun from under his cape, and fired two shots into the patrol car. One officer received minor injuries. The second officer survived only because of the quick actions of his partner in getting him medical attention and the fact that he was wearing a bulletproof vest.

The defendant has asserted the insanity defense. He was originally found incompetent to stand trial in September 2015. In September 2016, pursuant to mandatory review of his case as required by Nita General Statutes, he was found to be competent.

The defendant has been examined by Dr. Arthur W. Randall at the request of defense counsel. Dr. Randall's report and vita follow this problem.

The case is now at trial. The position of the defendant is that the defendant was not legally sane at the time of his assault on the police officer. The position of the government is that Hamilton knew what he was doing at the time of the shooting, and knew that it was wrong by society's view, but that he shot the police officer as a result of his extremist views. The government has retained an expert witness who will so testify in the government's rebuttal case.

For the defendant, conduct a direct examination of Dr. Randall.

For the State, conduct a cross-examination of Dr. Randall.

For the defendant, conduct any necessary redirect examination.

Arthur W. Randall, MD

19 South 21 Street
Nita City, Nita 46556
564–1031

October 3, 2016

William Bower, Attorney at Law
Defenders Association of Nita
1526 Chestnut Street
Nita City, Nita 46556

Dear Mr. Bower:

At your request I examined Mr. Richard Hamilton at the Nita City Jail on 10/1/16. The following is a report of my neurological and psychiatric examination.

Identification

Richard Hamilton is a twenty-year-old, single, Caucasian male who lives with his mother and stepfather at 623 Worth Street, Nita City, Nita. On or about 7/28/15, he was arrested and charged with the shooting of a Nita City police officer. He tells me that he has been incarcerated at the Terford Prison for the past three months.

Statement of the Presenting Problems

The defendant has a history suggesting mental disability. The circumstances around the shooting were quite bizarre and suggest mental disability. The defendant's statements and behavior since his arrest and at the present time are also suggestive of mental disability. For all of these reasons, counsel for the defendant deemed it quite appropriate to secure neuropsychiatric examinations from independent board-certified neuropsychiatrists in order that they might offer their expert opinions to the court as to the issue of the defendant's mental status at the time of the alleged felony with special reference to legal responsibility under the M'Naghten Rule, which is followed in the State of Nita.

Past History

The defendant was born in Nita City to a widowed mother. His father died in a car accident before he was born. Reportedly, the pregnancy was uneventful and the delivery uncomplicated. His infantile development was entirely normal. He experienced the usual childhood diseases without complications, and his health during childhood was normal.

He was reared in a lower middle-income socio-economic environment in the absence of a father who died before his birth, but blessed with the love of his mother. When he was thirteen years of age his mother remarried. The boy always resented his stepfather, whom he describes as unfair and dictatorial.

He entered first grade in a parochial school, but, unable to keep up his marks, was transferred to public school.

It is important to note that the defendant has always been a loner, spending most of his leisure time by himself, and that he never developed a close relationship with any female except his mother and grandmother.

At the age of fifteen, he was arrested and charged with the shooting of another youth, also fifteen years of age. He was adjudicated as delinquent, but was given probation and was released to his mother.

After graduating from high school he matriculated at a small military college in the South. He tells me that he earned a 3.7 average during the first semester, but was not awarded an A in any subject. Because of this he became resentful and, feeling persecuted by his teachers, refused to study during the next semester, and his marks dropped to 2.4. At this point he became disgusted and left that college and transferred to Nita University. There he felt that the teachers were not teaching the subject matter properly and decided that he could learn just as much by reading alone as he could by going to class. He therefore stopped attending his classes. However, he protected himself from finding out he was wrong by not taking the end of the semester finals. In this way, his delusional system was not threatened.

It is important to note that he had become involved in a white supremacist group and became engrossed in studying the history of race relations, both in this country and the world. The more involved he became in these studies, the more he would tend to brood about the treatment of "his people" in this country, and the more bitter, resentful, and seclusive he became.

Upon leaving Nita University, he returned to his parents' home in Nita City. There he secluded himself in his room and became more and more involved with reading about the history of race relations. His parents attempted to pull him away from this activity, urging him to get a job, but he refused, feeling that, "If I were to get a job and work I would only get screwed because of quotas and affirmative action by those socialists, so why bother." He became more and more involved with these studies. He became more and more bitter and more and more resentful. He also became increasingly seclusive. In January of 2014, he left his parents' home to visit a friend in Memphis, Tennessee. He remained there for approximately three weeks, and he tells me that he had a good time during that visit. He then returned to Nita City to continue his reading and brooding. He began to feel that he should do something to actively redress the grievances of "his people." He returned to Memphis a few months later, and he remained with his friend for approximately two months. During that time he got into an altercation with the local police, and he was beaten about the forehead. He showed me a scar on his right eyebrow, which he said he sustained at the time of the beating. In the meantime, his hatred for the culture in which he found himself became more and more intensified and more and more he began to feel himself engulfed in a divine mission to strike back at the culture, and the authority figures who perpetuated the culture.

Interviews with the defendant's mother indicate that when the defendant returned to Nita City about a month before the incident, he spent $2,000 for furniture, which he gave away. She also stated that during the month before the incident her son was reading the Bible six to eight hours per day, began talking to himself, was increasingly seclusive and insisted that he was Jewish, which he was not.

One day he said that he had a vision, and in this vision he saw two beams of light, which he interpreted to be the Holy Ghost. He began to feel at this time that the Holy Ghost was commanding him to act in a militant fashion. On July 28, 2015, he dressed in combat boots, white pants, a white shirt and a white hooded cape, took a shotgun, walked up to a police car in which two police officers were sitting, and shot one of the officers.

Several hours after the incident he was placed under arrest after a brief struggle with Nita City police officers at his parents' home. He originally denied any involvement in the shooting, but, after two hours of questioning, he stated that he shot the police officer because the "Holy Spirit told him to execute the police officers."

The defendant was interviewed by Dr. Wactle, the staff psychiatrist at Terford Prison on August 19, 2015. Dr. Wactle reports: "Direct questioning regarding his (defendant's) previous assault, his attack at the time of the alleged shooting, or his struggle with the arresting officers, caused the defendant to refuse to respond. When asked about his communication with the Holy Spirit, the defendant responded, 'I made that stuff up so they'd stop beating me (there was absolutely no medical evidence of a beating). I wanted to get the trial over with. I don't trust anybody. I'm not crazy. I'd rather be in prison than in the hospital.'"

In September 2015, the defendant was found incompetent to stand trial. In September 2016, the defendant was found competent to stand trial.

Examination

When seen in the Nita City Jail on October 1, 2016, the defendant was a tall, slender, athletic looking twenty-year-old right-handed male, ambulatory, oriented, alert, verbal, and cooperative. His vital signs were within normal limits.

The routine physical and neurological examination revealed no unusual findings except for the scar over the right eyebrow.

The significant findings in the psychiatric examination were as follows: his intellectual endowment was normal and there was no evidence of intellectual retardation or of intellectual deterioration.

His emotional reactions were somewhat flat, and he expressed little emotional reactivity at any time during the interview. The significant findings in the examination were as follows: his thinking was characterized by paranoid delusion, which included both delusions of grandeur, delusions of persecution, and religious delusions of having been sent on a divine mission. His ability to critically appraise his situation was quite impaired. He states, "I know that society feels that I am in trouble, but I do not feel that I am in trouble." He went on to say that he had done what God had told him to do and that he was in God's hands. At one time during the interview he seemed not a part of the interview, and he appeared as if he might be hallucinating. He seemed quite paranoid in the presence of a guard who was watching from a window into the interview room, and he refused to open up until I persuaded the guard that we were fine and that I would appreciate it if he not be visible to Mr. Hamilton. The defendant did open up with me after that. On several occasions I tried to get the defendant to say he was sick. However, at no time would he admit that he was mentally ill. Each time he denied that he was mentally ill. It was quite obvious that he had no insight into his mental disability. His judgment, too, appeared to be severely impaired.

Diagnosis

Schizophrenic reaction, paranoid type. He remains quite psychotic at this time in spite of the fact that he is taking medications. I agree, however, that he is competent to stand trial.

Opinions

In my opinion the defendant was mentally disabled at the time of the above shooting. He was unable to appreciate the nature of his behavior, and he was unable to determine that what he was doing was wrong.

Respectfully submitted,

[*Signed*]

Arthur W. Randall
Diplomate of the American Board of Psychiatry and Neurology

Nita Statutes

Nita Criminal Code. Chapter 40

40-8-101. Criminal Responsibility. No person shall be tried, sentenced, or punished for any crime while mentally ill or mentally deficient so as to be incapable of understanding the proceedings or making a defense; but he shall not be excused from criminal liability except upon proof that at the time of committing the alleged criminal act he was laboring under such a defect of reason, from one of these causes, as not to know the nature of his act, or that it was wrong.

N.R.S. 611.026, as amended by Laws 2002, CH. 352, Section 1, effective May 18, 2002.